MUSLIMS IN BRITAIN

The m ment of social, religious and ethnic diversity is a key social policy concern in Brit nd Muslims in particular have become a focus of attention in recent years. This ti nd topical volume examines the position of Muslims in Britain and how they ar nging and making social, political and religious space.

Wi tributions from world-renowned scholars on British Muslims and from policy- ists writing on issues of concern to Muslims and others alike, the book explor w British Muslims are changing social and religious spaces such as mosqu the role of women, engaging in politics, creating media and other resour d thus developing new perspectives on Islam and transforming Muslim society within. Chapters cover issues of religion and politics, Britishness, governanc der issues, religion in civic space and inter-ethnic and religious relations, as the role of intellectuals, chaplains and activists in reforming Islam and re g the British political landscape.

Pro a broad and comprehensive examination of the key issues surrounding M the United Kingdom, this book will be a valuable resource for studen rers and researchers in sociology, social policy, geography, politics, Islamic studies and other related disciplines.

Waqar I. U. Ahmad is Deputy Vice-Chancellor of Research and Enterprise at Middlesex University. Formerly Chief Social Scientist at the Office of the Deputy Prime Minister, he is an Academician of the Academy of Social Sciences, a member of the Higher Education Funding Council for England's Research and Innovation Advisory Committee, and a Fellow of the Muslim Institute.

Ziauddin Sardar is Professor of Law and Society at Middlesex University. Considered a pioneering writer on Islam and contemporary cultural issues, he is author of some fifty boc C. Hurst, 2011). A former columr Critical Muslim.

MUSLIMS IN BRITAIN

Making social and political space

Edited by Waqar I. U. Ahmad and Ziauddin Sardar

Routledge
Taylor & Francis Group
LONDON AND NEW YORK

First published 2012
by Routledge
2 Park Square, Milton Park, Abingdon, Oxon OX14 4RN

Simultaneously published in the USA and Canada
by Routledge
711 Third Avenue, New York, NY 10017

Routledge is an imprint of the Taylor & Francis Group, an informa business

British Library Cataloguing in Publication Data
A catalogue record for this book is available from the British Library

Library of Congress Cataloging in Publication Data
Muslims in Britain: making social and political space/edited by Waqar I. U. Ahmad and Ziauddin Sardar.
p. cm.
Includes bibliographical references and index.
1. Muslims–Great Britain. 2. Muslims–Great Britain–Social conditions.
3. Muslims–Great Britain–Politics and government. I. Ahmad, W. I. U. (Waqar Ihsan-Ullah), 1957– II. Sardar, Ziauddin.
DA125.M87M878 2012
305.6'970941–dc23

2011045121

ISBN: 978-0-415-59471-4 (hbk)
ISBN: 978-0-415-59472-1 (pbk)
ISBN: 978-0-203-12146-7 (ebk)

Typeset in Bembo
by Wearset Ltd, Boldon, Tyne and Wear

Printed and bound in Great Britain by the MPG Books Group

CONTENTS

List of illustrations vii
Notes on contributors viii

Introduction 1
Ziauddin Sardar and Waqar I. U. Ahmad

1 Religion and public space 17
Ziauddin Sardar

2 Britain and Britishness: place, belonging and exclusion 33
Rosemary Sales

3 Exploring social spaces of Muslims 53
Lucinda Platt

4 Muslim chaplains: working at the interface of 'public' and 'private' 84
M. Mansur Ali and Sophie Gilliat-Ray

5 Young Muslims in London: gendered negotiations of local, national and transnational places 101
Louise Ryan

6 Multiculturalism and the gender gap: the visibility and invisibility of Muslim women in Britain 120
Heidi Safia Mirza

7 Everyday making and civic engagement among Muslim women in Scotland 141
Rahielah Ali and Peter Hopkins

8 Negotiating faith and politics: the emergence of Muslim consciousness in Britain 156
Nasar Meer

9 'Creating a society of sheep'? British Muslim elite on mosques and imams 171
Waqar I. U. Ahmad

Index 193

ILLUSTRATIONS

Figures

3.1 Homophily among Muslims and non-Muslims 63
3.2 Predicted probabilities of social mixing among the majority, Muslims and non-Muslim minorities 72
3.3 Predicted probabilities of having no close friends among Muslims and non-Muslims, by sex 78

Tables

3.1 Distributions of Muslims across samples and key characteristics 60
3.2 Patterns of social activity: percentage of each group engaging in each activity, across Muslims and non-Muslims, 2001 61
3.3 Results of log-linear models of ethnic and income homophily among Muslims and non-Muslims 66
3.4 General social mixing and domestic social mixing across Muslims and non-Muslims 68
3.5 Probability of social mixing: results from logistic regression models of general social mixing and mixing in own or another's home 70
3.6 Numbers of close friends: percentages with different numbers of friends, 2008/2009 73
3.7 Probabilities of having close friends: binary logistic and ordered logistic model estimates 76

CONTRIBUTORS

Waqar I. U. Ahmad, previously Chief Social Scientist at the Office of the Deputy Prime Minister, UK, is Deputy Vice-Chancellor Research and Enterprise at Middlesex University. Professor Ahmad's books include, with Hannah Bradby, *Ethnicity, Health and Health Care: Understanding Diversity, Tackling Disadvantage* (Blackwell, 2008) and *Ethnicity, Disability and Chronic Illness* (Open University Press, 2000). He is an Academician of the Academy of Social Sciences, a member of the Higher Education Funding Council for England's Research and Innovation Advisory Committee, a one-time member of the Economic and Social Research Council's Strategic Research Board and a Fellow of the Muslim Institute.

M. Mansur Ali is a post-doctoral researcher at the Centre for the Study of Islam in the UK, Cardiff University. With Sophie Gilliat-Ray and others, he is working on a study of Muslim chaplaincy in Britain. His research interests include *'ulama* and Muslims in the West, and Islam in Bangladesh.

Rahielah Ali is a doctoral research student in the School of Geography, Politics and Sociology at Newcastle University. Her work focuses upon the everyday experiences of Muslim women in Scotland, exploring ways in which they practise Islam in spaces of the social, the embodiment of dress and community participation following national and global events.

Sophie Gilliat-Ray is Reader in Religious and Theological Studies and Director of the Islam-UK Centre at Cardiff University. She has authored numerous books, articles and chapters relating to Muslims in Britain. Her latest book is *Muslims in Britain: An Introduction* (Cambridge University Press, 2010).

Peter Hopkins is a Senior Lecturer in the School of Geography, Politics and Sociology at Newcastle University, UK. He is author of *The Issue of Masculine Identities for British Muslims* (Edwin Mellen, 2008) and co-editor of *Geographies of Muslim Identities: Diaspora, Gender and Belonging* (Ashgate, 2007) and *Muslims in Britain: Race, Place and Identities* (Edinburgh University Press, 2009).

Nasar Meer is Senior Lecturer in the School of Arts and Social Sciences at the University of Northumbria. During 2012–13 he will be a Minda de Gunzberg Fellow at Harvard University and a Visiting Fellow with the Institute for Advanced Studies in the Humanities (IASH) at the University of Edinburgh. His recent book-length publications include *Citizenship, Identity and the Politics of Multiculturalism* (Palgrave, 2010); (with Anna Triandafyllidou and Tariq Modood, eds) *European Multiculturalism(s): Cultural, Religious and Ethnic Challenges* (Edinburgh University Press, 2011); and *Race and Ethnicity* (Sage, forthcoming).

Heidi Safia Mirza, of the Institute of Education, University of London, UK, has published extensively on gender and race, including studies on ethnicity and educational attainment, multiculturalism and the experiences of Muslim and ethnic minority women. Professor Mirza's current research includes involvement in the ESRC-funded Understanding Society Survey (with Lucinda Platt and others) and the European Union project Young Migrant Women in Secondary Education. Among her recent publications are *Race, Gender and Educational Desire* (Routledge, 2009) and *Black and Postcolonial Feminisms in New Times* (Routledge, 2010).

Lucinda Platt is Professor of Sociology at the Institute of Education, University of London, and Director of the Millennium Cohort Study. Her main research interests are in poverty and inequality and in ethnic minority disadvantage, with a particular focus on longitudinal analytical approaches. Her latest book is *Understanding Inequalities: Social Stratification and Difference* (Polity Press, 2011).

Louise Ryan is Reader in Gender and Migration and Co-Director of the Social Policy Research Centre at Middlesex University, UK. She has published widely on issues relating to gender, ethnicity, social networks and family migration. She is co-editor (with Wendy Webster) of *Gendering Migration: Masculinity, Femininity and Ethnicity in Post-war Britain* (Ashgate, 2008).

Rosemary Sales is Emeritus Professor of Social Policy at Middlesex University, UK. Her recent research projects have examined immigration theory and policy and new migration flows, focusing particularly on London. Her publications in this field include *Understanding Immigration and Refugee Policy: Contradictions and Continuities* (Policy Press, 2007).

Ziauddin Sardar, writer, broadcaster and cultural critic, is Professor of Law and Society, the School of Law, Middlesex University. He is the author of numerous books, including the highly acclaimed autobiography *Desperately Seeking Paradise: Journeys of a Sceptical Muslim* (Granta, 2004), and co-author (with Merryl Wyn Davies) of the international bestseller *Why Do People Hate America?* (2002). A collection of his writings is available as *Islam, Postmodernism and Other Futures: A Ziauddin Sardar Reader* (Icon Books, 2003) and *How Do You Know? Reading Ziauddin Sardar on Islam, Science and Cultural Relations* (Pluto Press, 2006). He co-edited the prestigious critical arts journal *Third Text* from 1996 to 2006, served as a Commissioner on the Equality and Human Rights Commission from 2006 to 2009 and as a member of the National Security Forum from 2008 to 2010, and was a columnist on the *New Statesman* for over ten years. Currently he is co-editor of *Critical Muslim* and Chair of the Muslim Institute. He is widely known as a public intellectual and appears frequently on radio and television.

INTRODUCTION

Ziauddin Sardar and Waqar I. U. Ahmad

'When you come back to England from any foreign country,' George Orwell wrote in a perceptive essay, 'you have immediately the sensation of breathing different air. Even in the first few minutes dozens of small things conspire to give you this feeling' (Orwell 1941). Much of what Orwell identified as typically British, or rather English, is still in evidence: 'the beer is bitterer, the coins are heavier, the grass is greener, the advertisements are more blatant'. But he will find identity less easy to define in an 'England' that is not the sole preserve of 'the English' any more: the population now is much more heterogeneous, with 'Englishness' (however it is defined) as only one segment in a multi-ethnic society. Orwell would find the air somewhat strange in a Britain awash with products of multiculturalism, from hip hop to bangra, chicken tikka masala to doner kebab, *Asian Network* to *The Kumars at No. 42*, and a plethora of black and Asian faces on television. Moreover, the history and tradition associated with Orwell's 'Englishness' – the Empire, the House of Lords, fox-hunting, the national anthem – are either questionable or meaningless to the vast majority of new-English who now live in England (although Orwell found them just as nauseating in the 1940s).

'As I write,' Orwell says in the opening lines of 'England Your England', 'highly civilized human beings are flying overhead, trying to kill me.' Nowadays, 'highly civilized human beings', while continuing with the traditional pastime, have discovered a new preoccupation: demonising minorities. And one minority in particular has become both the subject and the object of their wrath: British Muslims. Apparently, Muslims in Britain are undermining the core values of Britishness. They are responsible for perpetuating, according to the former prime minister Gordon Brown, 'a crude multiculturalism where all values became relative' (2004). According to his successor, David Cameron, they are the disseminators of a worldview based on 'real hostility towards Western democracy and liberal values' (2011). The natives, complains David Goodhart, former editor of *Prospect* magazine, are now 'forced to share with strangers' – those alien, immigrant and unsavoury Muslims among us (2004).

Questions of identity in Britain have always been focused on otherness. In the 1950s and 1960s, Muslims and other 'immigrants' were described as 'aliens'. What is 'alien' represents otherness, the site of difference and the repository of fears and anxieties. It was the noticeable colour, accent and general demeanour of 'immigrants' that was the source of fear expressed so vividly in the notorious 1968 'rivers of blood' speech by Enoch Powell. The clarion call was for assimilation, which gave way to integration in the 1970s, which in turn was replaced by multicultural pluralism in the 1980s, leading to the celebration of difference and diversity under New Labour in the 1990s. Towards the end of the twentieth century, otherness became fashionable and cultural difference became a hot commodity that made Britannia 'cool' and sold multiculturalism at home and Britain abroad. Difference ceased to be threatening; and otherness was now sought for its exchange value, its exoticism and the pleasures, thrills and adventure it could offer. But in both cases, indeed in all cases, the racial dichotomies of Self and Other are retained, along with power relationships of domination and inequality.

In the plethora of labels used to describe the minorities – 'blacks', 'Indians', 'Asians' – there was a general assumption that they had a single, or at least principal and dominant, identity. Submerged underneath these labels, Muslims were generally seen during the 1950s and 1960s as law-abiding, docile folks. It was their colour and ethnicity that were a problem. The first time Britain became aware of Muslims, and Muslims became a cause for concern to wider British society, was during the OPEC oil boycott in the early 1970s. Suddenly all 'Muslims' became 'Arabs', and all 'Arabs' were shifty, dangerous people determined to undermine civilisation as we know it. We can thank European history for such perceptions. Throughout history, Europe, and hence Britain, has seen Muslims as a function of its fears and desires. During the Crusades, Muslims presented Europe with religious, intellectual and military challenges, so they were portrayed as infidels, ignorant and bloodthirsty, the barbarians at the gate of civilisation (which didn't actually exist in Europe!). During the eighteenth and nineteenth centuries, Muslims became treacherous, rebellious subjects of the Empire. In the early part of the last century, Arabs were regarded as oversexed sheikhs ready to whisk white women off to luxurious desert tents, as portrayed by Rudolph Valentino. How Muslims were portrayed depended on the desires and fears that the West projected onto them (Sardar 1999). So, it was hardly surprising that in the aftermath of OPEC and the Iranian revolution, Muslims were regarded as despotic ogres, dangerous revolutionaries and violent, treacherous thugs bent on undermining decency and democracy. However, while British Muslims were seen as inalienably different, they were not seen as dangerous. All this changed after the Rushdie affair. The expression of the outrage at the publication of *The Satanic Verses* suddenly transformed the Muslims from a law-abiding, compliant community into a volatile group with little appreciation of good old British values such as freedom of expression (Sardar and Davies 1990). Just over a decade later, the atrocities of 11 September 2001 introduced a new dimension: Muslims now came to be widely seen as the danger within. So, British Muslim identity not only carries a historical baggage but is also framed by global events. What happens in the rest of the world – like the 'war on terrorism' and the invasion of Iraq – defines and frames the relationship between Muslims and others in Britain and has a direct bearing on how British Muslims are perceived in Britain.

But British Muslims are also problematic in other ways. In a secular society like Britain, where religion is largely marginalised and relegated to private spheres, people find it seriously difficult to see religion as a badge of identity. As Sardar notes in his contribution to this volume (Chapter 1), in secular Britain religion is seen as largely a private affair focused on rituals as a 'reductive relic' and kept to the narrow confines of 'Thought for the Day' and *Songs of Praise* because 'God can be allowed to have a few good tunes'. But religion has no place in public space. And an identity that is specifically based on religion is, by definition, problematic. At the very least, it raises questions of loyalty: if Muslims owe their allegiance to a universal community – the Ummah – what are they first: British or Muslim (Hussain 2004)?

Identity based on religion is particularly problematic when all British notions of identity, as Orwell points out, are expressed in hierarchies of race and class. It is a little too glib to argue that British identity had the luxury of seeing race as external, the definition of difference beyond its shores. But the exercise of power that created an empire on which the sun never set, and a notion of class that defined and shaped modernity and was not a stranger anywhere in the world, are essential attributes of the conventional notion of Britishness. Without it, the British could not be simultaneously xenophobic, internationalist and parochial – the sort of people who go on Spanish holidays to eat fish and chips and drink warm bitter ale. British identity is based on an assumption of authority that makes the world a familiar place, a proper theatre in which to continue being British. It also produced its own internationalist perspective: Britain has had its share of 'old India hands', 'Africa men and women' – urbane cosmopolitans who know Johnny Foreigners better than they know themselves.

The problem with this notion of being British is that Johnny Foreigner is now within. All those other categories through which Britain defined and measured itself – the 'evil Orientals', the 'fanatic Muslims', the 'inferior races of the colonies', the Irish, the immigrants, the refugees, the Gypsies – are now an integral part of Britain. It is not just that they are 'here' but that their ideas, concepts, lifestyles, food, clothes now play a central part in shaping 'us' and 'our society'. How can good ol' Middle England be comfortable with accepting the identity of villains? What happens to conventional notions of Britishness when there is no yardstick to measure difference and define the (white) British as over and above everyone else?

It is not just that 'Britishness' is exclusive and contested to be a source of unity, as Rosemary Sales (2012) suggests in Chapter 2 of this book. The promotion of Britisheness itself has been 'ambivalent and contradictory'. While some attempts have been made to push a progressive and inclusive agenda, Sales argues that the failure to 'address the inequalities and undemocratic aspects of British life' has tied 'Britishness to a version of national identity that privileges certain sections of the population and excludes others'. Orwell would have concurred. Indeed, even the claim that democratic values are uniquely 'British' is 'reminiscent of colonial attitudes in which the "civilized" were distinguished from the uncivilized "other"', writes Sales. Moreover, Britain's foreign adventures in the Middle East, Iraq and Afghanistan – which Orwell would have condemned without hesitation – are seen as 'a highly selective approach to democracy and human rights'. In other words, definitions of democracy and human rights are more a product of political expediency than universal norms Britain embraces and cherishes.

Unique British values are indeed frequently invoked in excluding Muslims from the national equation, and describing them as exclusivists. Which raises a couple of natural questions: besides the much-vaunted democracy, what values does one identify with Britishness? And: what is the British element in the identity equation of British Muslims that would be acceptable to all? The litany about fairness, democracy, justice and decency just would not do – for all cultures accept these as their inherent values. Such values cannot be claimed by any one nationality. They are general human values; they belong to all humanity and occur in all traditions. They can be claimed by Muslims as Islamic values rather than British values. Identified at such a level of abstraction, British values do not bring people together with a sense of something unique, particular and special they share; they do not provide the kind of strong affective bonds of emotional attachment. Orwell provides us with another set of 'common' values: the British 'are inveterate gamblers, drink as much beer as their wages will permit, are devoted to bawdy jokes, and use probably the foulest language in the world'. That too, although correct, is hardly a set of unique national characteristics!

There is in fact nothing about alleged British values – except perhaps those suggested by Orwell – that Muslims do not already subscribe to. This is why the whole notion of isolationist Muslims is such a red herring. As research presented by Lucinda Platt confirms in Chapter 3, Muslims mix with other communities and groups in Britain as easily as everyone else; they share 'with other minorities in increased chances of cross-group friendships and social "mixing"'. Muslims are distinctive, Platt concludes, 'in that they are more likely to have intergroup contacts than the majority population, and they are not distinctive, in that they share this propensity with non-Muslim minorities'. These findings, Platt rightly asserts, 'fly in the face of common claims that Muslims are different, exclusive or isolationist'. It may be surprising for some, but for all their problems, Muslims are human after all. Muslim patterns of social contact are not located in some parallel universe but are based on sociability – the fundamental basis of shared understandings.

Platt's research confirms Sales' analysis. Sales argues that evidence suggests that British Muslims have a strong attachment to 'their local area and to the democratic values that have been claimed as British'. This means that 'there is a strong basis for the building of citizenship, based on democratic values that are widely shared'. But the emergence of a viable notion of citizenship based on a 'shared understanding' requires us to re-examine British history and acknowledge 'the undemocratic elements that have, as much as its progressive achievements, been part of the construction of the British state'.

States rely on myths of 'nationhood' which, as Sales declares, promote 'the dominant group, often marginalising or rendering invisible others who may also occupy the national territory'. The main instrument of building nationhood is history. British identity, whatever values it may aspire to, is ultimately based on the acknowledgement of a common past. Sharing and having been shaped by this common past is what makes the British identity different from all others. The trouble is, history is a deliberate human creation, itself another wilful act of power, artificially constructed to support an artificial identity. The national story on which the notion of Britishness is based deliberately excludes the unsavoury foreigners and is constructed on the basis of selective processes of memory. Europe engineered a cultural identity based on a common descent from the supposed traditions of ancient Greece and Rome and two thousand years of Christianity. British history books always begin with the arrival of the Romans. So, British history begins by submerging, barbarising and differentiating itself from Celtic history. 'Celt' and 'Welsh' are words whose linguistic roots, one Greek, the other Saxon, mean stranger. The history of Britain, as written in the age of devolution, records not a common shared past but continuous contest and conflict within the British Isles. Whatever Britain is, it is the creation of dominance by kings and barons and upwardly mobile yeoman who practised colonialism at home and, after perfecting the technique 'on the playing-fields of Eton', Orwell argues, moved abroad.

It really is quite dumbfounding how much of Britishness, and by association Englishness, is based on fabricated history. Consider the whole notion of Anglo-Saxon Britain. Winston Churchill and Rudyard Kipling were devotees of Anglo-Saxon history for a reason. It enabled them to avoid how genuinely European British history has always been. The Norman kings spent hardly any time in Britain, spoke French rather than English, and were most concerned with dominating Europe from their French possessions. Of course, the 'Saxon' bit of the Anglo-Saxon has its own problems. After the Welsh Tudors and Scots Stuarts, a brief quasi-native interlude, German monarchs were bussed in to reign over Britishness that was to be marked by Englishness alone, and that wanted nothing to do with Europe.

The selectivity of historic memory, promoted in endless television series, is part of its inventiveness. History always seeks ancient roots, the better to justify its innovations. Ancient Anglo-Saxon liberties were purposefully invented on a number of occasions to fashion the British Parliament. This foundational institution was not a true popular democratic institution until 1929, the first election based on universal adult suffrage. The statue of Oliver Cromwell quite properly stands outside Parliament. His insistence that ancient Anglo-Saxon liberties rested on property-owning was the novel twist that secured class hierarchy, made the Restoration of monarchy easy, and enabled manufactured history to continue its work. The pomp and ceremony of the British monarchy was a late Victorian invention. The Royal Family as the model for the normative family, an ideal for a nation, is a post-Edwardian invention, Victoria's son Edward hardly being a suitable candidate for model husband and father. And so it goes on.

Thus, the notions of race and class are intrinsic to the self-definition of the English. Without the idea of race there is little left for English identity to hold on to: only being a disadvantaged minority within Britain, the complete inversion of received history. Not surprisingly, 'the English' feel threatened. But they feel threatened not simply because they see their identity being eroded. What they are more worried about is the evaporation of the power that that identity confers. But an all-powerful identity is like an all-powerful tree in the garden: it sucks the life out of all other plants. When power is skewed in this manner, it is not possible to develop a shared understanding or a viable notion of citizenship.

If Muslims are to feel truly at home in Britain, and at ease with their British identity, then their story must be seen to be an integral part of the national history. Muslims have had a sizeable presence in Britain for centuries and have made valuable contributions in shaping Britain. As Nabil Matar (1998) has shown, the presence of Islam in Britain goes back to the middle of the sixteenth century. The Welsh encounter with Islam, as Grahame Davies's brilliant study (2011) reveals, goes back some 900 years. And as Rahielah Ali and Peter Hopkins point out in Chapter 7 of this book, 'Scotland's relationship with Islam and Muslims extends as far back as the seventh century', although Muslims did not 'become noticeable until well into the nineteenth century and after the Second World War with the increase of labour demands and economic opportunities'. All this history can no longer be ignored; it has to be part of the national history of Britain so that it can become a source of pride for, and generate a sense of belonging among, British Muslims.

But there is more. For over seven hundred years, between the Battle of Tours and the fall of Constantinople, Islam played a vital role in shaping Europe. All of this history, which is crucial in understanding the symbiosis between Islam and Britain, and making Muslims feel at home in Britain, has been rendered invisible. It is during this period that Islam actually transformed Europe and turned it into a world civilisation. The conventional history, defining this period as the Dark Ages, sees the long gestation of embattled Europe forged by the antipathy that sustained the Crusades. Unwittingly, the enemy prompts the rekindling of the flame of civilisation when, phoenix-like, classicism arises from the fall of Constantinople. The warlike intervention by the Turks permits a flood of Greek manuscripts to come to the West. This inspires the Renaissance obsession with all things classical, permits Europe to recover its Greek roots, invent modernity, discover the rest of the world and recover the destiny of world domination implicit in its Roman ancestry. It is, of course, all a fabulous fabrication. In reality, the Renaissance would have been unimaginable without Islam, Greek thought would have remained a stranger to Europe without Muslim philosophers, and even liberal humanism, which we cherish so much in Britain, would have remained a pipe dream without classical Islamic thought and learning (Makdisi 1981). This history is an integral part of British heritage and should be an essential component of our national story.

It is also a history that demonstrates the common origins of Muslim and British values. In Islamic humanism we see the overarching emphasis on universal education and a free health service, science and learning, free thought and pluralism, responsible and accountable governance. These values are difficult to distinguish from British, liberal values – which is hardly surprising, since Britain took them from Islam in the first place (Makdisi 1990)! However, these similarities only become visible when we see Britishness as an open and pluralistic identity, a form of becoming rather than a fixed notion, an amalgam of identities rather than a monolithic one.

A national story that incorporates Islamic history would enable Muslims, particularly young Muslims born and bred in Britain, to appreciate just how much of their – Islamic – values are an integral part of British values. This would be positive way for the coming generations to acquire a viable British Muslim identity. But there is an even bigger dividend to be had from Britain's embrace of its Islamic roots and the acknowledgement by British Muslims that British values are an integral part of Islam. Diasporas have always played a very important part in shaping the Muslim civilisation. The Prophet Muhammad himself migrated from his home town of Mecca; and the civil society and civilisation he built in Medina were fashioned by a diaspora. The classical civilisation of Islam was built not by Arabs but by communities of diasporas from central Asia, the Indian subcontinent and Africa. The Abbasid caliphate, commonly seen as the zenith of Muslim thought and learning, was the outcome of the efforts of a diaspora. The independent Muslim states that emerged in the second half of the twentieth century, such as Pakistan and Malaysia, were often conceived and created in Britain by a politically active diaspora. British Muslims can take a leaf out of this book of history and seize the opportunity to reform Islam and, in the process, change societies in the Muslim world itself.

They are already doing so. As Waqar Ahmad's interviews with British Muslim elites and intellectuals show, British Muslims are writing and articulating contemporary interpretation of Islam, beginning with a re-imagining of mosques as 'community hubs, seats of learning, spaces for dialogue and contestation, and vital bridges to people of faith and no faith' (Chapter 12 of the present book). It may still be a 'distant dream', as Ahmad notes, but it is an essential step in rethinking Islam as a system of ideas for living in the contemporary world. In fact, all his respondents criticise the reduction of Islam to a set of rituals and a list of dos and don'ts, while emphasising the importance of an open and empowering reinterpretation of Islam. The British Muslim elite see Britain as an ideal place for experimentations with reform and 'important provocations' that test 'the limits and pace of acceptable change' within Islam.

Ahmad's analysis makes it clear that British Muslim elites have a vision of an alternative, pluralistic, inclusive and democratic Islam. But this vision is not limited to a select few – 'people in position of influence because of their formal roles, status with civil society, political or representational power, or involvement in professions or governments'. As Nasar Meer shows in Chapter 8 of this book, it can be found throughout the entire spectrum of British Muslim society. There are important internal developments, Meer argues, that suggest 'the fruition of a tangible Muslim consciousness among Muslim communities'. Muslims play with faith-based and sociologically constructed identities, and choose their self-definitions carefully. They have used the specific history of Britain to argue for their own particular positions such as on Islamic schools, they have developed their own specific resources for public representation, and they have mobilised themselves politically to ensure their voice is heard in the corridors of power. The Muslim identities are not a passive or monolithic phenomenon, Meer asserts, but 'contain many social layers that are independent of scriptural texts': across Britain, Muslims can be found participating in political parties, engaging in and promoting ethical models of business, demonstrating commitment to equalities and working with anti-discrimination movements. Every engagement involves a critical appreciation of what it means to be a British Muslim – and a consequent attempt to discover a broader meaning of Islam.

The study of Muslim chaplains in Chapter 4 by Ali and Gilliat-Ray provides us with further examples of how Islam is being reinterpreted. Throughout Britain, Muslim chaplains provide a religious-based service in prisons, hospitals, universities and other institutions. This is both a new profession and a new phenomenon, 'a new and important category of social actor in British public life'. After mosques and Islamic centres, Ali and Gilliat-Ray point out,

> the Ministry of Justice/Prison Service is now probably the largest single employer of Muslim religious professionals in Britain. Over 200 Muslim chaplains work in British prisons on either a full-time or a sessional basis, and within this figure there are 12 women, mainly serving in all-female establishments. Similarly, there has been a substantial increase in the number of Muslim chaplains in the National Health Service (NHS), and the emergence of these opportunities has provided a further avenue for women to take up professional religious roles in public institutions.

Ali and Gilliat-Ray provide a fascinating example of how 'new theological reflection' among Muslim chaplains is leading to a new 'interpretation of Islamic traditions'. Chaplains are often confronted with situations that force them to think and act in new ways. For example, they frequently have to deal with women from within and outside the Muslim community. But 'most schools of Islamic law', write Ali and Gilliat-Ray, 'regard any physical contact between unrelated men and women (even a simple handshake) as sinful, and contrary to the teachings of Islam'. However, this prohibition can pose 'particular challenges in the mixed-gender context of a British prison or hospital, where conventional norms of formal greeting are likely to include shaking hands', and not taking part in the ritual can be seen as 'discriminatory and misogynist', leading to formal disciplinary action. When one chaplain, who had already suffered disciplinary action, pointed out that his understanding of Islamic law did not permit contact with members of the opposite sex, his senior colleague rejected this narrow interpretation of Islamic law:

> He explained that in a public workplace a theology of pluralism should prevail. This is because chaplains at times have to encounter people with many different religious, philosophical and ideological beliefs which may be at odds with their personal worldviews. The more experienced chaplain explained how his own approach, developed over some years, involved a consideration of the different weight and significance of individual sin as against collective sin. He argued that if the newly appointed chaplain deemed shaking hands with the opposite gender as sinful, it would nevertheless only constitute an individual sin. In contrast, if the outcome of not shaking hands was the portrayal of a negative and bigoted picture of Islam, this would become a far more serious collective sin. He suggested that in such circumstances, preference must always be given to maintaining a positive impression of Islam and the avoidance of collective sin, even at the expense of worries about compromising personal piety.

This innovative and eminently sensible interpretation constitutes *ijtihad* – a new understanding of what it means to be a Muslim in a pluralistic society. However, the chaplains themselves refrained from using the term. But Ali and Gilliat-Ray insist that

> Muslim chaplains in Britain are involved in different levels and forms of *ijtihad* as they exercise interpretive effort to translate the principles of Shariah into the practice of chaplaincy. This might sometimes involve new interpretive judgement, as the example concerning handshakes demonstrates; in other cases it might entail the decision to search for alternative Islamic legal opinions on a particular issue, even if that means choosing interpretations derived from a different school of Islamic law. The legal tradition in Islam is far from homogeneous, and this is regarded by some chaplains as an enabling opportunity, not a difficulty.

In a pluralist society, other religious communities can also sometimes be of immense help. Under Islamic law, Muslims are required to bury their dead as soon as possible. Muslims also have an aversion to invasive post-mortems. The Jewish community has similar concerns. So, to address the concerns of both communities the Jewish community has piloted projects in Salford and Rochdale, Greater Manchester, to examine the 'feasibility of non-invasive magnetic resonance imaging (MRI) of the deceased body, instead of invasive pathological post-mortems'. The Bolton Council of Mosques has also been involved, working with the coroner on MRI scanning. 'Using scanners at night', say Ali and Gilliat-Ray, 'when they are less likely to be in use for the living, means that the cause of death can usually be ascertained quickly, and in some cases this can enable burial within the prescribed period.'

Working in a multi-faith, pluralistic society, Ali and Gilliat-Ray conclude, Muslim chaplains are

> forced to think about their faith *reflexively*. They are required to examine how their worldviews and religious truths relate to those of others, as well as to the principles of public life – especially the ideas of egalitarian individualism and the universalism of modern law and morality.

Given the quality of debate on Islamic issues in Britain, it would not be surprising if British Muslims, on the physical periphery of the Muslim world, reform and transform the centre.

But who are these people, undertaking the 'arduous work of hermeneutic self-reflection', who describe themselves as 'British Muslims'? Platt suggests that those who assert their British Muslim identities tend to be 'UK-born minorities attempting to make sense of ongoing minoritization'. But we are dealing with complex, multiple identities, 'often highly localized' in terms both of where Muslims are located in Britain and of 'regional identifications in the parental country of origin'. Louise Ryan, in Chapter 5 of this volume, shows just how important are 'spaces and places' in shaping British Muslim identities. Her respondents have multiple 'homes' and frequently use 'it depends on the area' as a signifier of both their sense of belonging and their identities. She argues that multicultural London is perhaps where young people can best 'express their diverse Muslim identities'.

The 'highly localized sense of belonging' is quite evident if one travels through Britain visiting various Muslim communities. In Scotland and Wales, for example, Muslims appear to feel more at ease than in England. The label 'British' is seldom used in the devolved nations, where Muslims tend to describe themselves as 'Scottish' or 'Welsh' Muslims (Sardar 2008). But what is Scottish about a Scottish Muslim? The answer lies in the fact that Scottish identity is more open and amenable than its English counterpart – something in which Muslims can actively participate and become part of. Scots and Welsh identity harks back to a different history; the Scots and Welsh conceive of identity in broad cultural terms founded on the heritage of different language, poetry and music. And this sense of heritage is defined in opposition to England and ritually performed in sporting encounters and celebrated in the gladiatorial combat these permit, whether they win, lose or draw. In contrast, however, English identity lays claim to all that Britain is, has and has done, with little (in fact, virtually no) acknowledgement of regional participation, and consequently offers few consoling cultural signs and symbols that are open and inclusive. As Orwell notes, when the English speak of the 'the nation' or 'England', they mean Britain! And England's narrative, he asserts, is of dominance, and as such it is about that class which rules the roost and comprises the makers of history. England downplays its own diverse cultural heritages and in consequence seems to lack passionate intensity as well as the capacity to offer an open invitation of inclusion to migrants. Moreover, Muslims tend to see Scottish and Welsh history in terms of their own history: as being persecuted and marginalised. This common bond of a strong sense of marginalistion encourages an equally strong identification with Wales and Scotland.

This is why, as Rahielah Ali and Peter Hopkins argue in Chapter 7, Muslims 'have a strong association with political parties and there are a number of Scottish

Muslims who are heavily involved in formal politics'. Many support the Scottish National Party. This backdrop also encourages women to participate in public life. Ali and Hopkins demonstrate that in Scotland, 'Muslim women are not simply passive and disengaged victims of a patriarchal religion'; rather, they engage 'actively in contributing to their local communities and to political processes while simultaneously responding to their persistent misrepresentation in the media'. The negative representation has led Muslim women 'to reassert themselves within the public sphere and to redefine spaces of civic engagement. In doing so, the participants make it clear that they are empowered in identifying as Muslim women in Scotland.' Muslim women develop social and political agency and collaborate with non-Muslim and Muslim communities in Scotland, 'with the specific aim of improving perceptions about Muslims and diminishing negative media stereotypes, becoming proactive both by challenging public discourse and stereotypes, and through the ongoing construction of reflective spaces of civic engagement'. Their 'everyday making', assert Ali and Hopkins, 'constitutes an important set of engagements with political processes in their local communities and in the Scottish polity more broadly'.

It is within the multicultural spaces and places in Britain that Muslims feel more at home. Ryan's interviewee Sofia provides us with a good example of young Muslims who are at ease with their plurality and multiple identities. Sofia uses the term 'home' to apply to London, Britain and Somalia. But her notion of 'home' is both complex and ambivalent. London may be home, but not all parts of the city are equally so regarded; Sofia finds some parts of London more welcoming than others; and some difficult and uncomfortable. This suggests, Ryan argues, that 'racism is experienced in specific places rather than being a general experience'. Space is not 'an innocent backdrop to position, but rather is filled with politics and ideology'. When faced with negative experience, young Muslims tend to explain them in 'terms of an ignorant minority who are contained within specific pockets of the city', while the city as a whole remains 'a place of possibilities, an imaginary space where belonging can be negotiated and proclaimed'.

Moreover, 'religious identity', argues Ryan, 'may give these young people a space within which to reflect upon and critique specific ethnic cultural practices. For young women, in particular, Islam provides a lens through which to challenge practices such as forced marriages.' The knowledge of 'real Islam', based on their own studies of the Qur'ān, 'enables them to question the authority of the older generation'. The complex web of identities and the interconnections between local and global are 'often articulated in terms of visits to the country of origin. Here their religious identity, far from denoting belonging, may have heightened the young people's sense of being "out of place"'. Hence, Ryan concludes, 'Muslimness is simultaneously boundless and grounded, universal but also particular, transcendent as well as situated'.

The work of Ryan, Platt, Sales, Ahmad and Ali and Hopkins suggests that British Muslims are discovering that while identity has historic anchors, it is not fixed to a limited, unchanging set of traditional signs and historic symbols. Both 'Muslim' and

'British' segments of 'British Muslims' are a changing feast. And, Britain itself is a product of various, diverse and changing traditions – including the centuries-old tradition of British Islam. A British Muslim identity is not something we can buy ready-made, or something that can be imposed on an unwilling community. It has even less to do with loyalty tests – such as Norman Tebbit's cricket test – based on mindless jingoism, which, according to Orwell, is minority stuff: 'all the boasting and flag-wagging, the "Rule Britannia" stuff', has little to do with the 'patriotism of the common people'. Ordinary Muslims may or may not wave flags, or cheer England's cricket team as it beats Australia to win the Ashes, but these acts do not confirm a British Muslim identity. Rather, it is something that evolves from confidence and symbiosis. It is something from which Muslims learn to change and stay the same, to be true simultaneously to their Islamic roots and British lives, learn how to live and shape their communities, and discover what has genuine value in a pluralistic, multicultural society.

So where does this leave the assertion that multiculturalism is the root of all contemporary problems in Britain? Or, as David Cameron put it, the 'doctrine' of 'state multiculturalism' has 'encouraged different cultures to live separate lives', produced behaviours that 'run completely counter to our values' and allowed Islamic militants to promote 'extreme ideologies' and radicalise young Muslims. As Sale makes so clear, 'the specific policies deemed to have led to this result have rarely been identified or examined, and critics have often relied on anecdotal, sometimes fictitious, evidence. In reality, multicultural policies have never been implemented systematically in Britain.' Even when New Labour championed multiculturalism, it was little more than rhetoric. Visible signs of difference may be celebrated but deep, structural inequalities, despite a plethora of anti-discrimination legislation, remain as intact as they were during the days of Orwell. On the whole, multicultural policies in Britain, as Heidi Safia Mirza points out in Chapter 6, have been piecemeal, based on concessions, extensions and exemptions such as scheduling exams to avoid key festivals for religious groups, or Sikhs being exempt from wearing helmets, or slaughterhouses for Jews and Muslims. But 'inclusive multiculturalism in the British context has been deeply racialized' and 'in its many shifting manifestations, including the most recent form, community cohesion, has consistently functioned to privilege "race" and ethnicity, and now religion, over gender'. In particular, Mirza asserts that multiculturalism has been 'gender-blind' and has failed to 'recognize the gendered power divisions within ethnic groups dealing with problems *between* communities, and turns a blind eye to problems *within* communities'. She writes:

> In the face of growing racist political rhetoric, Islamophobia and anti-asylum and immigration policies in Britain, we are witnessing a retreat from multiculturalism and a move towards civic integration. In a multicultural 'post-nation', integration and active citizenship are now seen as the solution to economic inequality, political under-representation and structural segregation in housing and education in the ethnic enclaves that serve our cities.

That 'active citizenship' is actively promoted by Muslims, men and women alike, is all too evident from the work of Sales, Platt and Ryan. Integration may be the new panacea, but that does not mean that we should write off multiculturalism. Indeed, most gains made by Muslim communities over the past few decades have largely been due to (negotiated) multicultural policies. Multiculturalism has actually reduced the isolation of Muslims and increased their integration. As Ludi Simpson has shown so consistently, separation, measured commonly as the Index of Dissimilarity, has been decreasing slowly in recent decades for every ethnic group – including the Muslims (Simpson 2004; Simpson *et al.* 2008). Where separation still exists, it is a product not of multiculturalism but of bigotry. Oldham provides a good example. This Greater Manchester town is frequently cited as a citadel of separation, with the Pakistani, Bangladeshi and white communities existing in splendid isolation. But it is not the Pakistani and Bangladeshi Muslims who are refusing to integrate; it is the white community. Indeed, the white communities are the most separated in Britain, in the sense of living in areas with themselves – most notably in Middle England, the land of *Midsomer Murders*, 'the last bastion of Englishness'. Integration is not a one-way process; it involves at least two sides. One cannot insist that Muslims should 'integrate' while the white communities refuse to do so. Integration involves a mutual process of transformation by all communities. Where the white communities have embraced pluralism, as Ryan demonstrates about London, integration is a lived reality.

There are, of course, numerous hurdles to Muslim integration. Some emerge from lack of economic opportunities, some are to do with disadvantages in housing and education, some are based on historic patterns of immigration, some are related to religious and cultural needs such as locations of mosques and cultural centres, some are related to tribal issues such as *biradri* which force certain groups in places like Bradford to coagulate, and some are a product of old-fashioned racism. But none of these can be placed at the door of multiculturalism.

The fears of secularists mentioned by Mirza notwithstanding, the introduction of religion in the multicultural mix, and equality legislation, has been good for the Muslim community. It has brought Muslims' concerns to the forefront, and provided an instrument for tackling Islamophobia. Moreover, there is nothing in multiculturalism which suggests that 'respect for difference' procures, as Cameron puts it, a 'hands-off tolerance' that permits 'unacceptable views or practices'; or, as Mirza suggests, leads to 'patriarchy and gendered oppressive practices'. These practices were there before multiculturalism became a 'state policy'; so blaming multiculturalism, as Cameron does, for the failure 'to confront the horrors of forced marriage, the practice where some young girls are bullied and sometimes taken abroad to marry someone when they don't want to', and other equally obnoxious practices such as honour killings, genital mutilation or polygamy among Muslims, is disingenuous. Furthermore, multiculturalism does not exist in isolation from such concerns as human rights and gender equality (Parekh 2005). Rather, it promotes them. The very fact that laws exist against such practices is largely due to multiculturalism; and these laws were introduced when 'state multiculturalism' was a state policy.

There is another point worth noting here. Multiculturalism does not suggest that we are total prisoners of our culture. Cultures evolve and change; traditions reinvent themselves. Obnoxious practices exist in all cultures – but this does not mean that these practices cannot be overcome and transcended. The function of multiculturalism is to provide spaces for cultures to transcend their unsavoury practices, and change for the better. This is precisely what the Muslim women in Scotland described by Ali and Hopkins are doing!

This brings us to one of the most common charges, laid from both the left and the right, against multiculturalism: it promotes radicalisation among Muslim youth. But if so, why do we find similar radicalisation among Muslim youth in, say, the United States and the Netherlands, where 'state multiculturalism' is conspicuous by its total absence? One can confidently say that multiculturalism in any form has not touched France, yet Muslim youth in France are as radicalised as in Britain. Logic would suggest that it is not multiculturalism but another common thread that is promoting radicalisation.

That common thread was clearly identified by Orwell: the 'hypocrisy of Empire', by which Orwell meant ignoring the havoc caused by colonialism and the perpetuation of this hypocrisy in British foreign policy. The devastation that British foreign policy has caused in the Muslim world during the first decade of the twenty-first century is worth noting. We invaded Iraq, where an estimated million innocent civilians have been killed. We invaded Afghanistan, handed it to the corrupting grasp of contending warlords, and reduced the already appalling living conditions of the mass of the population to biblical levels. We have connived in 'extraordinary rendition' and torture of Muslims. We have propped up dictatorships and authoritarian regimes throughout the Muslim world. Our weapons have been used to kill and maim peaceful demonstrators. Isn't this enough reason for young Muslims to be seriously upset and lead them towards radicalisation?

To suggest that multiculturalism, whose main value, according to *The Future of Multi-ethnic Britain* (Runnymede Trust 2000), the Parekh Report that started the whole debate, is to 'treat people with due respect for difference', does not promote British values is dumbfounding. To suggest that a vision of society that promotes pluralism and dignity for all is responsible for radicalisation of dissatisfied and alienated youth is akin to suggesting that Conservative Party philosophy is responsible for the outlook and behaviour of the National Front.

'An illusion can become a half-truth, a mask can alter the expression of a face', says Orwell. The constant illusions to multiculturalism as the source of all the major problems of British society is a mask that hides what Orwell sees as the true face of Britain. The country, he says, is 'notoriously two nations, the rich and the poor' – a division as evident nowadays as in Orwell's time, still sustained by race and class to such an extent that we imagine 'the whole population dwelt in London and the Home Counties and neither north or west possessed a culture of its own'. The ultimate goal of multiculturalism, the reason why it has been a target of constant criticism, is to undermine the privileges of race and class and allow cultural plurality of Britain – 'the most class-ridden country under the sun', according to

Orwell – to come to the fore. Its main target is the very 'muscular liberalism' that critics of multiculturalism defend and seek to perpetuate. Multiculturalism exists to challenge liberalism's power to define what it is to be human, different, free, rational or ethnic, what is valuable, worthwhile, successful and proper. Multiculturalism categorically rejects the pathologically arrogant assumption that there is only one – liberal – way to be human. It is all about other, different ways to be human. It insists on seeing good in other cultures and their enduring values; and is a necessary quest not just for any self-respecting society, but for human social evolution itself.

'Policies that could be described as multicultural', notes Sales, 'have generally arisen from local initiatives and been piecemeal rather than comprehensive, often an accommodation to the claims of local groups organized along ethnic lines.' But these multicultural initiatives have not been simply about giving voice to a faith community like the Muslims; they are also about understanding the core role of faith in identity, understanding what we need to give and what we need to take to grow and prosper together. That understanding must begin by appreciating that people are more than a racial category. It's the more that makes us a fully cultured personality and gives us something distinctive to offer – different ways of seeing things, expressing ideas, responding to issues.

As this anthology demonstrates, Muslims are articulating what makes them British in innovative and creative ways. Of course there are a few extremists within the community. There are some who see themselves purely in terms of victimhood. But the majority, who must be the focus of our attention, are taking responsibility for themselves, participating fully in and making their mark on every aspect of British life, changing themselves and their outlook on Islam in the process, and making themselves more comprehensible and better understood to their fellow citizens. What more could one ask of a minority community?

What would Orwell have thought of veiled women in Bradford, weird and wonderful mosques dotted around Britain, and the screaming *Daily Mail* headline: 'Mohammed has become the most popular name for newborn boys in Britain'? We can only imagine. But we can be sure that Orwell did not think much of the *Daily Mail*'s 'England'. There are, however, some 'English traits' he approved of. A 'minor trait which is extremely well marked though not often commented on', and is 'one of the first things that one notices when one reaches England', is 'a love of flowers'. Another trait you notice 'the instant you set foot on English soil' is 'the gentleness of the English civilization'. We love to queue, don't mind if we are shoved off the pavement, and the 'power-worship' that has 'infected the English intelligentsia' has 'never touched the common people'. Our democracy may be corrupt, our electoral system 'all but open fraud' that is 'gerrymandered in the interest of the monied class', but we can rest assured that 'it cannot become *completely* corrupt'. Then there is an 'all-important' trait: 'the respect for constitutionalism and legality', the belief in 'the law' as 'something above the State and above the individual'. That's the closest Britain gets to a 'world-view', says Orwell. This is a worldview that most Muslims will readily embrace.

References

Brown, G. (2004) Annual British Council Lecture, reprinted in the *Guardian* (London), 8 July.

Cameron, D. (2011) PM's speech at Munich Security Conference. Online, available at: www.number10.gov.uk/news/speeches-and-transcripts/2011/02/pms-speech-at-munich-security-conference-60293.

Davies, G. (2011) *The Dragon and the Crescent: Nine Centuries of Welsh Contact with Islam*, Bridgend: Seren.

Goodhart, D. (2004) 'Discomfort of strangers', *Guardian* (London), 24 February.

Hussain, D. (2004) 'British Muslim identity', in M. S. Seddon, D. Hussain and N. Malik (eds) *British Muslims between Assimilation and Segregation*, Leicester: Islamic Foundation.

Makdisi, G. (1981) *The Rise of Colleges: Institutions of Learning in Islam and the West*, Edinburgh: Edinburgh University Press.

Makdisi, G. (1990) *The Rise of Humanism in Classical Islam and the Christian West*, Edinburgh: Edinburgh University Press.

Matar, N. (1998) *Islam in Britain, 1558–1685*, Cambridge: Cambridge University Press.

Orwell, G. (1941) *England, Your England and Other Essays*, Stuttgart: Reclam. Online, available at: http://orwell.ru/library/essays/lion/english/e_eye.

Parekh, B. (2005) *Rethinking Multiculturalism: Cultural Diversity and Political Theory*, Basingstoke: Palgrave Macmillan.

Runnymede Trust (2000) *The Parekh Report: The Future of Multi-ethnic Britain*, London: Profile Books.

Sardar, Z. (1999) *Orientalism*, Buckingham: Open University Press.

Sardar, Z. (2008) *Balti Britain: A Provocative Journey through Asian Britain*, London: Granta.

Sardar, Z. and Davies, M. W. (1990) *Distorted Imagination: Lessons from the Rushdie Affair*, London: Grey Seal.

Simpson, L. (2004) 'Statistics of racial segregation: measures, evidence and policy', *Urban Studies* 41 (3): 661–681.

Simpson, L., Gavalas, V. and Finney, N. (2008) 'Population dynamics in ethnically diverse towns: the long-term implications of immigration', *Urban Studies* 45 (1): 160–183.

1

RELIGION AND PUBLIC SPACE

Ziauddin Sardar

Introduction

That religion has been marginalised in Britain's public space, reduced to a muffled whisper if not exactly a dying whimper, we can take for granted (Hosen and Mohr 2011). It is not just that there is an absence of moderate Muslim voices in public discourse. Rather, Muslims are part of a more general collective failure by all religious communities. People of all faiths – Christians, Jews, Muslims, Hindus – have failed to raise their voices on crucial issues of ethics and morality, society and international relations, and to talk and educate the great British public sufficiently or appropriately on the meaning of faith. The void thus created is only too evident. As the entire world was seduced by the ethics of 'greed is good', where was the religious duty of care? Did faith communities in Britain raise their voices about conspicuous wealth or the need to purify wealth by delivery of social justice and real resources to the poor? As the globalised economy reaps what has been sown, and cuts to social services begin to overwhelmingly affect the poor, and bonuses for bankers reach an obscene level, where are religious voices demanding that the first priority is the option for the poor and detailing what in conscience must be done to protect those in dire straits? The only religious voices we hear are the voices of extremism: Muslim cults shouting inhuman slogans, Christian groups refusing vaccination, messianic Muslims and Christians proclaiming the end of time!

But my concern is with the mainstream, not extremism. I believe the most secure route to eradication of the seduction of the extreme is ministering to the God-shaped void in the daily lives of the mass of the population. The task is to become relevant to the issues, concerns and circumstances of the society in which we coexist, asserting the need for an acknowledged role for faith, whatever that faith may be, in the public life of our society. This challenge raises its own questions. Some of these questions – should we celebrate diversity, or are matters of truth at stake? Can we maintain our love of freedom, while cutting it off from religious roots? Should all religions be equally welcomed in the public sphere? – have been ably raised by Roger Trigg (2008). We could raise others. What part in the activity of the faithful, or even the mildly interested, should religion take in public life? What does society gain, what has society lost by the retreat of religion from public life? What can and should religion contribute to the life of society? Are the religious a reliable, safe pair of hands to be entrusted with a role in public life? In what ways can and should the religious and various faith communities contribute to public life in Britain? Of course, we also have to confront the elephant in the room. How can religion occupy a place in the public space of a multi-faith and genuinely multicultural society? These are urgent questions for religious communities to address.

The need for religious voices

We live in a time when our social fabric is unravelling and unprepared to confront the hardships that await us, a particular period in history that I have elsewhere characterised as 'postnormal times' (Sardar 2010). Generations have grown up knowing only ever-expanding material horizons. These generations have been abandoned to the untender mercilessness of a system of values that equates human worth with what material goods we have and display. We live in a consumer culture where personal identity is shaped by the advertising glitz that gives a lifestyle profile to the brand names of the products, goods and services one selects and owns. The xyz alphabet of the me generations must now face hard choices not only of economic recession but of saving the planet from our history of extravagance, finding solutions for the obscenity of entrenched national and global poverty and inequality that blights the lives and confounds the hopes and opportunities of billions at home as well as abroad. Then there is an abundance of moral and ethical conundrums we have accumulated through the exponential growth in our knowledge and ability to manipulate the processes of the life of humans, animals, plants and the very substance of our planet. With knowledge, we have amassed accompanying ignorance, not least of how to reason in conscience with the difference between what can be done and what should or ought to be done, and whether our power to know and to do is applied for true betterment of the human condition or contributes to debasing our humane capacities and indeed could even end by making us less human. It is not merely nurturing the development of and concern for conscience that is the proper duty of religion. Religions are in many ways the last bastions of the language and terms in which to reason with and think through the dilemmas that become ever more common in our daily lives. What do generations bred to endless possibilities know of sacrifice, endurance, acceptance, self-denial, duty of care and prudential considerations? These are religious issues. It is the responsibility of religious communities to make positive contributions to sustainable humanity so that those who have no religious formation are not conned by the ethos of the marketplace or left with the erroneous impression that all we have to offer them are joyless 'thou shalt nots'. Faith communities cannot leave unchallenged the dominant philosophy of our time that all life amounts to is individual and personal satisfaction, the fulfilment of self. Rather, they have to offer alternatives to all whose journeys of personal indulgence leave them asking, 'Is that all there is?'

Before considering the complex challenges, let me begin with some commonplace details. According to all measures, British society still considers this to be a Christian country. True, church attendance has been in long, gradual decline. Yet a majority of British people consider themselves Christian irrespective of whether they participate in formal organised acts of worship or not. Of the 92 per cent of British people who answered the voluntary religious affiliation question on the 2001 census (Office of National Statistics 2001), nearly three-quarters (72 per cent) declared themselves to be Christian, as opposed to 16 per cent who stated that they had no religion. The 'no religion' category included atheists, agnostics, heathens and self-proclaimed Jedi. And I would make the point that the general presumption that minority non-Christian religions fare better in maintaining the affiliation, attendance and practice of their adherents is a generosity too far. The truth requires unpicking of the distinction between cultural identity, faithful practice and informed, educated participation in the fellowship of an interpretive community. The distinction is a complicated manoeuvre, but one which would reveal a situation comparable to that among the generality of the Christian population. There are numbers of what might be termed latent Muslims, Hindus or Buddhists comparable to the numbers of latent, or should that be residual, Christians. The extremist voices do not represent, and can never speak for, this silent majority.

The point, however, is that the figures for self-identification with religion endure while the public acknowledgement of religion is becoming further and further marginalised. When I was a lad, the Sunday morning television programmes for Asians – all geared to encouraging us, especially women, to learn English – were always followed by a televised act of Christian worship, which I understand was allocated proportionally among the various denominations over the course of each year. The *Radio Times* reserved two front covers per year, one of which was invariably at Easter, for religious imagery and plugging religious programmes. Radio 4 broadcast a daily act of worship to all permutations of bandwidths or frequencies and audiences. According to the original charter of the BBC, there were only three persons who had to be employed by the corporation and one of them was the head of religious programmes! Good Friday saw a reserved place for a televised act of observance between noon and 3 p.m. Christmas stamps used to reflect the nativity story, rather than Santa appearing to poo down a chimney. Television schedules gave prominence on Christmas Day itself to acts of worship and a number of programmes with explicit religious themes. These are just a few of the signs and symbols whose disappearance represents the retreat of religious observance from the public space. They are harbingers and consequences of a general shift in the temper of society.

Radical secularism

The process that gradually but inexorably has carried religious observance to the margins is a product of radical secularisation (Asad 2003). A great deal of the spiritual, over the course of centuries, was transferred to temporal control without noticeable effect on public acknowledgement of the importance of organised religion. But for some time now we have passed the point of critical mass. Secularisation has become synonymous with something quite distinct: secularism. Secularism is an organised philosophy even when not an outright ideology. It has claimed the centre ground because it has persuaded many of its superior ability to serve the real needs of society. Allegedly, it is the neutral, dispassionate and disinterested outlook that alone is capable of maintaining a peaceful conversation between all the competing voices, factions, interest groups, ideas and ideologies contending in the public space of an increasingly complex and heterogeneous society. What fits secularism for a dominant role is its trademark: doubt, perpetual doubt that debunks, overturns and interrogates all grand narratives claiming to explain the human condition. The clear implication of secularism is that conviction, convincement of almost any kind, is the product of a closed, unreasoning and potentially irrational, not to say fanatical, mind and hence by implication bad and most certainly a limited and inferior outlook. As a consequence, priests and bishops prefer to remain silent rather than speak out against gross inequalities in society. Mosques cannot look like real mosques; they have to look like opera houses or warehouses to be acceptable to the secular tendency. Faith communities, it is assumed, have nothing to say about the great economic, social or political issues of our time.

All this has led to a severe God problem in society. God has become the great unmentionable. For the faithful, God is an absolute reality, whether found through mystery and clouds of unknowing or revealed in lucid clarity. This defies the uncertainty principle that is the essential feature of secularism. Religion in any and all its manifestations can be only a subject for scrutiny, interrogation and tests of justification and legitimacy – never simple affirmation or mere acceptance. Under such a dispensation, religion is best understood and treated as a quaint personal and private predilection. Its claims on the public space are at best traditional, purely ornamental and ceremonial, getting a polite indulgence on the margins for a few high days and holidays but not given routine prominence, the kind of educative exposure that would unduly impact on popular consciousness. So, the television programme *Songs of Praise* endures, because God can be allowed to have a few good tunes. But 'Thought for the Day', on the BBC's radio programme *Today*, is much too much for the secular lobby: a slot for only religious views is supposed to be a dark blot on secular Britain. The fact that almost all other slots are devoted to secularism is, of course, neither here nor there. On the whole, religious programming becomes comfy sofa magazine shows of unbearable niceness and a complete absence of anything challenging or argumentative, let alone disturbing to the conscience of the times, and virtually never mentioning God. Alternatively, it may appear in investigative trawls through the perverse and perversions advanced in the name of religion by the extremes. The perception grows in society that true and authentic expression of religion is to be found among the extremists, making the plaintive whimpers of the mainstream ever harder to hear and more subject to equivocation and outright incomprehension.

The result is not only an absence of religion in the public space but also the growth of a profound religious illiteracy (Moore 2007) that spreads like a virus through society. Fewer and fewer people become acquainted with what religion actually says and does. Religious education by the faithful is something children must be shielded from because it is tantamount to brainwashing, a foreclosure of choice – though how one learns anything without education is a question best not asked. Do not classical musicians start their training at a tender age? And, one is forced to ask, why education in the doubt of secularism, or its curriculum surrogate comparative religion, is not merely another form of indoctrination that prejudices the capacity for belief and commitment is again a question that dares not state its case. We exist in a climate where all religions must struggle against the tide of inquisition which usually focuses on monumentally irrelevant questions and misses the salient points of what genuinely matters to people of faith. Self-description, self-portrayal by the faithful becomes more and more difficult, further compounding the rise of general religious illiteracy. We end with a situation where those who do not believe assume the right to define what is authentic in religion and therefore who and what is typical, representative of religious belief and believers. While this is an acute problem for minority non-Christian religions – and I speak as one of the most sorely afflicted – it is by no means exclusive to us. I would suggest it now affects what passes for common knowledge of Christianity itself.

Society has accumulated both a distorted and a reductive idea of what constitutes religion, any religion. It has only a minimal understanding of the beliefs, practice and contemporary interpretations of any and all religions. And all religions are best known through their least appealing historic failures. Religion has gone beyond being what believers say and do in the name of religion, the sociological reformulation of the comparative religion explanation. It has become identified by the very worst that believers have ever done to themselves and others in history. That is why it is little wonder that religion is not exactly welcome in the public space – for none of us, or only the most select few, can claim to be without taint, to be entirely innocent of grievous faults, always to have lived up to our best calling either in the practice of our own faith or in relations with those of other faiths.

Reductive perceptions of religion

The generalities of the conception of religion, any religion, at large in Britain today present us with a bleak and depressing picture. Before we can consider what is to be done, we need to take stock of what is left of the presence of religion in the public space. The reductive redoubt falls into two categories: religion is ritual; and religion on its best behaviour is about niceness, a vague, non-specific, woolly sense of some sorts of moral and ethical parameters.

Ritual is the most obvious relic of religion and not surprisingly has come to be seen not only as what religion is about but as the prism through which it is best understood. Ritual observance is about high days and holidays and the rites of passage of human existence: the occasions marking birth, marriage and death. Individually, this is how people make the significance of major events in their lives memorable, utilising the facility of formal religion as an integral part of the opportunity for 'a bit of a do'. I am not one of those who spurn this kind of encounter. I would argue that it can be one of the few occasions when religious outreach is possible. And there is another face of such ritualised religious observance in Britain that we ought to think about. The grand state occasions, which integrate or revolve around acts of religious observance, have become increasingly important in the bleak landscape we face. I think of things like the funeral of the late Queen Mother – vicariously the memorialising and laying to rest we would all like to give to a beloved grandmother, and expressed through the solemnity of religion, where we hear the words that signify what belief is about, even if we do not necessarily grasp the fullness of their meaning. Ritual is not redundant; ritual is important as an occasion for collective shared meaning if we can learn how to use it constructively. I remember, for example, being in Malaysia at the time of the Dunblane school atrocity, when a gunman shot and killed children in their primary school. I was deeply impressed and moved to find that BBC World Service television broadcast the entirety of a church service from Dunblane. One could pick out other such instances. True, we can complain that such instances are reductive; religion is not solely about celebration or consolation. However, both are significant starting points, points of entry to public consciousness. If state occasions and public memorials are the only time we get to acknowledge the existence of something beyond the material, so be it. Our challenge is how we find a way to go further.

If religion as ritual is a reductive relic, the growth of the presentation of religion as niceness is what I would term a disaster. It is little more than a placebo for a society that no longer either understands what religion is or knows how to cope with what religion should or ought to be. All those dread magazine programmes which are about the nice things religious people do but run a mile from engaging with why, what these actions signify and how they have meaning and implications for the whole of one's outlook on life, the universe and everything are a sad reflection of what vestigial religion has become. On the one hand, it suggests that religion pertains to morality in the broadest sense without ever seriously engaging with why or how such moral behaviour derives from or relates to religion. And, of course, niceness precludes the asking of any kind of tough questions to disturb the composure of the religious, the latently religious or the openly non-religious.

Religion as moral reflection is the 'Thought for the Day' factor. It is the fiendish challenge to be engaging, personable, relevant, pithy and profound in less than four minutes. The considerable constraints of the medium mean a general acceptance that mention of God is, by and large, a switch-off for the audience. The thought that occurs to me is that while this vestigial and truncated nod in the direction of religion testifies to a thirst for moral consideration, what is actually offered to the audience is morality without context. For people of faith, moral reflection is rooted in its only proper context, the belief that we are all answerable to a power far beyond the human. For the religious, it is God consciousness alone that makes moral imperatives important in our individual and social life. Being witty and wise, a good raconteur, may make the population think more kindly of the religious on a daily basis. It does not amount to a bridgehead for spreading education and understanding of the content and meaning of any particular faith. The rotation of multi-faith voices which is now the order of the day makes its contribution to the identikit interchangeable world religion gloss that is little different from the New Age, eclectic, make-your-own religion for your own personal world philosophy. The message gets us little further than the proposition: be nice and be good if you can, should circumstances permit. Most of the thoughts I hear on such daily outings leave me with an enduring feeling of sadness and remorse, however wise and apposite their content.

I would suggest that this prevalence of niceness is a feature of another problem, the real dilemma we need to consider. The placebo effect is a function of what society considers the intractable problems of how to placate the greatest number in what is now a multi-faith rather than just a multi-denominational society. It is that very British response of being polite. It seeks out the lowest common denominator by which everyone seems to have some mention while leaving all the big issues determinedly ignored. I happened upon an instance recently which illustrates the point. On a Sunday morning magazine programme I watched a film report in which one nice white English family was dispatched to spend one day sharing the Ramadan fast with an equally nice Muslim family. The two families clearly had never met before; a certain reticence and stiffness was evident all round. Other than the fact that Muslims do not eat during the fast – though even the exact specifics of this rather significant element managed to be glossed over – we learned little apart from the fact that the children of the white family did not fancy the idea much. Virtually nothing of what it means to fast – not, I agree, a very visual subject – was included. And no sooner had they arrived than the white family departed laden with packages of cooked food. What that has to do with fasting was not explained either. This, I am sure, is what the producers of the programme considered to be doing their bit for cross-cultural understanding: let niceness prevail and we will somehow muddle through. But niceness will just not do.

It seems to me we are toying with the thin edge of the wedge that is the American solution. In a country awash with religion, Americans have a public space where all religions can participate and be noticed – within caveats and reason – but only on the basis of being minimised (Beal 2008). So, one can publicly wish people 'happy holidays' but for goodness sake don't mention Christmas. Thus, the entire basis from which Christianity derives can be privately understood and represented in the public space only in the secularised form of a mass excuse for questionable un-Christian consumer excess. American houses are dressed up, illuminated with Santas, reindeer, snowmen, helpful elves and even the occasional angel, doing who knows what damage to the global environment, all for the sake of a religious celebration. Meanwhile, people dedicated to secularism under the guise of the separation of church and state determine that display of nativity scenes in public spaces will cause offence to non-Christians and should not be permitted. It is not only a Martian who would find it impossible to understand what's going on. Put me down as totally befuddled! The cultural influence of the United States is such that similar lunacy is on the rise in Britain.

Offending others

And so, at last we need to consider the elephant question. Is it really the case that Muslims, Hindus or Sikhs are or would be affronted by public display of nativity scenes? Or indeed, would they be offended by more robust and abundant public reference to and acknowledgement of Christian worship and observance? My assessment, from all I know and have experienced, is that they certainly would not. It would be taken as an encouraging sign by minorities that religion matters, and would invariably lead to pleas for 'me too' – and that is the elephant we need to hunt down. What afflicts religion in the public space in Britain begins with what afflicts Christianity in a Christian country. The dilemmas of the public space have not been created by the arrival of non-Christian faiths; that is an excuse, a rationalisation after the fact. But while Christianity is in retreat in the public space, there is no hope that the question of how the public space can or should be made available to minorities, to non-Christian faiths, will be sensibly discussed, let alone resolved. All faiths, therefore, face a common shared dilemma. For the public space is important in establishing balance, setting benchmarks that affect the teaching of what religion is, what it requires and, most importantly, what it neither requires nor permits among its followers. The public space is vital for the self-representation of religions to ensure that there can be informed public debate about how we construct an equitable, just and honourable mutually respectful society that is good for welcomes and includes the best contributions of all its citizens. I would argue that we all have a great deal to gain from mutual support in finding answers to problems that already do and will continue to affect us all, though perhaps in different ways.

Let me briefly explain why the arrival of non-Christian faiths is not basic to the problem. The popular image of the inability of various religions to get along with one another does not start, as a lived experience here in Britain, with Christian–Muslim relations, though the history of Christian–Jewish relations is a different matter; it does not begin with Christian–Hindu or Christian–Sikh or Christian–Buddhist relations. In honesty we have to recognise it begins within Christianity itself. Intolerance, religious wars and persecution are internal to the history of the Christian religion in Britain. The question of tolerance, mutual tolerance among Christian denominations, is a long struggle not entirely ended. We all have a great deal to learn from that history: first, how not to repeat it ever again; and second, how to extract from it constructive elements that can create a route map to a genuinely tolerant society where faith is mutually understood and mutually respected, and where religions are collectively strengthened to portray themselves in their own terms and take on an active role in public life.

Tolerance is a virtue, but it is far from easy. True tolerance is not merely being nice; it is making the difficult choice to respect and give access to beliefs and practices you are sincerely convinced should not exist. If indeed the religious can achieve this task, they can truly lead the way for the rest of society. What I am seeking is not an abrogation of the identity and distinctiveness of each religion, not a mélange, the 'all religions are the same' option – clearly they are not. What I am seeking, and hoping can come to pass, is something much more taxing, but ultimately rewarding. I want to consider the possibility that we transcend not our distinctions but our faulty understanding and application of exclusivity. If religions can overcome this propensity and envision an inclusive public space of informed respectful mutual coexistence, I believe they can lay the groundwork for what I call transmodernity.

So what is the job the religious should set as their prime target? Simply put, and with such profound complexity as the idea of 'simple faith', the return of a respect for sacredness as the underpinning of social values. And the commitment to social values as the necessity for ensuring human dignity, social justice, equity and the opportunity for all to fulfil their God-given talents and be included in the project of bettering the condition of our society and the whole world for all people. The betterment I seek can only be found through efforts to build sustainable peace and mutual tolerance. It is the task of religious communities to explain how God consciousness is what I would term the secure handhold that should lead us on this path and help us to make better choices, to assess and make judgements about how we are progressing in the right direction or not. It is no small task. But it is quintessentially *the* religious task. What we share, in all our diversity, is the common sense of our createdness. We are not merely sentient beings in charge of our own destiny. We are agents of a Creator, beholden to the source from which we receive the great gift of life, beholden for how we use our endowments and talents, beholden for how we exercise the responsibilities of the freedom of our existence, beholden for how we treat all others who are equally created beings, beholden for how we make use of the material world into which we are born, beholden and answerable beyond this life and this world for all our actions in this life. For people of faith, all things are not relative, not endlessly open to the dictates of circumstance or human fads and fancy. The questions of life, about how we live, individually and collectively, are questions of choice and accountability to be weighed and reasoned with on scales of judgement: good, better, best as compared with bad, worse and worst, selecting as best we are able the options that promote and sustain human betterment for all and the earth we share. This is the meaning of religion.

The substance of agreement that unites religious communities is considerable. However, these basic propositions come to us through diverse histories, different founding texts and different traditions of human interpretation, both within and between different religions. We have different terminology and ways of saying what we mean on the same subject. Moreover, shared values come in different guises, analogous yet often so differently expressed, differently structured and bound into different cultural systems that the commonalities are not immediately obvious. And culture is not the meaning of religion, only its flawed man-made vessel, so culture can become a byword for distorting religion into customs and practices that in effect countermand the teachings of religion and the delivery of religious values. Not everything that comes down to us through history makes finding commonality and common cause easy. The commonalities are things we have to search for through and beyond the human history which divides us into distinct identities and groupings. Values, morals and ethics are where we can meet, if we make the effort to find our common ground. Values, morals and ethics matter because they are our road map and compass bearings for living a God-conscious life. They are not endlessly flexible, but they are ways of asking questions, reasoning with and determining how to negotiate the circumstances of our times in the best possible way.

The transmodern synthesis

The diversity that appears to divide us provides an important lesson. All our differences substantiate that there is more than one way to seek righteousness. At our best we all have diverse, multiple ways of organising and delivering shared values. We each have to find our own way to be relevant to the circumstances and conditions of contemporary times, to be modern. In our different ways the process of reasoning with our times to find the common ground of shared values can be a positive force. A dialogue concerning our differences has the potential to illuminate new possibilities for us all. In our separate yet mutual efforts to be relevant we can learn from each other and come to find and apply new insights on our own understanding of our own beliefs. Living together, confronted by shared circumstances, we have much to learn from each other. I do not mean by this that we embark on a process of becoming each other, that we negate the differences among and between us. I mean we can find ways in which we can transcend our differences by using our religious and cultural values to enhance our capacity to live peacefully together with mutual respect and tolerance. Such transcendence places its emphasis on how we put our faith into action rather than focusing on our theological differences. I am not saying such differences become irrelevant but I am suggesting they are not insuperable obstacles to collective effort. I am certain they could and should help us all, each in our own way, to rise to the very best that we are called to be. Instead of obstacles, we have to make them hurdles we surmount to achieve peaceful coexistence and mutual promotion of harmonious community through diverse fellowship of faiths. This is the condition I call transmodernity.

Transmodernity is a concept designed to address the positive element of self-renewal and self-reformation that exists in all diverse world cultures. I should explain that initially I used this concept to address the global problem of dominance, the dominance of perspectives derived solely from the history of western civilisation (Sardar 2006). Dominance is a fact of history, but one that has had a pernicious effect on our world. It constrains non-western cultures and identities, shackles them with the slur of presumed inferiority and in consequence deforms the possibility of a genuinely plural world, a world that liberates and includes the constructive contribution of all communities and human imagination. Dominance is a doctrine of exclusivity which insists that those who do not subscribe to, align themselves with and conform to its strictures are marginalised. As I have tried to make clear, the dominance of our day is a secularist ascendancy that has turned its back not just on the cultural diversity but also on the religious diversity within western civilisation itself. If this has been accepted by British society, and I am by no means sure it has, it ill suits the worldview and cultural formation of minority communities in Britain. It inhibits them by disorienting their commonly accepted lifeways and social antennae. It works to make genuine inclusive, full participation in British society an intractable problem. It makes difference the only function of multiculturalism – whereas what we need to locate and bring into the mainstream is what culture, the extensive expression of religious identity, is actually for: an adaptive mechanism that enables cooperation and collaboration in mutually shared effort to make society as a whole a better place for everyone. It is for this reason that I think we need the idea of transmodernity to help us transcend the limitations of the multiculturalism we have practised to date.

Dominance is also inherent in our own religious outlooks. The missionary zeal of monotheistic religions leads to an aspiration to convert or conquer the world. Each faith – Judaism, Christianity and Islam – not only has an exclusivist notion of truth but insists that truth is the same for everyone and at all times. Transmodernity means we transcend such conventional notions of religious truth and traditional ideas of religious dominance. I think monotheistic faiths need to move forward and recognise that each faith is true in its own terms, and Truth is so complex, so Infinite, that it cannot be totally enclosed within a single religious outlook. Truth may not be contingent but it can be seen in a different light, at different times, by different people, with different perspectives. There are different truths; but each truth is important and immutable for those who hold it. Everyone must be allowed to live by the worldview that seems true to them. This will be a painful realisation for certain religious communities but it is an essential step forward if the monotheistic faiths are to transcend their history of antagonism and conflict.

If the problem is dominance, then transmodernity is arriving at a social compact that does not privilege any one standpoint, including religion, secularism or liberal humanism. This will seem a troubling prospect for some. A statement of faith is the ultimate privileging of one way of viewing the world. But there are none among us who in conscience would not acknowledge that our faith includes, demands and requires a duty of care, extending the benefit of our values, enacting our moral and ethical framework on behalf of all humanity whether of our faith or not. We are all called to care for human beings as a whole as they are. We are all called to care for the well-being of all God's creation, human, animal, vegetable and mineral. What transmodernity asks of religion is perhaps more even than it asks of secular liberal humanism. Yet what it asks is already inherent in the faiths we profess. And that is why, if the religious can make this transformation, they can lead the way to a better human future for all. What transmodernity asks of us is to give to others our very best; but to offer our best according to the needs of others in such ways as they can truly receive its greatest benefit – to do what is right according to our faith and understanding not irrespective of what other people believe but irrespective of whether they believe as we do. It is a considerable distinction. And it can only be achieved by a negotiation through difference; it requires a search for consensus across and respecting our differences. It is a negotiation about how we live together in the world as people with different identities, identities derived from faith which remain distinct yet find their truest meaning in creating a peaceful, harmonious, sustainable society that is just, equitable, concerned with meeting the needs, realising the potential and including the contribution of all. In making such a society we may all be changed. My argument, however, is that we will all be changed into better representatives of our different faiths. What will change most is the society in which we live together. We can create the opportunity of remaking it more in the image and according to the dictates of faithful conscience. If we open ourselves to such a future, we construct the possibility of more open futures grounded in the example of living faiths. We offer society the potential of realising the main product of transmodernity: mutually assured diversity.

The faith communities need to consider that religion has lost hold of its place in society by seeming to be more concerned with the claims to exclusivity and dominance of our theology, the particularities of our doctrine, than with working for what we are called to bring forth as a result of faith. Instead of 'Thy kingdom come, on earth as it is in heaven', we have given too much attention to making my kingdom as I say it should be on the human authority of my religious interpretation. In this insistence on orthodoxy we have encouraged secularisation as the way to make the peace among and between us. Thus, we jettisoned both baby and bathwater! Religion has played its part in empowering a society that no longer knows the meaning of faith and struggles to define any parameters or limitations to constrain, guide and counsel individual human desires. Together we can bemoan that condition. The question before us is, can we transcend our insularity to achieve a transmodern society infused with the open and shared example of living faiths?

For all the energy expended in the search for exclusivity, the truth is that there never have been successful monocultures. Our societies have always been diverse and complex. Culture and society have never been discrete, exclusive, static, bounded, uniform, orthodox entities. Internally, all cultures and societies have always been heterogeneous, speaking with multiple voices. They have been and are interpretive communities. What I am suggesting is that we turn away from the historic fact that it is easier and less demanding to sit on pinheads defining what pure faith should be than to plunge into the complexities of the world searching conscientiously for right action and righteous workable solutions to actual human predicaments. It is certainly more difficult to take the option for society when we have to acknowledge and find consensus with people with whom we do not agree. I simply make the case that society is now in such a dire state, so imperilled by the absence of faiths in the public space, that we cannot in conscience stand aside, no matter how difficult we conceive the task to be.

Beyond theory

Theory is one thing. What can and should we do in practice to revitalise our faith and usher it back into the public space of British society? Unless Christianity in all its diversity reclaims its place in the public space, I would argue, there is little chance for minority non-Christian religions to advance their claims. However defiant some voices among minorities may be, in my experience people like me, members of minorities, feel the lack of a vibrant Christian presence in public life. We think that if Britain is a Christian country, it should continue to be so, demonstrably and publicly. Our concern is that we too, as minorities, are then permitted and welcomed to public notice of our high days and holidays, to express our conscientious beliefs as a motive force for engaging in British society and to be part of inclusive ritual commemoration and observance on occasions that speak to the collective identity of the Britain we can build together.

There are implications for Muslims too. Not only do Muslims need to become more politically engaged, but they need to ensure that their voices are heard on the major debates in Britain, such as those on public accountability and democracy, human rights and social justice, economic cuts and social welfare, equality and pensions, and assisted suicide and the care of the elderly. For them to actively participate in these debates, it is necessary to point out that Muslims do have a view and position on these issues, one that, while not always different from other perspectives, can sometimes be quite distinct. On issues of condoms and abortion, for example, the general Muslim position differs markedly from the Catholic one: the former are allowed; the latter is permitted (up to four months, depending on which school you follow) under certain circumstances – when the mother's life is in danger, or if the child is conceived after rape. The point to emphasise is that while religious positions have a common ground, they are not always the same. It is not just that religious thought needs to be in the public space, but the public space must also register the diversity of religious positions.

Muslims also need to transcend the mental ghetto in which they are trapped. It is somehow assumed, both by Muslims and by the wider public in Britain, that Islamic values and British values, however they are defined, are somehow antagonistic to each other. Nothing could be further from the truth. But it is important for Muslims to go beyond the narrow confines of Shariah law, gender relations based on medieval customs coated with an Islamic gloss, and tribal norms that are best consigned to history to emphasise the universal concepts and values of Islam. Whatever their ethnic background or sectarian affiliation, all British Muslims subscribe to a rich repertoire of concepts that define the foundations of Islam and with which many in Britain, people of belief and of no belief, will find a common resonance. I am thinking of such Qur'anic concepts as *adl*, *ilm* and *shura* (I have consistently argued that these and other basic concepts of Islam can be used to shape policy and make Islam relevant to contemporary and future times; Sardar 1979, 1985), which have a direct bearing on what is happening to British society and need to be aired, discussed and elaborated in the public space. The concept of *adl*, for example, with its emphasis on social justice, equality and equal opportunity for all, is central to the discussion about cuts to public spending, social mobility, salaries of executives, and the debates about multiculturalism and the 'Big Society'. The concept of *ilm*, the notion that the pursuit of knowledge, learning and thought is the basis of a civil society, and education is the right of all members of society, is directly relevant to the argument on tuition fees, the financial squeeze on, and virtual abandonment of, certain social science and humanities disciplines (such as history and philosophy) and research funding. The idea of *istislah* – a basic source of Islamic law – that public interest should be the basis of policy and legislation is equally central to the debates about climate change, reforms to the National Health Service, green belts around cities, inner-city development as well as more specific issues such as what should happen to the Olympic stadiums after the games are over. When alternatives to the current first-past-the-post electoral system are uppermost in the public mind, and the responsibilities and accountability of members of Parliament are in the public eye, surely the Islamic concept of *shura*, the principle that society should function on the basis of wide-ranging consultation and accountability, must be relevant to such public debates. And above all this is the general Islamic principle of 'inviting to all that is good': Muslim voices have to make their presence felt on issues of public good, social and cultural virtues, and policies that enhance the welfare and well-being of Britain. Muslims must loudly claim all that is good and humane, and promotes human welfare, as Islamic wherever and by whomsoever it has been devised. This ultimately is the acid test of Muslim openness and the pluralistic possibilities of Islam.

On the symbolic level there has been progress. Prayers offered by representatives of various faith groups have become part of certain state occasions. We have established the principle of state funding for faith schools for a diversity of faiths. As the father of a son who attended a Catholic secondary school, I can attest how appreciative of the ethos and unafraid of the concept members of minority communities are. But faith schools are not unalloyed benefits, nor the only possible answer. I am thinking of a project in Liverpool to establish a mainstream state community school with an Islamic ethos. As the project unfolded, with cross-party and multi-faith support, it became evident that the principles of an Islamic ethos in action in our education system delivered values that won the endorsement and support of non-Muslim parents too because they expressed shared values that can coexist and serve everyone in the mainstream. It seems to me entirely healthy that state-funded state schools should be required to diversify their intake. Is it really the case that I am more prepared to entrust my son to a Catholic school than other British parents would be to send their children to an Islamic or Hindu state-funded school? It would be the transmodern thing to do; it would set benchmarks, standards and oversight for Islamic and other schools I am anxious should be enforced. If it is an option few can imagine, then it defines a serious problem that we need to work together to address. I can tell you that my son, the only Muslim in his school, won two prizes in his first year: one for the Christmas and the other for the Easter religious quiz. To live in Britain as active and engaged British citizens, I and my children must be informed and aware of the beliefs and history of religion in Britain. It has not made my son less a Muslim, but, I feel, it ensures that he will be a better-informed, more thoughtful and conscientious Muslim who is a better partner to his non-Muslim neighbours and fellow citizens. The symbolic presence of multi-faith representatives at state occasions leads me to point out that unless we reclaim Christmas and Easter as Christian festivals there is little chance we can offer public recognition to minority communities. I would like to see public recognition of Eid ul-Fitr, which marks the end of the fasting month of Ramadan, of Divali and Guru Nanak's Birthday or Wesak Day (marking the birthday of the Buddha) and so on.

Acknowledging and providing public recognition of diverse celebrations of faith is a beginning. Beyond that, faith communities need to be clearly heard on issues of poverty, human dignity and human rights, equality and good community relations, freedom and fairness. They need to stand up against structured injustice, naked greed and conspicuous consumption, the politics of corruption and class division. They have to champion the cause of the disadvantaged and the marginalised. There is no injustice out there that does not have an ethical or moral dimension and about which the religious can be complacent.

Conclusion

Faith communities do not stand apart from society. Their voices on issues of contemporary relevance are as important as the voices of secularism. But to arrive at the transmodern situation, where no single voice dominates the public space, and spaces where faith groups can engage in social action for and on behalf of not only sectional communities but all of society, it is necessary to find ways to enable open, mutually tolerant and respectful debates among and between the diversity of voices of faith in British society. Such debate does not and cannot belong solely to religious professionals: it has to become an engagement at the level of the generality of ordinary people. To be transmodern we have to prepare the groundwork and not inhibit the interest ordinary citizens have in what makes them different so that they can discover how alike, cooperative and collegial they can be, how common the ground is in terms of basic values they share. While making Britain a society where religions and the religious talk together about what is relevant to their lives must ultimately be a task for the mass of ordinary people, it is as institutional and organised religious communities that we bear the responsibility of leading the way, opening the spaces.

Faith communities need neither to shout nor to whisper. But they do need to talk in earnest among themselves, and to assert the fact that religion has a vital part to play in shaping public debates. People of faith have to try hard to be heard on a plethora of issues about the moral status and ethical action of British society. But it is time for all people of faiths to ensure that their voices are clearly heard for the cause of human betterment now and in Britain.

References

Asad, T. (2003) *Formations of the Secular: Christianity, Islam, Modernity*, Stanford, CA: Stanford University Press.

Beal, T. (2008) *Religion in America: A Very Short Introduction*, New York: Oxford University Press.

Hosen, N. and Mohr, R. (eds) (2011) *Law and Religion in Public Life: The Contemporary Debate*, London: Routledge.

Moore, D. L. (2007) *Overcoming Religious Illiteracy: A Cultural Studies Approach to the Study of Religion in Secondary Education*, Basingstoke: Palgrave Macmillan.

Office of National Statistics (2001) www.statistics.gov.uk/census2001/census2001.asp.

Sardar, Z. (1979) *The Future of Muslim Civilization*, London: Croom Helm.

Sardar, Z (1985) *Islamic Futures: The Shape of Ideas to Come*, London: Mansell.

Sardar, Z. (2006) 'Beyond difference: cultural relations in a new century', in E. Masood (ed.) *How Do You Know? Reading Ziauddin Sardar on Islam, Science and Cultural Relations*, London: Pluto Press.

Sardar, Z. (2010) 'Welcome to postnormal times', *Futures* 42 (5): 435–444.

Trigg, R. (2008) *Religion in Public Life: Must Faith Be Privatized?* Oxford: Oxford University Press.

2

BRITAIN AND BRITISHNESS

Place, belonging and exclusion

Rosemary Sales

Introduction

The idea of 'Britishness' became a key theme in public discourse during the New Labour period, continuing in a rather different form under the Conservative-led Coalition elected in 2010. Gordon Brown, whom Tom Nairn (2006) described as the 'Bard of Britishness', promoted it as an inclusive identity that supports social cohesion as people with diverse backgrounds – including those born outside Britain – are able to share a common space through their adherence to a common set of values. His notorious call for 'British jobs for British workers', however, was based on a more exclusive view of Britishness, a view reflected in immigration policy, which is increasingly preoccupied with controlling the entry of people from outside the European Union. The Conservative emphasis on the celebration of 'our monarchy, our armed forces, and our parliament as a vital part of what it means to be British'[1] suggests another concept of Britishness, drawn from a particular version of the history of the 'British nation'.

'Britishness' thus has many different, and often contradictory, aspects. These tensions are at the heart of the notion of the 'nation-state', which implies that 'nation' and 'state' are coterminous and the borders of the state mark the division between nationals and non-nationals, or 'insiders' and 'outsiders'. Nation-states are, however, constructed through concrete social processes and have many dimensions – political, geographical, historical, cultural, economic – whose boundaries may not fit neatly together. These relationships are particularly complex in Britain's case, with its history of internal and external conquest. Confusion extends even to the name of the state: the 'British' state is the United Kingdom of Great Britain and Northern Ireland and thus includes non-British territory. As Cohen suggested,

> the boundaries of British nationality, identity and citizenship are only very imprecisely drawn and understood. This indeterminacy can be thought of as

> a series of blurred, opaque or *fuzzy* frontiers surrounding the very fabrication and the subsequent recasting of the core identity.
>
> *(1995, my emphasis)*

The promotion of Britishness therefore raises fundamental disagreements about the nature of citizenship, belonging and what it means to be 'British'. Muslims have been propelled to the forefront of these discussions, as political events – from the 'riots' in northern English towns in 2001 to the London bombings of 2005 and the 'war on terror' – have often seen them stigmatized as cultural, social and political outsiders, as fundamentally 'un-British'.

This chapter addresses critically the promotion of Britishness and the ways in which Muslims have been positioned within this discourse. The idea of 'place' is fundamental to the notion of nationhood, and the discussion focuses on four interrelated issues: first, the relation between nation, belonging and place, especially in the British case; second, the different ways in which Britishness is constructed and understood; third, the unequal relations between the nations that make up the UK state and the implications for national belonging; and fourth, the ways in which the promotion of Britishness has led to tighter boundaries around citizenship, through immigration policies that exclude people from the national territory and have intensified the conditional nature of citizenship; and through policies, most notably the anti-terrorism agenda, that present many of those living in Britain as 'un-British'.

Nation, belonging and place

The ideas of national identity and the national interest claim to embrace all those living within the nation's borders. They embody, however, specific power relations based on, for example, class, gender and ethnicity. Indeed, the notion of the 'nation-state' contains a fundamental contradiction between a *state*, which holds sovereignty within a particular geographical space in which all citizens have access to certain universal rights; and the *nation*, which suggests a people with some common history and culture, an 'imagined community' that is 'both inherently limited and sovereign' (Anderson 1983: 15). Thus, citizenship involves universal principles, above cultural difference, yet it exists only in the context of a nation-state which is based on cultural specificity (Castles 2000: 188). The construction of nation-states involves the spatial extension of state power and the incorporation of previously distinct ethnic and linguistic groups. As Luhmann suggests, 'state formation can be understood in terms of the territorialization of political dominance' (quoted in Jessop 1990: 350), and this may involve the exclusion, assimilation or even genocide of minority groups.

Myths of 'nationhood' and national belonging embody those of the dominant group, often marginalizing or rendering invisible others who may also occupy the national territory. There is thus a disjunction between the place – the borders of the nation – and the ideology of nationhood, which may exclude some of those who reside within these borders as well as those who reside outside. At the same time, some non-residents may be included in the broader nation, through retaining the 'right to return' (as in the case of the Jewish diaspora in relation to Israel) or through ideological, cultural links and economic links.

The British state, the United Kingdom, was constructed through conflict and conquest and represents the dominance by England over the other nations now within its borders. British national identity is thus 'a relatively recent construct' that was 'superimposed on earlier national identities of English, Welsh, Scottish and Irish' (Heath and Roberts 2008). Attempts were made to obliterate their national languages, and Welsh, Scots Gaelic and Irish have struggled to remain living languages. Significantly, the national language is not 'British' but English, while England's power is also reflected in the supremacy of London as Britain's political, financial and cultural capital. Slippage between the terms 'Britain' and 'England' is widespread, and it is a commonplace that Scottish or Welsh people become 'British' when they are successful but remain Scottish or Welsh if they fail. More recently, black Britons have faced the same ambivalent acceptance.

The place of Irish people within the British nation is even more ambiguous. Britain's oldest colony, Ireland was partitioned in 1920 following a long struggle for independence, with the 26 southern counties forming the Irish Republic, while the 6 north-eastern counties remained part of the United Kingdom. Those living there were predominantly Protestant, mostly descendants of settlers from Scotland, who were granted privileged status relative to the local Irish (predominantly Catholic) population. The majority of Protestants wished to retain the ties on which their status depended and, espousing Unionism, resisted Irish independence. No side in the War of Independence won outright victory, and the Unionists finally settled for partition. The borders of Northern Ireland were constructed in order to entrench Unionist majority rule, a gerrymandering that was combined with systematic discrimination in housing and employment and manipulation of electoral boundaries within Northern Ireland (Farrell 1980). The state thus embodied deep divisions over national identity which were at the heart of the 'Troubles' from the late 1960s. The position of Irish people within Britain is also ambiguous. They face severe economic and social discrimination (Hickman and Walters 1997; Tilki *et al.* 2009), but Irish citizens – from both North and South – enjoy full rights of entry and citizenship within Britain, an anomaly that reflects complex strategic and political considerations on the part of the British state (Hickman 1998).

As well as England's domination over the other nations of the United Kingdom, the British state was forged in the process of colonialism and imperialism in Africa, the Indian subcontinent, America and elsewhere. This established 'a cultural and national superiority of world-wide proportions: an empire where, truly, the sun never set' (Cohen 1995). Britishness has thus been associated with conquest and dominance, an association that current foreign policy, including the war on Iraq, has done much to perpetuate.

The process of Empire-building and subsequent decolonization established a number of what Cohen calls 'fuzzy frontiers' of national identity; the citizenship rights accorded to Irish people in Britain is one such example. Another was caused by the settlement of British people in the dominions, which created a dominion-diaspora 'cemented by ties of kinship, economic interdependence and preferential trade arrangements, by sport, by visits and tourism' (Cohen 1995). The process of decolonization brought immigration from Asia, Africa and the Caribbean, and with the formation of the Commonwealth, citizens of these countries initially had full rights of entry to Britain. This symbolic universal equality was seen as 'a necessary price to pay for the role of parent' (Paul 1997: 12). When Commonwealth citizens attempted to take up these rights within Britain itself, however, they were met with hostility and discrimination, and indeed the prime minister of the time, Clement Attlee, described the arrival of 492 Commonwealth citizens from Jamaica on the *Empire Windrush* in 1948 as an 'incursion' (Holmes 1988: 257). The status of Commonwealth, rather than British, citizen had been introduced to appease India and Pakistan, whose people did not want to be seen as British subjects (Paul 1997: 17). Ironically, it was this status that opened the way for differential treatment of Commonwealth citizens in subsequent legislation (Sales 2007).

The succeeding decades have been marked by struggles for full inclusion by black and ethnic minority citizens, including those born in Britain. The entry of black British citizens disrupted notions of Britishness based on myths of the 'island race' and a common origin, and it became more difficult for white Britons to 'territorialise their identity' (Cohen 1995), but British society remains deeply divided along lines of race and ethnicity. Thus, tensions remain between the notion of Britain as a place and the concept of 'British people', which is often seen in more exclusive ethnic terms.

The agenda of Britishness

The resurgence of interest in Britishness is taking place within a very different context from that in which the idea of Britishness was constructed. Britain is no longer dominant on the world stage, although the Commonwealth, many of whose members retain the British monarch as head of state, allows it to retain some of the privileges of a major power. While it remains a global financial centre, its economy is much diminished relative to other leading economies, including newly emerging powers. The new economic and political landscape has forced it to develop closer ties with continental Europe through membership of the European Union but its involvement often remains reluctant and half-hearted, as shown by, for example, the refusal to join the Eurozone or the Schengen Agreement. Many on the Conservative right view EU institutions as fundamental threats to British rights and the 'British way of life', and opposition to EU policy has overwhelmingly been framed within an anti-European, and often xenophobic, discourse.

The new interest in Britishness has been precipitated by political, economic and social changes, including new forms of globalization, which reflect Britain's waning power on the international stage. These processes have created social fragmentation and dislocation. Economic restructuring has undermined traditional industrial –

particularly male – employment and with it social structures, such as trade unions, that promoted solidarity. This coincided with increased geographical mobility and changes in family structures, undermining the 'male breadwinner' model and the extended family. These changes were given enormous impetus in the Thatcher era with its agenda of promoting individualism and reducing the collectivist aspects of welfare provision. This agenda has continued under New Labour and the Conservative-led coalition government elected in May 2010.

The growth of individualism has also been associated with social and political change, including the declining importance of religion, especially the Protestant tradition, which was fundamental to the construction of British identity (Colley 1992). According to Bunting (2007: 86), the collapse of religious belief 'hollowed out the edifice of British national identity'. At the same time, other ideologies that provided alternative visions of the future, such as socialism, have become less powerful.

The structural changes of recent decades, some the result of deliberate policy, have made life more uncertain and precarious for many British people. The recent increase in immigration and ethnic diversity has, however, been widely blamed for these problems. The real causes of globalization are invisible and complex, but immigrants are its most visible sign (Castles 2000) and can thus become a focus of resentment and a target for hostility. Bloch and Solomos speak of a 'commonsense acceptance of the argument that many western societies have become "too diverse" for their own good' (2010: 1). Asylum seekers have become a particular focus of hostility (Lewis 2005), but the new discourse has also targeted longer-established migrant communities, including British citizens.

Multicultural policies have been a particular target of criticism, blamed by some for promoting relativism and undermining shared values. Gordon Brown, speaking in 2004, suggested that while there should be 'respect for diversity', Britain should never have justified 'a crude multiculturalism where all values became relative'. Trevor Phillips, then head of the Commission for Racial Equality (CRE), the body charged with combating racial discrimination, argued that multiculturalism had gone too far and that there was a need to hold on to 'a core of Britishness' (quoted in Cheong *et al.* 2007: 8). Some who position themselves on the left, such as those associated with the Euston Group, have condemned multiculturalism as pandering to reactionary elements within ethnic communities. David Goodhart, editor of the magazine *Prospect*, went further in suggesting that ethnic diversity itself is primarily responsible for the loss of shared values. He argues that we are now 'forced to share with strangers' but that 'such acts of sharing are more smoothly and generously negotiated if we can take for granted a limited set of common values and assumptions. But as Britain becomes more diverse that common culture is being eroded' (2004: 1).

Although multiculturalism was thus invoked as the author of contemporary problems, the specific policies deemed to have led to this result have rarely been identified or examined, and critics have often relied on anecdotal, sometimes fictitious, evidence. In reality, multicultural policies have never been implemented systematically in Britain and, as Joppke observes, no national 'government before New Labour had ever taken up multicultural rhetoric' (2009: 82). National policy on race relations has been developed within a liberal tradition that focuses on the individual rather than the group. The anti-discrimination legislation introduced from the 1960s provided a framework of formal legal equality in areas such as employment, while leaving untouched structural inequalities. At the same time, Britain's version of liberalism – based on tolerance of difference rather than a consensus of national values (ibid.: 118) – accommodated visible signs of difference such as the Sikh turban and Muslim headscarf and shalwar kameez within, for example, police uniform as well as within schools. The former was achieved through race relations legislation (Sikhs are classed as an ethnic group within the Act) and was thus based on individual rights to non-discrimination; the latter has been based on local agreement often involving parents and local communities.

Policies that could be described as multicultural have generally arisen from local initiatives and been piecemeal rather than comprehensive, often an accommodation to the claims of local groups organized along ethnic lines. As Kundnani (2001) suggests, many people were elected onto local councils during the 1980s as the 'surrogate voice for their own ethnically-defined fiefdoms'. This position allowed them to retain patriarchal relations within 'their' communities largely free from criticism by outsiders fearful of being seen as racist by attacking 'traditional culture' (Kofman *et al.* 2000).

The promotion by government of religiously based, or 'faith', schools could be seen as an exception to the general trend of national policy, allowing groups rather than individuals to secure acknowledgement of 'cultural rights'. The policy should, however, be seen in the context of the development of Britain's schooling system, in which the churches (predominantly the established Church of England and the Catholic Church) played a major role. This was retained as the national system of compulsory education was introduced in 1944, with church schools receiving state finance while churches retained effective control over the running of these schools. In 2008 there were 1,855 Catholic primary schools and 393 Catholic secondary schools in England and Wales. In England alone the Church of England had 4,468 primary schools and 201 secondary schools.[2] As other religious groups have become more organized, this situation has inevitably led to demands for funding to establish their own schools. In 2008 there were 26 Jewish, 3 Muslim and 1 Sikh primary school within the state system. This form of multiculturalism, however, rather than exposing students to different cultures, allows them to 'withdraw behind the walls of a (quasi) private school held by "their" group' (Joppke 2009: 87), reinforcing separation. New types of schools introduced under both the Thatcher and New Labour governments in the name of 'parental choice' further fragmented the school system, leading to segregation along ethnic and class lines (Burgess and Wilson 2004). This agenda is being dramatically escalated under the current Coalition government as education is increasingly treated as a private commodity rather than a public good.

Muslims and the agenda of Britishness

Political events of the past decade have meant that the agenda of Britishness has become increasingly preoccupied with Muslims. During the summer of 2001, 'riots' occurred in several northern English cities, with groups of white and Asian – predominantly Muslim – youths coming into violent confrontation on the streets. These events marked a turning point in the debate on multiculturalism, prompting official interest in social cohesion and shared 'British values'. The official report that investigated these events (Cantle 2001) claimed that Asian and white families were living 'parallel lives' with little meaningful interaction. The White Paper on immigration, *Secure Borders, Safe Haven,* which followed, suggested the need to 'rebuild a sense of common citizenship' (Home Office 2002: 10) and argued that minority communities needed to do more to learn the English language and about the British way of life. British values were compared to other 'cultural practices' which, it argued, 'conflict with these basic values', such as those 'which deny women the right to participate as equal citizens' (ibid.: 30).

Rather than examining structural causes, the official response to these events sought answers in the behaviour and values of the communities involved and in particular of Asian, predominantly Muslim, groups. As Kundnani (2002) put it, this 'seemed to be a case of "blame the victim"'. The divisions to which official commentators drew attention were, however, often symptoms of underlying trends rather than themselves causes. The immediate triggers were the increased activity by the racist British National Party in these areas and the one-sided response of the police to the conflict their presence produced. The long-term processes at work, however, allowed them to spark sustained conflict. Amin identifies three major factors that account for these tensions: deprivation, segregation and new youth politics (2002: 961).

Deprivation had been intensified by the collapse of the textile industry, which had been the backbone of employment for both Asian and white workers until the 1960s. The area is among the most deprived in the country, with unemployment reaching 50 per cent among Asians in Oldham (ibid.). Segregation has been blamed as the primary cause of the riots, but rather than being the result merely of groups' preferences for living apart, it arose from structural factors as well as deliberate policy (see also Platt, Chapter 3 of this volume). Economic collapse removed the workplace as a central site of integration and common fate (Amin 2002: 962), turning communities in on themselves (Kundnani 2001: 106). Ethnic separation in city centres was intensified by 'white flight' to the suburbs and systematic discrimination in housing allocation (Rattansi 2002). In Oldham, an investigation by the CRE found that the local authority had operated a segregationist housing policy (Kundnani 2001: 106). Moreover, segregation was reinforced by 'parental choice' in schooling, which allowed white parents to send their children to majority-white schools outside their catchment area, as well as the development of Muslim schools.

The frustrations of young people born and brought up in Britain, both with their exclusion from wider society and with their own self-appointed leaders, led to a new form of youth politics (Kundnani 2001: 108). Amin suggests that as British citizens, they wanted to claim full rights to belonging, including as both British and Muslim, and challenged those who 'want to keep them in their own minority spaces', unsettling the 'majority opinion that minorities should behave in a certain way in public' (2002: 964). They did not lack understanding of 'British values' or the English language. On the contrary, they were expressing frustration at 'widespread cultural inclusion followed by structural exclusion' (Young 2002: 15).

The terrorist attack on the Twin Towers in September 2001 and the London bombings of July 2005 were crucial in instigating the Britishness agenda. The attack on London's transport system, which killed 52 people, was carried out by four young British-born Muslim men. This atrocity suggested a profound rejection of the society in which they had been brought up and has been widely interpreted as evidence that some sections of the British Muslim population have loyalties which conflict with British values (CRE 2005: 10). As Khan suggested, 'The very Britishness of the "home-grown" bombers meant that all British Muslims came under suspicion. Somehow we were all responsible because we were expected to have known of the terrorists in our midst.'[3] In this atmosphere, the word 'multiculturalism' became a code for the 'problem' of Muslims and Islam (Parekh 2006). The prime minister, Tony Blair, speaking on the first anniversary of the bombings, demanded that Muslim leaders

> do more to attack not just the extremists' methods, but their false sense of grievance about the west. Too many Muslim leaders give the impression that they understand and sympathise with the grievances, an attitude that ensures the extremists will never be defeated.[4]

Thus, Muslims were viewed with suspicion if their political views conflicted with those of western governments. As these terrorist outrages were used as the pretext for a 'war on terror' that included the illegal invasion of Iraq, this 'sense of grievance' came to be shared by huge numbers of British people. It was the Muslim population, however, which became increasingly a 'suspect community' (a term originally applied to the Irish) in need of intervention and control. Ahmad and Evergeti (2010) suggest that this stigmatization has contributed to a 'racialization of Muslimness', with a shift from ethnic or national identity towards a predominant Muslim identity. The agenda of Britishness has thus increasingly focused on Muslims, who have been presented as the alien 'other'.

Britishness – conflicting agendas?

In promoting 'Britishness', individuals and groups have drawn on different notions of what constitutes 'Britishness' and the boundaries between who is British and who non-British. Jacobson distinguishes between

> the *civic boundary*, according to which citizenship is the primary criterion of nationality; the *'racial' boundary* which defines as British those individuals

> believed to have British ancestry or 'blood'; and the *cultural boundary*, according to which Britishness is a matter of . . . culture, values or lifestyle.
>
> *(2004, my emphasis)*

In practice, most versions draw on a combination of these different boundaries.

The celebration of 'British' identity has generally been associated predominantly with the right of the political spectrum. The core of far right ideology, such as that espoused by the British National Party and its predecessor the National Front, is a racialized notion of nationhood, although more recently this has generally been phrased in terms of opposition to 'alien' cultural, and specifically Muslim, values. The Conservative Party sees itself as the party of patriotism and focuses on what it sees as the culture of Britishness and its symbols. David Cameron wrote in a recent online discussion, 'As a political party, we Conservatives are patriotic to the core – I don't think anyone doubts that. Yes we have embedded the Union Flag into many of our banners and backdrops.'[5] Conservatives tend to emphasize Britain's cultural and historical uniqueness and to celebrate the trappings of its imperial power. As Cameron suggested,

> We won't get very far in promoting Britishness if people don't have a feel for Britain's history and heritage [and] more emotional connection with the institutions that define Britishness such as our monarchy, our armed forces, and our parliament. These institutions are a vital part of what it means to be British.

This approach is evident in a pledge by the current Conservative-led government to promote Britishness through a 'narrative' version of British history to be taught in schools. This will, as the new Education Secretary put it, tell 'our island story',[6] an approach that suggests an exclusive view of belonging. The Conservative Party under David Cameron has also attempted to promote a more inclusive notion of Britishness. A prominent element of the 'modernizing' agenda was the appointment of Baroness Warsi, a Muslim woman, as chair of the party. In a recent interview she explained how she believed Britishness could encompass Muslims through the conservative values of individual achievement:

> Britishness is a feeling of tolerance; it is a feeling of allowing people to live their lives the way they wish to live their lives. It's about fairness, it's about meritocracy, it's about a dream where somebody like me, a labourer's daughter, can be born in that country whose parents went there with 200 rupees in their pockets and they set up multi-million businesses there.[7]

Faced with the dominance of conservative views of what Britishness means, some on the centre and left have claimed the need for a progressive version of nationalism. Labour MP Sadiq Khan suggests that 'the left has allowed its rightful hatred of jingoism to spread to a distaste of anything nationalist, allowing the right to define

Britishness' (2007: 27). Gordon Brown, referring to the far right's appropriation of the Union Jack, argued that it 'does not belong to a vicious minority, but is a flag for all Britain – symbolising inclusion, tolerance and unity' (2004). A number of reports by 'progressive' bodies have investigated how people identify with Britishness (e.g. Rogers and Muir for the IPPR 2007; CRE 2005). The Smith Institute investigated different conceptions of Britishness (Johnson 2007), with most contributors arguing for a new and progressive form of national identity based on civic values. This marks a departure from the British form of liberalism, which has been based on 'modus vivendi' rather than ethical consensus as in France (Joppke 2009: 118), and with private rather than public values predominating.

Moreover, the proponents of this new form of Britishness have sought to identify some specifically British identity that can bind people, including newcomers, together. The then prime minister, Tony Blair, claimed in 2006 that Britain's 'essential values' were 'belief in democracy, the rule of law, tolerance, equal treatment for all, respect for this country and its shared heritage . . . [this] is what we hold in common; it is what gives us the right to call ourselves British'.[8] The values he speaks of are, however, universal and 'merely ideals to which anyone might aspire' (Winder 2007: 32). Moreover, if one is claiming a set of values as specifically British, these are necessarily counterposed to those deemed 'non-British'; values which outsiders are deemed to be in need of in order to become truly British.

In seeking to identify the essence of 'Britishness', both New Labour and Conservative proponents have combined this appropriation of universal civic values with a particularist version of British history and culture. Gordon Brown, while acknowledging that these values and qualities are found in many other cultures and countries, argued that there is a 'a golden thread which runs through British history of the individual standing firm for freedom and liberty against tyranny and the arbitrary use of power'. In writing of citizenship in the preface to *Secure Borders, Safe Haven*, David Blunkett drew on a historical narrative that is at best partial, suggesting that 'British nationality has never been associated with membership of a particular ethnic group. For centuries we have been a multi-ethnic nation. We do not exclude people from citizenship on the basis of their race or ethnicity' (Home Office 2002: 10). These accounts ignore the oppressive and undemocratic practices that were fundamental to the construction of the British state, some of which persist to the present day. For example, although Blunkett's statement holds true for the formal rules of British nationality, at least until recently, exclusion on the basis of ethnicity and religion were central to the construction of British national identity and to the rights enjoyed by British residents. It has been based on a Christian and, into the nineteenth century, Protestant identity. Full belonging was 'predicated upon belonging to the national church: Anglicanism and Englishness were fused together' (Cesarani and Fulbrook 1996: 7). Elements of that tradition remain, for example in the requirement in state schools to carry out a 'broadly Christian' daily act of worship, while the hereditary monarch, to whom new citizens must swear allegiance, is also head of the (Protestant) Church of England.

In spite of the claims for democracy as being essentially British, New Labour did not challenge these anachronisms and, in adding a new 'citizenship pledge' (below in italics) to the existing Oath of Allegiance which new citizens are required to swear, made the bizarre juxtaposition of adherence to 'democratic values' with allegiance to a hereditary monarch:

> I [swear by Almighty God] [do solemnly and sincerely affirm] that, from this time forward, I will give my loyalty and allegiance to Her Majesty Queen Elizabeth the Second her Heirs and Successors and to the United Kingdom. *I will respect the rights and freedoms of the United Kingdom. I will uphold its democratic values. I will observe its laws faithfully and fulfil my duties and obligations as a British citizen.*
>
> *(Home Office 2002)*

It may be suggested that the monarchy is an irrelevance, part of the world of celebrity rather than serious politics. It continues, however, to play an important role in British public life and retains considerable constitutional functions (Sales 2007) as well as a profoundly ideological role, entrenching 'privilege, deference and an elite's sense of entitlement' (Bunting 2007: 87). The prominent involvement of Princes Harry and William in support of troops engaged in the Iraq war – and in Harry's case actual combat – was a highly political intervention aimed at gaining legitimacy for an unpopular war.

Balancing 'shared values' and inclusion of difference raises further problems in the promotion of Britishness. As Stevenson (2007: 3) puts it in the preface to the Smith Institute collection, 'there are clearly potential tensions between the desire to celebrate common values, and the notion of Britain as a nation that is welcoming and accommodating of a wide range of cultures and belief systems'. These tensions are embedded in the liberal state, which permits the practice of a range of religious beliefs, some of which may include values that the majority do not share and may see as repressive or illiberal. The liberal version of multiculturalism that has predominated in Britain has extended this to accommodate other religious and cultural practices. Some commentators, however, have espoused an 'aggressive new liberalism' (Kundnani 2008: 41) to attack multiculturalism and diversity and to suggest that accommodation to the Muslim population has gone too far. In the name of promoting liberal values, this has led some to support illiberal policies such as the invasion of Iraq.

While there are clear differences between the racial, cultural and civic boundaries of Britishness, in practice many accounts combine some or all of these. Although all but the far right reject an explicitly racial view of Britishness, the writings of Goodhart, one of the most vociferous of the new liberal commentators, demonstrate how slippage can occur between civic notions of citizenship and more exclusive notions of national belonging. He claims on the one hand that citizenship is a 'not an ethnic, blood and soil concept but a more abstract political idea – implying equal legal, political and social rights (and duties) for people inhabiting a given national space' but goes on to suggest that 'for most of us [citizenship] is something we do not choose but are born into – it arises out of a shared history, shared experiences and, often, shared suffering' (2004: 3). This mixture of boundaries is reflected in the survey evidence analysed by Heath and Roberts (2008), who found that 'the predominant conception of national identity in Britain today is one that emphasizes ethnic as well as civic criteria'.

The racial and cultural boundaries of Britishness clearly exclude 'outsiders', including those born within Britain, who do not share this ethnicity or history. While the civic version claims to be inclusionary, the appropriation as British of values that are in fact universal denigrates other traditions and can provide legitimacy for illiberal acts (see Mirza, Chapter 6 of this volume). Moreover, the boundaries around citizenship are becoming more tightly policed, excluding those outsiders deemed not to have a right to belong, a policy vigorously pursued alongside the 'Britishness' agenda.

The disunited kingdom?

The British state was built on the dominance of England over the other nations in the United Kingdom and thus embodies inequalities of power and status between its component nations which are compounded by anachronisms such as the privileged status of the Church of England. These inequalities mean that the United Kingdom's borders continue to be contested by, for example, nationalist movements in Scotland and Northern Ireland.

These inequalities are reflected in the imbalance in the way in which people identify with 'Britishness'. Heath and Roberts (2008), in an analysis of evidence from national surveys, show that in the last decades of the twentieth century there was a decline in the proportion of people in Great Britain who thought of themselves as primarily or exclusively British, and a growing proportion who thought of themselves as Scottish, Welsh or English rather than British. They point out that in England the distinction between British and English is very 'fuzzy' and not as sharp as that between British and Scottish or Welsh. This reflects the 'conflation of English and British national identity', which has become the 'default public position on Britishness of the political elite' (Andrews and Marinetto 2010). Bechofer and McCrone (2007) suggest that this conflation has been reflected in official promotion of Britishness and that 'Brown's attempt to forge a "British way" relies over-much on English history and examples rather than genuinely British ones'.

Significantly, Northern Ireland has been largely excluded from contemporary discussions of Britishness. A report for the CRE states that 'the most basic, objective and uncontroversial conception of the British people' is one that includes 'the English, Scots and the Welsh' (2005: 22), ignoring Northern Ireland. Goldsmith's official report on citizenship (2008) also ignores Northern Ireland, suggesting that a sense of British identity is widespread in 'all three territories'. Gordon Brown himself left out Northern Ireland in calling for the acknowledgement of the Union flag in 'England, Scotland and Wales'.

Northern Ireland is, however, the region within the United Kingdom where the symbols of Britishness – Union Jacks, pictures of the Queen – are most visible in everyday life and where people identify most strongly as 'British'. It is also the region where national identity is most fiercely contested. Unionist, or British, identity has been linked to conservative politics based on the maintenance of the privileges built into the foundation of the state. Unionism remains an identity that many within Northern Ireland – predominantly Catholics – reject, and a substantial proportion have Irish citizenship. The dominance of Unionism has made it difficult for some Protestants to find a progressive Protestant identity (Sales 1997). Ironically, although Northern Ireland Unionists have jealously guarded their Britishness, on travelling to Britain they find that they are seen as indistinguishable from other Irish people, their Britishness neither appreciated nor understood.

The level and nature of identification with 'Britishness' is very different within the four 'nations' of the United Kingdom and it therefore cannot provide the basis for a common sense of belonging. Furthermore, research for the CRE (2005) shows differing forms of identification between white and black and ethnic minority citizens in England, Scotland and Wales. Among white participants, the English thought of themselves as indistinguishably English or British, while both Scottish and Welsh identified more strongly as Scottish or Welsh than British. Participants from ethnic minorities were happy to identify as either Scottish or Welsh but not with Englishness, which they did not feel included them. As one put it, 'There is a difference between being British and being English. English is being indigenous, being white and from this country. But being British, the primary thing that comes to my mind is that you have a British passport' (quoted in CRE 2005: 40). This statement reflects the findings of research with British-born Asian young men (Hussain and Bagguley 2005). Britishness was crucial for them not as an identity but as a source of rights. 'Britishness' and 'Englishness' were seen as racialized identities, while citizenship as an identity was not. Those born in Britain felt that citizenship is their 'natural right' (ibid.: 411) but did not feel part of a common culture, first language or robust set of values shared by British citizens (ibid.: 414). They felt strongly that they belonged but perceived that the dominant white population did not fully accept that belonging (ibid.: 421). More recent research with Muslim young people in London produced similar findings in relation to identity (Ryan *et al.* 2009). Most participants felt positive about living in Britain and the rights and privileges associated with citizenship, but did not 'feel' British. They did, however, feel a strong sense of belonging and attachment to London and to their local neighbourhood in north London (see also Ryan, Chapter 5 in this volume). They cited religious and racial discrimination as reasons for not feeling British. Heath *et al.* (2010: 204) also suggest that the perception of discrimination reduces the likelihood of identification with Britishness among Muslims.

Significant sections of the population thus find it difficult to identify with Britishness. The fuzzy boundaries around the nation and national identity give it an abstract quality, and local place provides a firmer basis for producing a sense of belonging. Research on the integration of refugees found similar identification with locality (see, for example, Spencer 2006). Moreover, the inequalities that the state embodies are reflected in the differential identification of people across the nations of the United Kingdom and between different groups within it (including Muslims), and Britishness can be an identity that people feel excludes rather than includes.

Exclusion, Muslims and the boundaries of belonging

The promotion of strong national identity is always developed in opposition to the 'other' and has been particularly important in times of war and conflict, as a way of producing a constructed unity that hides the inequalities and divisions within the 'nation'. The promotion of Britishness is thus inevitably tied to some form of exclusion at the expense of those deemed to be 'non-British'. The borders around the nation are being tightened both in relation to the formal rules governing entry and citizenship and through the policing of behaviour and values that are deemed unacceptable.

Access to the formal status of British citizenship and its accompanying rights has shifted historically to include and exclude different groups. The Nationality Act 1948, which codified nationality in the post-Second World War period, created an 'undivided class of citizens of the UK and Colonies' (Goldsmith 2008: 14). Subsequent immigration acts undermined this 'undivided' class, distinguishing between the rights of citizens of the Old Commonwealth (predominantly white) and the New (predominantly the Indian subcontinent, Africa and the Caribbean). This was embodied in the distinction introduced in the Immigration Act 1971 between patrials (those with a parent or grandparent born in Britain) and non-patrials. This established an ethnic basis for citizenship (or *ius sanguinis*, citizenship based on descent).

Britain's managed migration policy has operated on an increasingly narrow notion of Britain's interests, selecting those deemed worthy of entry and settlement on the basis of their use for the economy (particularly their skills) and their country of origin. The recently imposed cap on labour migration from outside the European Union is part of an agenda of shifting from traditional areas of recruitment such as the Indian subcontinent towards the European Union, particularly the new member states. These restrictions impact on Muslims since the majority seeking to enter Britain are from outside the Union.

Underlying the restrictive immigration agenda is the notion of a 'tipping point' beyond which it would be dangerous to increase numbers of immigrants. The notion of British people as fundamentally 'tolerant' towards immigrants has been a consistent theme in official thinking (Holmes 1998) and underlies the notion that good race relations are dependent on rigid immigration controls (Sales 2007). Introducing a new strategy on immigration in 2005, Tony Blair suggested that the British 'tradition [of] tolerance is under threat' (Home Office 2005) from unwanted immigration. The claim that outsiders are in need of toleration, however, presents them as a problem. As Khan (2006) put it, 'I don't want to be tolerated. You tolerate a tooth ache. I should be accepted – like all British citizens regardless of colour.'

This notion of a 'tipping point' also underlies the official approach to diversity. As well as the rules on entry having been tightened, the path to long-term residence and citizenship has become more difficult, and conditional on 'appropriate' behaviour and values. Acquiring citizenship through 'naturalization' – an ideologically loaded term implying that membership of a nation-state is laid down by 'natural laws' (Castles and Davidson 2000) – has never been a right for aliens living within Britain. With the agenda of citizenship developed in the white paper *Secure Borders, Safe Haven*, immigration control has become tied to the notion of integration, whereas they had previously been strictly separate (Joppke 2009: 117). Gaining British citizenship has become dependent on the ability to pass tests on knowledge of the English language and 'life in the UK'. These tests exclude certain groups: the less literate and those with less opportunity for interaction, particularly women. The failure rate in 2007 was 31.3 per cent (MIPEX 2007) and the pass rate for Bangladeshis only 46.3 per cent (Goldsmith 2008: 118). Knowledge of the language of the society in which one lives is essential to effective participation, but in official policy it is increasingly being seen not as a facilitator of integration but as a condition for rights to residence and citizenship. The points-based system of 'earned' citizenship, which New Labour planned to introduce in 2011, would have involved deducting points where 'an active disregard for UK values is demonstrated'. This could include participation in lawful demonstrations such as those against the wars in Iraq and Afghanistan (Webber 2009), which have placed the British state in direct conflict with predominantly Muslim populations.[9] Citizenship can also be removed from those deemed to have behaved in an unacceptable, and thus 'un-British', way.

While the physical borders of the nation have been strengthened, domestic policy towards Muslims is increasingly dominated by security considerations and the so-called terrorist threat. At the same time, the social cohesion agenda has sought to promote common values, but, as Cheong and co-authors suggest, this is to be achieved at the expense of the social alienation of 'others' (2007: 23), thus strengthening the nation's ideological borders. Policies have been aimed at separating 'good' Muslims from 'bad', or 'moderates' from 'extremists' (see also Sardar, Chapter 1 of this volume). Inevitably, however, policy measures and their accompanying discourses aimed at the 'extremists' impact on all people who identify as, or are identified by others, as Muslims, while many commentators blur the distinction between Islam and Islamism as a political ideology, as for example Martin Amis's call for collective punishment of Muslim communities (quoted in Kundnani 2008: 43).

The Home Office's counter-terrorism strategy has involved two strands, 'hard' and 'soft' policies, which aim to work with mainstream Islam to isolate extremism (McLaughlin 2010: 105). The 'hard' policies have involved a range of measures including legislation such as the Terrorism Acts of 2006 and 2008, which have increased the powers of the security forces to gather information, including powers of detention for suspects. There has also been a doubling of state resources devoted to anti-terrorism since 2001 (ibid.: 106). Since 'terrorism is no longer defined by the territorial boundaries of the nation state' (ibid.), domestic intelligence is now linked to border control with the securitization of the issues of asylum and immigration (Squire 2009).

The Prevent Strategy, the 'soft' arm of this policy, was launched in 2007 as 'the preventative strand of the government's counter-terrorism strategy' and aimed 'to stop people becoming terrorists or supporting terrorism both in the UK and overseas'.[10] It was based largely on local partnership involving public bodies and Muslim organizations (Ryan *et al.* 2009). These bodies have had a wide remit in using the agenda to 'enhance community cohesion' (ibid.). In seeking to promote a 'moderate' or 'compliant' version of Islam, the government has become entangled in making distinctions between different versions of religious belief. The then Home Secretary, Jacqui Smith, suggested in 2008 that terrorism was a 'misinterpretation of religion' (quoted in Kundnani 2008: 54). This distinction between different versions of religious belief is, however, 'entirely outside the competence of the liberal state' (Joppke 2009: 14). Moreover, securing moderate allies in the war against terrorism has not been straightforward. The Muslim Council of Britain, for example, was dropped as the favoured organization of British Muslims after voicing criticism of foreign policy. While its dropping was clearly a political decision, the fact could not be acknowledged and was presented as a preference for another version of Islam (Kundnani 2008: 55).

The attempt to engineer compliance to an official agenda, and in particular to deny any connection between foreign policy and the growth of extremism, has blurred the boundaries between those perceived as 'moderate' and those seen as 'extremists', making Muslims as a whole part of a 'suspect community'. Government minister Baroness Warsi warned against the tendency to divide Muslims along these lines, which, she contends, can fuel misunderstanding and intolerance.[11] The identification of the social cohesion work within the Prevent Strategy as counter-terrorism has led, as the Home Office recently acknowledged, 'to accusations that the government's interest in Muslim communities is related only to the risk of terrorism'.[12] Moreover, the programme has been used to amass huge amounts of information on the 'political and religious views, information on mental health, sexual activity and associates' of Muslim people, most of whom have no involvement in crime, according to the *Guardian* newspaper. Shami Chakrabati of the civil rights organization Liberty is quoted as describing it as an attack on civil liberties which was 'unBritish'.[13] Security measures aimed at identifying terrorists have often targeted whole areas viewed as Muslim and led to false arrests, for example of the Kalam brothers, who were freed in 2006 after one of them had been shot and wounded by police (see also McLaughlin 2010: 107–108).

While Muslims are increasingly the object of policy, targeted for their lack of Britishness, evidence from the Citizenship Survey interestingly suggests that Muslim groups, like ethnic minorities in general, largely share the five civic values that Blair associated with Britishness (duty to vote, respect for the law, tolerance towards outsiders, equality of opportunity and patriotism) and that all ethnic minority groups are more likely to subscribe to values of equality (Heath *et al.* 2010: 203). The adherence to patriotism of the two groups that are predominantly Muslim, Pakistanis and Bangladeshis, however, was much lower than the average, indicating the lack of resonance of the 'Britishness' agenda.

Conclusion

Concern with Britishness has arisen both as a result of the impact of long-standing social and policy processes and from immediate events such as those connected with the 'war on terror'. The former have undermined social solidarity and often intensified segregation, on both ethnic and class lines, at local level. In the absence of policies to tackle the underlying causes of disenchantment and disconnection, the promotion of Britishness can do little to promote social cohesion.

The promotion of Britishness has been ambivalent and contradictory. While there have been attempts to promote a progressive and inclusive agenda, in failing to address the inequalities and undemocratic aspects of British life it inevitably ties Britishness to a version of national identity that privileges certain sections of the population and excludes others. The claiming of democratic values as uniquely 'British' is reminiscent of colonial attitudes in which the 'civilized' were distinguished from the uncivilized 'other'. Furthermore, the foreign policy pursued by successive governments, particularly in relation to the Middle East and the war in Iraq, have led many people, Muslim and non-Muslim, to become disenchanted with Britain's international role and what many would claim is a highly selective approach to democracy and human rights.

Britishness is too contested as an identity to be a source of unity. The construction of British national identity was based on inequalities between the different parts of the state and between different groups within its borders, and these inequalities are reflected in different levels of identification with 'Britishness'. The evidence does, however, suggest that British citizens, including Muslims, have strong attachment to their local area and to the democratic values which have been claimed as British. It appears, therefore, that there is a strong basis for the building of citizenship, based on democratic values that are widely shared. This needs to be accompanied by a critical examination of British history which acknowledges the undemocratic elements that have, as much as its progressive achievements, been part of the construction of the British state.

Notes

1 David Cameron, Conservative Party leader, on http://conservativehome.blogs.com/platform/2009/07/david-cameron-proud-to-be-british.html.
2 Campaign for State Education – Briefing, 'Faith Schools'. Online, available at: www.campaignforstateeducation.org.uk/Faith%20Schools%20March%202010.pdf.
3 'Being a British Muslim', speech to Fabian Society, 6 July 2006. Online, available at: www.fabians.org.uk/events/speeches/missing-a-positive-vision-for-british-muslims.
4 Tony Blair, speaking to the Commons Liaison Committee, 4 July 2006.

5 David Cameron, Conservative Party leader, on http://conservativehome.blogs.com/platform/2009/07/david-cameron-proud-to-be-british.html.
6 Michael Gove, speech to the Conservative Party Conference, 5 October 2010.
7 http://sheikyermami.com/2010/10/01/baroness-warsi-lectures-brits-on-britishness/.
8 Speech by Tony Blair, 'The duty to integrate: shared British values', 8 December 2006. Online, available at: www.politics.co.uk/news/2006/12/8/blair-warns-of-duty-to-integrate.
9 The Coalition government has abandoned the policy of earned citizenship but has not announced what will replace it.
10 www.homeoffice.gov.uk/counter-terrorism/. The Prevent Strategy is currently being reviewed and the new strategy will focus more explicitly on counter-terrorism and less on wider objectives of integration.
11 Speech at Leicester University, 19 January 2011.
12 See p. 48.
13 *Guardian* (London), 16 October 2009.

References

Ahmad, W. I. U. and Evergeti, V. (2010) 'The making and representation of Muslim identity in Britain: conversations with Muslim "elites"', *Ethnic and Racial Studies* 33 (10): 1697–1717.

Amin, A. (2002) 'Ethnicity and the multicultural city: living with diversity', *Environment and Planning A* 34 (6): 959–980.

Anderson, B. (1983) *Imagined Communities*, London: Verso.

Andrews, R. and Marinetto, M. (2010) 'No place like home? Britishness, multiculturalism and the politics of utopia', paper presented at the Political Studies Association Conference, Edinburgh, 29 March–1 April.

Bechhofer, F. and McCrone, D. (2007) 'Being British: a crisis of identity', *Political Quarterly* 78 (2): 251–260.

Bloch, A. and Solomos, J. (eds) (2010) *Race and Ethnicity in the 21st Century*, Basingstoke: Palgrave Macmillan.

Brown, G. (2004) Annual British Council Lecture, reprinted in the *Guardian* (London), 8 July.

Bunting, M. (2007) 'Faith and nation', in N. Johnson (ed.) *Britishness: Towards a Progressive Citizenship*, London: Smith Institute.

Burgess, S. and Wilson, D. (2004) *Ethnic Segregation in England's Schools*, CASE Paper 79, London: Centre for the Analysis of Social Exclusion (CASE), London School of Economics.

Cesarani, D. and Fulbrook, M. (1996) 'Introduction', in D. Cesarani and M. Fulbrook (eds) *Citizenship, Nationality and Migration in Europe*, London: Routledge.

Cantle, T. (2001) *Community Cohesion*, report of the Independent Review Team chaired by Ted Cantle, London: Home Office.

Castles, S. (2000) *Ethnicity and Globalization*, London: Sage.

Castles, S. and Davidson, A. (2000) *Citizenship and Migration: Globalization and the Politics of Belonging*, Basingstoke: Macmillan.

Cheong, P. H., Edwards, R., Goulbourne, H. and Solomos, J. (2007) 'Immigration, social cohesion and social capital: a critical review', *Critical Social Policy* 27 (1): 24–49.

Cohen, R. (1995) 'Fuzzy frontiers of identity: the British case', *Social Identities* 1 (1): 35–62.

Colley, L. (1992) 'Britishness and otherness: an argument', *Journal of British Studies* 31 (3): 309–329.

Commission for Racial Equality (CRE) (2005) *Citizenship and Belonging: What Is Britishness?* London: CRE.

Farrell, M. (1980) *Northern Ireland: The Orange State*, London: Pluto Press.

Goldsmith, P. (2008) *Citizenship: Our Common Bond*, London: Ministry of Justice.

Goodhart, D. (2004) 'Discomfort of strangers', reprinted in the *Guardian* (London), 24 February.

Heath, A. and Roberts, J. (2008) 'British identity: its sources and possible implications for civic attitudes and behaviour', Oxford: Nuffield College, Oxford University. Online, available at: www.justice.gov.uk/docs/british-identity.pdf.

Heath, A., Rothon, C. and Ali, S. (2010) 'Identity and public opinion', in A. Bloch and J. Solomos (eds) *Race and Ethnicity in the 21st Century*, Basingstoke: Palgrave Macmillan.

Hickman, M. J. (1998) 'Reconstructing and deconstructing "race": British political discourses about the Irish in Britain', *Ethnic and Racial Studies* 21 (2): 288–307.

Hickman, M. J. and Walters, B. (1997) *Discrimination and the Irish community in Britain*, London: Commission for Racial Equality.

Holmes, C. (1988) *John Bull's Island: Immigration and British Society, 1871–1971*, Basingstoke: Macmillan.

Home Office (2002) *Secure Borders, Safe Haven: Integration with Diversity in Modern Britain* (White Paper), London: The Stationery Office.

Home Office (2005) *Controlling Our Borders: Making Migration Work for Britain. Five Year Strategy for Asylum and Immigration*, London: Home Office.

Hussain, Y. and Bagguley, P. (2005) 'Citizenship, ethnicity and identity: British Pakistanis after the 2001 "riots"', *Sociology* 39 (3): 407–425.

Jacobson, J. (2004) 'Perceptions of Britishness', online version of *Nations and Nationalism* 3 (2): 181–199.

Jessop, B. (1990) *State Theory: Putting Capitalist States in Their Place*, Cambridge: Polity Press.

Johnson, N. (ed.) (2007) *Britishness: Towards a Progressive Citizenship*, London: Smith Institute.

Joppke, C. (2009) *Veil: Mirror of Identity*, Cambridge: Polity Press.

Khan, S. (2006) 'Being a British Muslim', speech to the Fabian Society, 3 July.

Khan, S. (2007) 'Is Britishness relevant?', in N. Johnson (ed.) *Britishness: Towards a Progressive Citizenship*, London: Smith Institute.

Kofman, E., Phizacklea, A., Raghuram, P. and Sales, R. (2000) *Gender and International Migration in Europe: Employment, Welfare and Politics*, London: Routledge.

Kundnani, A. (2001) 'From Oldham to Bradford: the violence of the violated', *Race and Class* 43 (2): 105–131.

Kundnani, A. (2002) *The Death of Multiculturalism*, London: Institute of Race Relations.

Kundnani, A. (2008) 'Islamism and the roots of liberal rage', *Race and Class* 50 (2): 40–68.

Lewis, M. (2005) *Asylum: Understanding Public Attitudes*, London: Institute for Public Policy Research.

McLaughlin, E. (2010) 'Community cohesion and national security: rethinking policing and race', in A. Bloch and J. Solomos (eds) *Race and Ethnicity in the 21st Century*, Basingstoke: Palgrave Macmillan.

Migrant Integration Policy Index (MIPEX) (2007) (www.integrationindex.eu).

Nairn, T. (2006) 'Gordon Brown: bard of Britishness', in T. Nairn *et al.*, *Gordon Brown: 'Bard of Britishness'*, Cardiff: Institute of Welsh Affairs.

Parekh, B. (2006) 'Europe, liberalism and the "Muslim question"', in T. Modood, A. Triandafyllidou and R. Zapata-Barrero (eds) *Multiculturalism, Muslims and Citizenship: A European Approach*, London: Routledge.

Paul, K. (1997) *Whitewashing Britain: Race and Citizenship in the Postwar Era*, Ithaca, NY: Cornell University Press.

Rattansi, A. (2002) 'Who's British?', in *Cohesion, Community and Citizenship: Proceedings of a Runnymede Conference*, London: Runnymede Trust.

Rogers, B. and Muir, R. (2005) *The Power of Belonging: Identity, Citizenship and Community Cohesion*, London: Institute for Public Policy Research (Executive Summary).

Ryan, L., Kofman, E. and Banfi, L. (2009) *Muslim Youth in Barnet: Exploring Identity, Citizenship and Belonging Locally and in the Wider Context*, London: Middlesex University, Report for London Borough of Barnet.

Sales, R. (1997) *Women Divided: Gender, Religion and Politics in Northern Ireland*, London: Routledge.

Sales, R. (2007) *Understanding Immigration and Refugee Policy*, Bristol: Policy Press.

Spencer, S. (ed.) (2006) 'Refugees and other new migrants: a review of the evidence on successful approaches to integration', report commissioned by the Home Office, COMPAS Working Papers, Oxford University.

Squire, V. (2009) *The Exclusionary Politics of Asylum*, Basingstoke: Palgrave Macmillan.

Stevenson, W. (2007) Preface to N. Johnson (ed.) *Britishness: Towards a Progressive Citizenship*, London: Smith Institute.

Tilki, M., Ryan, L., D'Angelo, A. and Sales, R. (2009) *The Forgotten Irish: Report of a Research Project Commissioned by the Ireland Fund for Great Britain*, Social Policy Research Centre, Middlesex University.

Webber, F. (2009) 'Subject to British values', Institute of Race Relations, 10 September. Online, available at: www.irr.org.uk/2009/september/bw000002.html.

Winder, R. (2007) 'Immigration and national identity', in N. Johnson (ed.) *Britishness: Towards a Progressive Citizenship*, London: Smith Institute.

Young, J. (2002) 'To these wet and windy shores: recent immigration policy in the UK', paper presented at the Common Study programme in Critical Criminology, University of Athens, April.

3

EXPLORING SOCIAL SPACES OF MUSLIMS

Lucinda Platt

Introduction

This chapter addresses questions of social contact and interaction among Muslims. It asks what is the nature of the social 'space' that British Muslims occupy – who do they associate with and in what ways? Despite a number of localized studies on the detailed interactions of specific groups of Muslims, an overview of the patterns of interaction and sociality that pertain across British Muslims is largely missing. These issues are important because much discussion of Muslims in Britain hinges on the assumption that experiences of connection and participation are significant for both their welfare and the welfare of the societies in which they live more broadly. However, participative behaviours cannot be read off from geographical distributions, values or experience of socio-economic advantage and disadvantage. This chapter therefore aims to be a first step towards describing patterns of friendship and association among British Muslims, ascertaining opportunities for participation and inclusion, and identifying differences both between Muslims and non-Muslims and among British Muslims.

Minorities, difference and social networks

British Muslims are subject to an increasing level of research and policy attention and, indeed, research into that policy attention (Ansari 2002). Studies of British Muslims have covered employment (Open Society Institute EU Monitoring and Advocacy Program 2004), education and educational aspirations (Ahmad 2001), family and fertility (Georgiadis and Manning 2011), values, and political mobilization (Birt 2009). The transformation of identities in the context of key moments such as the Rushdie affair and the 7 July bombings have been highlighted, with some suggesting that (global) Muslim identities that were latent at that point, or were subordinate to alternative or more localized identities, emerged as a consequence (Ahmad and Evergeti 2010), or, alternatively, that private religious identities became politicized by these events (Nagel and Staeheli 2009). At a European level, Muslim identities are typically regarded as singular; and thus it is anticipated that investigation of different national minorities in the United Kingdom or other countries will tell us something about Muslim values, identities and activities more generally (Diehl *et al.* 2009; Modood 2009; Verkuyten 2007). This chapter focuses on British Muslims, but it does consider the issue of whether it is meaningful to think, even for British Muslims, of an overarching identity or whether it is more important to focus on the heterogeneity of British Muslims (Ansari 2002). A question for the future is how this discussion can be amplified in a cross-national perspective.

As has been pointed out, there has also been a transformation of public discourse in recent years, with British Muslims being constructed as 'others' (Modood 2009), and as possessing divergent values and acting separately, distinct from the rest of the population. Such messages echo Cantle's comment on communities leading 'parallel lives' (Community Cohesion Review Team 2001). For some, distinction is an essential part of cultural maintenance and re-imagination (Werbner 2005), while others have focused more crudely on the extent to which Muslims are simply 'different'; see, for example, Bisin *et al.* (2008), and see also the discussion in Georgiadis and Manning (2011). The implication has been that British Muslims' beliefs and values set them apart, geographically and socially, from other Britons.

This has been reinforced in the social capital literature with its distinction between 'good' and 'bad' capital, understood as the extent to which association reinforces or bridges particular group boundaries (Geys and Murdoch 2010; Lin 2001; Putnam 2000). The emphasis has been on ethnically based networks and in-group association as representing 'bad social capital' (Cheong *et al.* 2007); yet it is an argument that is used more often to draw attention to minority patterns of association than to question the exclusive or solitary nature of majority-group intercourse. Patterns of association are, typically, not measured directly but in relation to geographical distribution and concentration. We know, therefore, a certain amount about the extent to which differential social capital (measured in a range of ways) is linked to different types of areas (Letki 2008), but much less about what different minority groups actually do with their time and whom they spend it with. Propinquity and social intercourse among Muslims has been regarded as both negative and exclusive, while at the same time the actual contours of different groups' social activity is little understood. Such understanding, I would argue, is a necessary precursor to a consideration of the significance – or otherwise – and valuation of patterns of social interaction.

Social contact as social support

As well as ethnically bounded networks being regarded with suspicion, social capital has also been invoked to fill the gaps, and deflect focus from the material conditions of minorities and new migrants (Zetter *et al.* 2006). Social capital and community support come to be seen as the solution as well as potentially the cause of marginalization of minorities. There has thus been a parallel strand of investigation exploring the extent to which networks, especially faith-based networks, provide particular forms of resource and support that aid, rather than obstruct, inclusion (Furbey *et al.* 2006; Jayaweera and Choudhury 2008). The protective nature of social support deriving from concentrations of one's own group – religious, ethnic or ethno-religious – has been found in terms of reduced levels and impact of racism (Bécares *et al.* 2009), and as supporting participation in, for example, voting (Fieldhouse and Cutts 2007) or higher education (Thapar-Björkert and Sanghera 2010). Thus, there are reasons to consider forms of social networking and support as having positive consequences, regardless of the composition of those networks. To the extent that particular groups have greater or stronger networks, we would expect them to have greater welfare. Yet though we know something of the geography and spatial proximity of British Muslims (Peach 2006), and about the relationship between religious affiliation or religiousness and a range of outcomes (as noted above), we know remarkably little about the actual nature of British Muslims' social contacts, their extent as well as their diversity (or homogeneity).

Moreover, it is important to consider social contact and social activity not just instrumentally – as a means to mobility through social capital or as leading to other positive consequences – but as goods in themselves. The importance of social contact as of value per se, and as an indicator of inclusion and well-being, has been noted in the social exclusion and multiple deprivation literature (Burchardt 2002; Levitas 2006). It goes back to the debate on the meaning and emphasis on the socially relative nature of poverty (Townsend 1979). It is now widely accepted that the ability (or inability) to participate relative to society's standards is central to the definition of poverty. This means that it is of interest to a wider conception of group welfare, one which moves beyond the dominant focus on labour market participation to identify whether minorities experience differential levels of social participation. There is much discussion of whether Muslims are isolationist (Battu *et al.* 2007; Battu and Zenou 2010; Blackaby *et al.* 1997; and see also the discussion in Saeed 2009), but much less attention is paid to whether they are in fact isolated – or relatively isolated.

Such a focus on social participation as welfare requires exploration of whether patterns of social contact are as extensive as for those from other groups. Are Muslims missing out, relative to other Britons – or even absolutely – on the core human experience of social contact? Or, instead, do faith-based networks help to foster extensive social engagement? Given the exclusionary discourse relating to Muslims, this becomes a moot point about their experience in the United Kingdom. In fact, recent analysis of sociability suggested that the two main British Muslim groups, Pakistanis and Bangladeshis, show a tendency to high levels of social contact, and a lower probability of isolation than some groups (Platt 2009), though patterns are distinctive, are somewhat gendered and are also shaped by economic resources. We do not, however, have any understanding of how social exclusion or inclusion is patterned across British Muslims as a whole, nor whether there are differences in friendship networks.

Muslims, heterogeneity and ethnic differentiation

This brings us to the issue of heterogeneity. So far, the discussion has focused on British Muslims; and there has been a tendency within the literature to assume a superordinate Muslim identity as subsuming heterogeneity among Muslims, for example by ethnic background or, indeed, across Europe. An alternative approach has been to describe the experience of the two main British Muslim groups, Pakistanis and Bangladeshis, as summarizing the experience of British Muslims (Open Society Institute EU Monitoring and Advocacy Program 2004), and it has been noted how British Muslim identities have become heavily ethnicized or identified with South Asian minority groups. Much of the qualitative literature on the experience of British Muslims also focuses on either South Asian Muslims or Pakistani Muslims (e.g. Ahmad 2001; Dwyer 2000). There are, of course, exceptions, but the emphasis within these on their distinctiveness emphasizes the general point. This is in part because the identities considered in the various studies are located at the intersection of ethnicity and religious identity (Archer 2009). There is a growing literature that is beginning to emphasize the importance of ethno-religious groups as constituting more meaningful social units for analysis than undifferentiated ethnic groups (Brown 2000; Karlsen and Nazroo 2010; Lindley 2002; Longhi *et al.* 2009; Platt 2005). However, these studies have generally been used to reveal heterogeneity within ethnic categories rather than to enhance our understanding of the diversity of British Muslims. The heterogeneity of British Muslims, and the experience of specific groups of Muslims, including their sometime unwillingness to be defined as 'British Muslims' (Nagel and Staeheli 2009), merits, it has been argued, at least recognition and preferably further attention.

When one is considering British Muslims' patterns of social interaction and sociability specifically, it might make sense to see these social contacts as ethnically embedded. Overarching Muslim identities might be expected to be particularly salient in the context of political mobilization (Birt 2009) or when expressing an embattled sense of personal identity. In addition, Muslim identities have been asserted by those UK-born minorities attempting to make sense of ongoing minoritization. British Muslim identities can be contrasted to often highly localized regional identifications in the parental country of origin, which are more a feature of, and more pertinent to, migrant generations (Alam and Husband 2006; Dhindsa 1998; Jacobson 1997). Indeed, it has been pointed out that in fact Muslim identification may take place as a very locally constituted demarcation of belonging and ownership of place (Ahmad and Evergeti 2010; Archer 2009; and see also Ryan, Chapter 5 in this volume, and Ahmad, Chapter 9). A global (rather than transnational) identity can thus be linked to a highly localized sense of belonging.

When it comes to specific practices of engagement and interaction, these might be expected to remain strongly embedded in ethnically specific practices of commensality and exchange. Activities such as shared eating and the maintenance of eating practices associated with – or recreated as – those of the country of origin emphasize ethnic identities (Bush *et al.* 1998; Lawton *et al.* 2008; Warde 1997). At the same time, fasting, the breaking of fasts and the observation of particular food proscriptions pattern informal exchange and sociability along religious lines. Additionally, faith-based institutions provide opportunities for social support, and a context for coreligionist contact. Nevertheless, religious institutions, even if not ethnically exclusive, tend to be distinguished by ethnicity (Salway *et al.* 2007). And shared language of ancestry or upbringing provides a significant basis of shared interaction, even if it is only one of several languages and the basis is one of attachment rather than practical necessity. Patterns of settlement are also more strongly distinguished by ethnicity than by religious affiliation (Peach 2006). Thus, overall, we might expect Muslim identity to be much more salient qua identity among British Muslims, but that ethnic distinctions will be observed when we look at patterns of friendship and social activity. We can explore this question of heterogeneity in two ways: by examining variation across Muslims by ethnic group, and by investigating whether there is homogeneity among those of Indian ethnicity regardless of religious affiliation. Indians are the only ethnic group for which there are sufficient proportions from different faiths to make this exercise viable with existing data.

The aims of what follows are, then, threefold. First, the chapter sets out to address the question of the actual levels and nature of Muslim social contact. In the words of the chapter title, what are the social spaces of British Muslims? If social contact both is important individually and provides group support, how far do British Muslims have access to friendships and social resources? Are their patterns of interaction distinctive, compared to those of non-Muslim Britons? Given that social resources are likely to be especially important for marginalized groups and those who face widespread antagonism and discrimination, do we find evidence of relative exclusion or of opportunities for social support?

Second, the chapter aims to explore the extent to which Muslims' patterns of social interaction cross religious or ethnic boundaries. To what extent are patterns of interaction homogeneous or heterogeneous in terms of the 'others' they involve? And how do these compare with those of non-Muslims, both the non-Muslim majority and non-Muslim minorities? Do British Muslims appear to be social 'mixers', or gain social contact from those 'more like themselves'? This also involves exploring the question of the extent to which different forms of homophily reinforce or challenge each other. How does 'connectedness' play out in relation to different forms of boundary-crossing? And, again, are British Muslims distinctive in the extent to which different forms of networks reinforce each other?

The third aim is to investigate the extent to which Muslims themselves are differentiated or similar. British Muslims come from a range of different ethnic origins and relationships with the United Kingdom. These ethnic groups have distinctive histories and patterns of exclusion. Does exploring Muslim experience hide patterns of ethnic diversity? Are Muslims better understood in terms of ethnic origins and antecedents, or, conversely, does it make sense to speak of British Muslims as a whole when examining patterns of social interaction specifically?

These questions are addressed in interlinking fashion in the analysis of representative survey data for England and Wales. The next section describes the data before reporting the findings.

Data and methods

To explore these questions effectively, this chapter uses the Citizenship Survey and investigates patterns of friendship drawing on the most recently available (2008/2009) survey, supplemented with specific questions on social activities only asked in the 2001 survey.

The Citizenship Survey started out as a biennial cross-sectional household survey of around 15,000 individuals living in England, with sweeps in 2001, 2003 and 2005. From 2007/2008 it moved to continuous fieldwork with annual data releases. The survey was explicitly designed to capture information about the involvement of individuals in a range of community and civic activities, their experience of their neighbourhood and attachment to it, as well as their experiences of local services, their networks and their experiences of discrimination. Since the survey is intended to capture ethnic-group differences in 'citizenship' and community experiences, it comprises a core 10,000-person main sample with a booster sample of approximately 5,000 members of minority ethnic groups. Recent surveys have also included a 1,200-person Muslim boost sample. The data are supplied with survey weights that adjust for survey design and for response probabilities, and these have been employed throughout the analyses.

In 2001 (Home Office and BMRB 2003), questions were asked on frequency of visits from friends, visits to friends, going out, and participation in organized activities. These were used in Platt's (2009) study of social isolation and ethnicity. Here they are coded into binary variables distinguishing those who have visits from friends at least once a fortnight, those who visit friends at least once a fortnight, those who go out socially at least once a fortnight, and those who take part in some form of organized activity at least once a month. These therefore describe the different forms and patterns of social engagement among Muslims and can be investigated for the extent to which they differ.

Questions on composition of friendship networks are taken from the 2008/2009 survey (Department for Communities and Local Government and National Centre for Social Research 2010). These cover the proportion of friends from the same ethnic group or with similar incomes, and the number of close friends. These measures are used in the ensuing analysis.

There are also a series of questions on 'social mixing', capturing information on interaction with those from other ethnic or religious groups in public or social situations, but going beyond purely economic interactions such as buying something from someone. The questions cover both the frequency of mixing and the contexts of mixing, such as at home, work, school, a café and so on. Here we use the general measure of whether the respondent has mixed in any context at least monthly, and also a much more specific measure of whether the respondent has 'mixed' in their or another person's home at least monthly. This latter variable therefore covers forms of contact in the private setting of the home, which might be considered more significant (and more protected) than external settings.

The ethnic group and religious affilation of all respondents were asked in each sweep of the survey and coded using the standard ONS categories. These measures are used to distinguish Muslims from non-Muslims, to distinguish those non-Muslims forming the white British majority from other non-Muslims, and to distinguish within religion by ethnicity and within the Indian ethnic group by religious affiliation. The numbers in each subpopulation and in both surveys can be seen in Table 3.1, along with some key characteristics for each survey.

Simple tabulations of distributions on the key measures of social activity and social contact are supplemented by log-linear analyses to capture the relationship between diferent forms of homophily (economic and ethnic); and binary and ordered logistic regressions are estimated to explore social mixing and friendship patterns in a multivariate context, controlling for other key variables.

The multivariate analyses of social mixing and close friendship use measures of whether born in the United Kingdom or outside the United Kingdom, family status (whether married/living with a partner or single or widowed/divorced/separated), number of children in the household, number of adults in the household, own and partner's income, and sex. All the tabulations have been broken down by sex and I discuss any differences in the text, but only report in the tables the results for men and women combined.

In exploring patterns of friendship and homophily, we do not, unfortunately, have precise information on the religious composition of networks or on religious mixing. Instead, we have information on composition of friendship by ethnicity, and the extent of mixing across either ethnic or faith lines. It will not therefore be possible to answer questions specifically about interfaith contact; rather, the chapter focuses on the size of, and general variation in, friendship networks.

Results

Patterns of socialization

I start by considering the basic questions of what British Muslims' patterns of social participation look like. Table 3.2 illustrates the proportions of Muslims and non-Muslims engaging in different forms of social activity at particular frequencies in 2001. Inspection of the table indicates that there do seem to be somewhat distinctive patterns of sociability, though it is not clear that these are greater or lesser for Muslims compared to non-Muslims, as the direction of the differences varies according to the activity. Muslims are more likely than both all non-Muslims and non-Muslim minorities to have friends round and to visit friends. These differences are statistically significant. Tests show that for these forms of activity there are no

TABLE 3.1 Distributions of Muslims across samples and key characteristics

		% women	*Average age*	*% UK born*	*N (unweighted)*
2001	Muslims	44	34	31	2,195
	All non-Muslims	51	47	93	13,107
	Minority-group non-Muslims	51	44	41	4,339
	Indian Hindus	45	40	30	652
	Indian Sikhs	51	37	51	349
	Indian Muslims	53	35	42	188
	Pakistani Muslims	44	34	42	917
	Bangladeshi Muslims	48	32	22	566
	Black African Muslims	42	33	9	115
2008/2009	Muslims	42	35	32	2,135
	All non-Muslims	52	47	90	12,746
	Minority group non-Muslims	49	40	30	4,763
	Indian Hindus	39	39	24	902
	Indian Sikhs	49	40	44	355
	Indian Muslims	42	40	28	254
	Pakistani Muslims	43	35	40	968
	Bangladeshi Muslims	40	34	25	345
	Black African Muslims	46	36	15	188

Source: Citizenship Surveys 2001 and 2008/2009. Proportions and means are weighted to population proportions.

TABLE 3.2 Patterns of social activity: percentage of each group engaging in each activity, across Muslims and non-Muslims, 2001

	Muslims					*Non-Muslims*	
	All	*Indian*	*Pakistani*	*Bangladeshi*	*Black African*	*All*	*Excluding majority*
Visits friends at least once a fortnight	63	71	65	71	49	58	54
Has friends round at least once a fortnight	68	82	69	74	62	61	61
Goes out at least once a fortnight	40	50	41	42	29	48	47
Participates in an organized activity at least once a month	45	48	46	43	43	53	53

Source: Citizenship Survey 2001. Weighted percentages.

significant differences among Muslims between men and women: both sexes are just as likely to engage in these activities. This might be unsurprising if these are family-level activities that tend to involve both partners in a couple. Nevertheless, if we compare by sex between Muslims and non-Muslims, we find that the differences are statistically significant only for men, and not for women. That is, Muslim women appear to be little different from other women in their patterns of reciprocal, domestic visiting, whereas Muslim men engage in this form of social behaviour more than other men.

When we turn to the other forms of activity – going out and participation in organized activities – Muslims are less likely than non-Muslims to engage in these forms of activity. However, here Muslim women and men differ significantly from each other, with Muslim men more likely to engage in these forms of activity than Muslim women. Muslim women are also significantly less likely to engage in these activities than non-Muslim women. But Muslim men are also significantly less likely to go out than non-Muslim men. Given that a majority of Muslim men belong to the two poorest ethnic groups, Pakistanis and Bangladeshis, and a substantial proportion of the remainder are black Africans, who also have high rates of poverty, this is likely to be in part a matter of resources. An earlier study of ethnic group isolation using these data (Platt 2009) showed that this was indeed the case, with income constraining the nature of the participation of Pakistanis and Bangladeshis. When it comes to participation in organized activitities, Muslim men are no less likely to participate than non-Muslim men, even though Muslim women are significantly less likely to participate in organized activities. There would thus appear to be both somewhat distinctive patterns of sociability among Muslims and also some gendering of more public activities, with Muslim women less likely to participate in these forms of activity.

It was posited earlier that patterns of sociability might be expected to be rooted in ethnic patterns of reciprocity and commensality – though this discussion has also drawn attention to the potentially important role of resource constraints in shaping specific patterns of social activity. Thus, while we might expect to see differences between ethnic groups on the basis of the first contention, we might also expect to see differences among Indians according to religious affiliation, given the differences in economic position across Indians, when grouped by religion (Longhi *et al.* 2009). When we look across Muslims by ethnic group, we see that there are indeed distinctive differences. Interestingly, on every measure Indian Muslims are most likely to participate and black African Muslims least likely. These differences are statistically significant for reciprocal visiting and significant at the 10 per cent level for going out. There are no significant differences in relation to participation in organized activities across Muslim groups. Thus, among Muslims there is not the complementarity of activities that we might have expected from the study of ethnically specific patterns (Platt 2009). Instead, the patterns of domestic sociability (having friends round and going to visit friends) that were noted for Pakistanis and Bangladeshis seem to be enhanced among Indian Muslims. These two aspects of social activity also render Indian Muslims distinctive compared to other Indians. Indian Muslims are also more likely than other Muslims to go out or participate in organized activities; but in terms of going out, they are insignificantly different from Hindu or Sikh Indians, although they are significantly *less* likely than Sikhs to participate in organized activities.

Obviously, these comparisons use religious affiliation and ethnic group as tools with which to structure and observe patterns of social participation. They are simple measures and do not take account of all the other ways in which these categories differ (for some of these differences, refer back to Table 3.1). Locating the source of the difference within the categories across which differences are revealed has been shown to be a dubious undertaking and, in particular, can obscure the importance of class or income differentials (Nazroo 2003). Social activity also varies with age and with family situation. This descriptive analysis is not intended to suggest that patterns of social participation differ between Muslims and non-Muslims *because* they are Muslim or non-Muslim, nor that the ethnic differences among Muslims are culturally determined. However, it does reveal something of the distinctive social landscape of British Muslims. Sociability would appear to be a core element of that experience, even if the forms that sociability takes are shaped by income and influenced by gender. It is fair to say that British Muslims' social world is distinctive. However, at the same time, the distinctiveness is not common across all British Muslims: there is substantial diversity.

The relatively low level of participation in organized activities among British Muslims suggests that organized faith-based activity may not form a particular resource for Muslims, and perhaps less so than for other groups. Alternatively, given relatively high rates of mosque attendance, respondents may not have identified the question as reflecting activities linked to the religious community. Black Africans overall were more likely to participate in organized activities than other groups in

Platt's (2009) study, and this was attributed in part to church-based activity, which has been shown to play an important role in the networks of black African Christians (Salway *et al.* 2007). Religious participation may still provide a resource, but perhaps less so – or be less recognized as doing so – than patterns of exchange based on local connectedness and shared income constraints. The role of similarity in networks, and the extent to which different froms of homophily (ethnic and income) are implicated in one another, are, therefore, the subject of the next section.

Homophily

Here we explore those questions that ask about the extent to which the respondents' friends have the same ethnic group or similar incomes to the respondent. As can be seen from Figure 3.1, non-Muslims are significantly more likely than Muslims to have friends entirely from the same ethnic group, by a factor of about 2 (50 per cent compared to 25 per cent). However, this can in large part be understood as an exposure issue. Non-Muslims are dominated by the majority, where opportunities for friendships with those from the same group are easily available and conversely where exposure to those from other groups is relatively low. If we compare non-Muslim minorities with Muslims for proportions with friends entirely from own ethnic group, the distribution of friendships across ethnic boundaries is not significantly different. Thus, all minorities, whether Muslim or not, are more

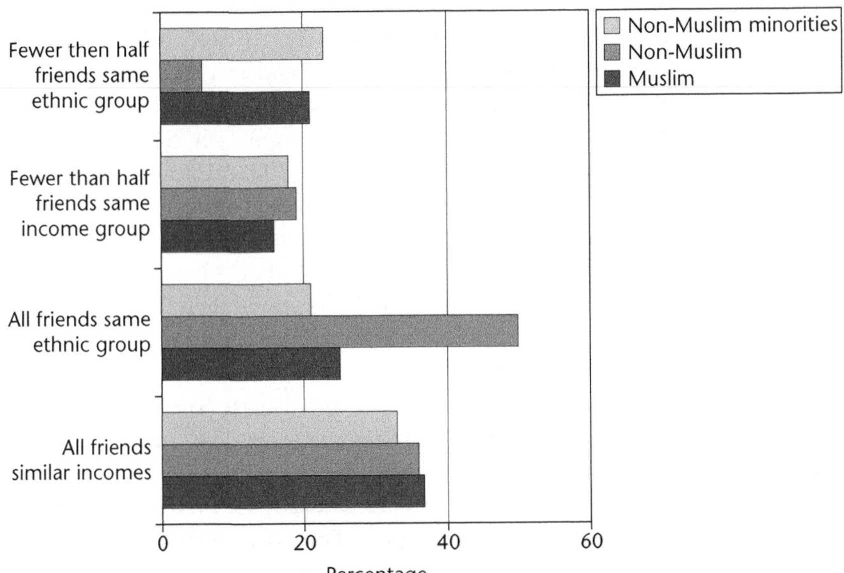

FIGURE 3.1 Homophily among Muslims and non-Muslims (source: Citizenship Survey 2008/9)

likely to have friends from other groups and more likely to have a majority of their friends from groups other than their own, compared to the population as a whole. In the context of discussions about isolationism, this obvious point is nevertheless an important one.

Intra-group friendships tend to be higher than random sorting of groups across the population would suggest because different forms of stratification, including geographical sorting processes, make contact with one's own group more likely (McPherson *et al.* 2001). Thus, taking account of distributions across a range of characteristics (such as income and class) can show how relative concentration of in-group friendships would take place without any additional factors deriving from preferences or exclusion. We can always expect to find that minority group networks over-represent members of the same minority group relative to what their population proportion would suggest, since different forms of stratification, such as income or class and ethnicity, tend to mutually reinforce one another. Nevertheless, that does not necessarily imply that minority groups' within-group networks enhance their exclusion – relating to the emphasis on 'bad' social capital, discussed above. We can explore this question empirically by looking at one additional dimension of homophily within friendship networks. In this way we can examine whether ethnic homophily tends to reinforce income homophily (and vice versa), as is typically the case, but also, perhaps more germanely, whether that is the same or different for Muslims and non-Muslims.

Income-based homophily is not as strong as ethnically based homophily, partly, no doubt, because others' (even friends') incomes are less easy to judge directly, and partly because incomes are more widely distributed than ethnic groups. Thus, while the majority are likely to come in contact predominantly with other majority-group members, there are more chances of contact with other income groups when explored purely from the point of view of potential exposure. Nevertheless, income homophily is still relatively high. Among non-Muslims, 36 per cent regarded all their friends as having similar incomes to themselves. This compares with the 50 per cent who regarded all their friends as coming from the same ethnic group. It is clearly lower than ethnic homophily but still represents a high level of income-based homophily. Among both Muslims and non-Muslim minorities the rate is similar, at between 33 per cent and 37 per cent, for having all their friends from the same income group. However, in this case it is higher than their rate for ethnically based friendships, which was around 21–25 per cent. Thus, minorities are more likely to share their income group with all their friends than to share their ethnicity; and this is true of Muslim and non-Muslim minorities alike. The United Kingdom is clearly heavily stratified by class and income across the population.

However, it is also the case that the forms of stratification are interrlelated, as the literature on homophily would lead us to expect. Thus, among those with all their friends from the same ethnic group, 47 per cent of non-Muslims overall, 54 per cent of non-Muslim minorities and 59 per cent of Muslims also shared their income group with all their friends. Among those for whom fewer than half their friends were from the same ethnic group, 25 per cent of non-Muslims, 27 per cent of non-

Muslim minorities and 31 per cent of Muslims shared their income group with all their friends. Conversely, among those who shared the same income group with all their friends, 65 per cent of non-Muslims overall, 34 per cent of non-Muslim minorities and 39 per cent of Muslims also had all their friends from the same ethnic group. This reduced to 44 per cent, 16 per cent and 15 per cent respectively when the income group was shared with fewer than half of their friends. It is, then, possible to argue that ethnically based friendships reinforce stratification; but this is true across the population. It is even more obvious, moreover, that income stratification increases ethnic exclusivity of friendships. To explore these relationships in somewhat more detail, I estimate log-linear models to ascertain how income homophily and ethnic homophily vary together or are independent across Muslims and non-Muslims. The results are given in Table 3.3.

We can see from Table 3.3 that the model of independence (model 1) is strongly rejected, as are the models of block independence where only one of the three relationships is constrained (models 2a–c). Model 3b, a model of conditional independence, which constrains the relationship between income and ethnic homophily and between Muslim or non-Muslim affiliation and ethnic homophily, fits the data well. It does not fit as well as the model of uniform association which constrains all the three-way relationships (model 4); but since it is more parsimonious and provides an adequate fit, with only 1 per cent of cases being misclassified, it is an appropriate summary of the data.

From this model we can calculate the odds ratio for having all friends in the same ethnic group rather than fewer than half from the same ethnic group for those with all friends in a similar income group compared to those with fewer than half from the same income group. Those with friends from the same income group had 3.2 times the odds of having friends from the same ethnic group. That is, those with all friends from the same income group were much more likely to have friends from the same ethnic group (rather than few friends from the same ethnic group) than those with few friends from the same income group. And this relationship holds across Muslims and non-Muslims. However, there is no difference in the odds of having friends in a similar income group for Muslims relative to non-Muslims.[1] This analysis sheds some light on the ways in which homophily in terms of income and homophily in terms of ethnicity are mutually constitutive. It also shows that these patterns are common across different groups, even if the probability of having friends of different ethnicities itself varies.

There is an extent to which these results provide some support for the contention that networks which are bounded on one dimension may close off access to more varied networks in another, the notion of 'bad' social capital (Cheong *et al.* 2007). However, they do not provide any evidence that this is more an issue for some groups – and specifically Muslims – than for others.

As was noted in the introduction, the focus on the heterogeneity of social networks still misses some of the crucial point about social networks that, over and above the instrumental perspective that sees networks as routes to mobility, jobs and so on, they can be considered as having value in their own right, regardless of

TABLE 3.3 Results of log-linear models of ethnic and income homophily among Muslims and non-Muslims

Model		*G2*	*df*	*p*	*Comparison*	*Change G2 (df)*	*% misclassified*
1	M + E + I	1,977	27	0.000	–		29
2a	M + E + I + [MI]	1,066	21	0.000	1–2a	811 (6)	24
2b	M + E + I + [EI]	1,063	24	0.000	1–2b	814 (3)	24
2c	M + E + I + [ME]	845	21	0.000	1–2c	1122 (6)	23
3a	M + E + I + [MI] + [EI]	232	12	0.000	2c–3a	513 (9)	3
3b	M + E + I + [MI] + [ME]	19	12	0.101	2c–3b	826 (9)	1
3c	M + E + I + [MI] + [ME]	843	18	0.000	2c–3c	2 (3)	23
4	M +E + I + [MI] + [EI] + [ME]	3	9	0.976	3b–4	16 (3)	<1

Source: Citizenship Survey 2008/2009.

Note

M = Muslim compared to non-Muslim; E = levels of ethnic homophily; I = levels of income homophily.

composition. For those with no friends, after all, it is irrelevant to discuss issues of homophily. In the final section, therefore, we go back to a consideration of the welfare implications of friendship by exploring the extent to which Muslims have close friends and how that compares with other groups and how it differs among Muslims of different ethnicities. Before that, however, we examine the question of diversity of networks from another perspective by looking at more general social 'mixing'.

Social mixing

The Citizenship Survey, concerned with questions of social interaction, asks a number of questions about the frequency and context of mixing socially with those from other ethnic or religious groups. As Table 3.4 shows – and perhaps unsurprisingly – rates of mixing are high, though, as with friendships, the chances of mixing across ethnic or religious boundaries are higher for minorities than for the majority. The second row of Table 3.4, however, shows that rates of mixing in own or another's house on at least a monthly basis are somewhat lower. The rates are still significantly higher, though, for minorities than for the non-Muslim majority; and there is no difference in the distributions for men and women by group. There are no significant differences between Muslims and non-Muslim minorities, or among Muslims. While the patterns accord with those identified for heterophilic friendships, they are nevertheless interesting since they show that cross-group contacts are not restricted to the public sphere. Having greater social contact but restricting that contact to outside the home could be consistent with an argument that social contact is primarily based on exposure. Within-home contacts seem to involve a more conscious inclusion of others. At the same time, for white majority members, ethnically homogeneous social contacts are more likely to be cross-religion contacts, given the higher proportion with no religion among the white majority. This would facilitate higher rates of cross-group contact even without crossing ethnic boundaries. By contrast, and particularly for Pakistanis and Bangladeshis, own-ethnic-group contacts will also be religiously homogeneous in the vast majority of cases. Cross-religious contacts will therefore also be cross-ethnic contacts in most cases. Thus, the majority can achieve religious mixing within ethnic boundaries, but minorities are much less likely to be able to do so. Nevertheless, what we see from Table 3.4 suggests that minority group members' homes are less likely to be ethnically or religiously exclusive areas than those of majority group members. If we refer back to Table 3.2 and the earlier discussion on social activities, this would suggest that such activities may not be so ethnically embedded after all, even if the patterning is ethnically distinctive.

As with the earlier tabulations, these descriptions of social activity may disguise as much as they reveal, in the sense that intensity and nature of social activity may be related to a range of characteristics that happen to vary between Muslims and non-Muslims. To explore whether we can understand patterns of social mixing in relation to distributions of age, family structure and other

TABLE 3.4 General social mixing and domestic social mixing across Muslims and non-Muslims

	Muslims					*Non-Muslims*			
	All	*P'stani*	*B'deshi*	*African*	*Indian*	*Indian Sikhs*	*Indian Hindus*	*All*	*All minorities*
General social mixing	94	94	95	92	97	95	97	80	94
Domestic social mixing	59	57	54	59	56	62	60	34	57

Source: Citizenship Survey 2008/2009.

Note
'General social mixing' = mixing socially with people from other ethnic or religious groups at least once a month. 'Domestic social mixing' = mixing socially with people from other ethnic or religious groups in own or others' home at least once a month.

potentially relevant characteristics, logistic regression models were estimated for the probability of any social mixing at least once a month and for mixing in own or others' homes at least once a month. Table 3.5 shows the results of these models. For this analysis, the non-Muslim majority was distinguished from non-Muslim minorities to give three mutually exclusive categories. The same variables were included in both models, even though some were found not to be significantly associated with each of the outcomes. In order to distinguish potential generational differences, a dummy for whether or not UK born was included. Furthermore, since this might be expected to differ in its effect for the UK majority and across minority groups, it was interacted with both the Muslim and the non-Muslim minority dummies.

Table 3.5 shows that there are no significant differences between men and women in their probability of mixing but that women are more likely to mix in their own or others' homes. Age decreased the probability of mixing, but it did so linearly for mixing at home and exponentially for mixing in others' homes. Interestingly, single and separated or widowed respondents were more likely than couples to mix socially. On the other hand, the number of adults in the household increased the probability of social mixing, presumably by increasing the range of potential contacts. Children, who might be anticipated to act as links to different families and therefore increase mixing, in fact made no difference. Combined own and respondent's income was positively associated with both mixing in general and mixing in own or others' homes. Thus, we see again the relevance of resources for opportunities for engagement more generally. Being born outside the United Kingdom increased the probability – for the reference category, of white British – of mixing in the home, though it was insignificant for general mixing and was therefore excluded from the revised specification (in the second column). Being non-UK born would appear to increase diversity of interchange within homes among the majority.

Turning to the differences between Muslims, non-Muslim majority and non-Muslim minorities, even after controlling for these differences, Muslims and non-Muslim minorities were substantially more likely both to mix socially in general and to mix in their own or others' home. Minorities, whether Muslim or non-Muslim, were not, however, significantly different from each other in their probability of social mixing. Interestingly, for mixing in the context of the home, the interaction between country of birth and minority status effectively cancelled out the greater probability of the non-UK born to engage in this sort of domestic social interaction. Thus, both UK- and non-UK-born minorities were more likely to engage in mixing socially in own or others' home than the majority, and the non-UK born were no more likely to do so than the UK born. We can see this more clearly by looking, in Figure 3.2, at the predicted probabilities of mixing either generally or in own or another's home from these models. These probabilities are evaluated for those in couples and with mean values on other characteristics. As the probabilities are not significantly different for men and women, or, for minorities, between UK and non-UK born, they are illustrated just for UK-born men.

TABLE 3.5 Probability of social mixing: results from logistic regression models of general social mixing and mixing in own or another's home

	(1)	(2)	(3)
	Any mixing at least monthly Model 1	*Any mixing at least monthly Model 2*	*Mixing at home*
Sex: Men (reference)	0	0	0
Women	0.0132	0.0136	0.125*
	(0.0673)	(0.0673)	(0.0575)
Age	–0.00786	–0.00803	–0.0274**
	(0.0112)	(0.0112)	(0.00915)
Age squared/1,000	–0.235*	–0.234*	0.0561
	(0.100)	(0.1000)	(0.0888)
Couple (reference)	0	0	0
Single	0.602***	0.594***	0.723***
	(0.123)	(0.123)	(0.0848)
Separated/widowed/divorced	0.443***	0.447***	0.510***
	(0.0988)	(0.0988)	(0.0853)
Number of adults in household	0.186**	0.188**	0.112**
	(0.0578)	(0.0576)	(0.0354)
Number of children	–0.0444	–0.0462	–0.00752
	(0.0456)	(0.0456)	(0.0328)
Income	0.0153***	0.0153***	0.00807***
	(0.00188)	(0.00187)	(0.00109)
UK born (reference)	0		0
Not UK born	0.226	–	0.579**
	(0.267)		(0.199)
Non-Muslim majority (reference)	0	0	0
Muslims	1.759***	1.487***	1.019***
	(0.374)	(0.149)	(0.166)

Non-Muslim minorities	0.731**	1.199***	1.017***
	(0.224)	(0.147)	(0.122)
Not UK-born by Muslim	–0.574	–	–0.602*
	(0.475)		(0.267)
Not UK-born by	0.503	–	–0.704**
non-Muslim minority	(0.394)		(0.247)
Constant	1.430***	1.437***	–0.502+
	(0.362)	(0.360)	(0.258)
Observations	12,454	12,465	12,454
Pseudo R^2	0.125	0.124	0.086
ll	–5,176.1	–5,182.6	–7,529.9
chi^2	836.8	849.9	732.8
df_m	13	10	13

Source: Citizenship Survey 2008/2009.

Notes
Standard errors in parentheses. $^{+}$ $p < 0.10$, * $p < 0.05$, ** $p < 0.01$, *** $p < 0.001$.

We see from Figure 3.2 that mixing with those from other ethnic or religious groups is much more likely for those from minority groups, even after controlling for relevant characteristics, and that this extends to social contact within the private sphere of the home, which might be considered a more exclusive domain.

We have seen, then, that there are relatively high levels of social contact among British Muslims across a range of measures, but at the same time these contacts are clearly shaped by opportunity structures. In the final subsection we explore the extent to which British Muslims can draw on the particular forms of support and well-being that are typically offered by close friendships.

Close friends

Here we explore the extent to which British Muslims have opportunities to forge and maintain close friendships, and to what degree. We explore this issue from the perspective that close friends are a 'good', capable of providing opportunities for activity, supportive resources or simply enriching life and preventing isolation. Given the extent of social activity in terms of visits to and from friends that we saw above, we might anticipate that levels of close friendship were relatively high among British Muslims. However, Table 3.6 shows that the proportions with no friends seem to be somewhat higher and the proportions with 6 or more friends

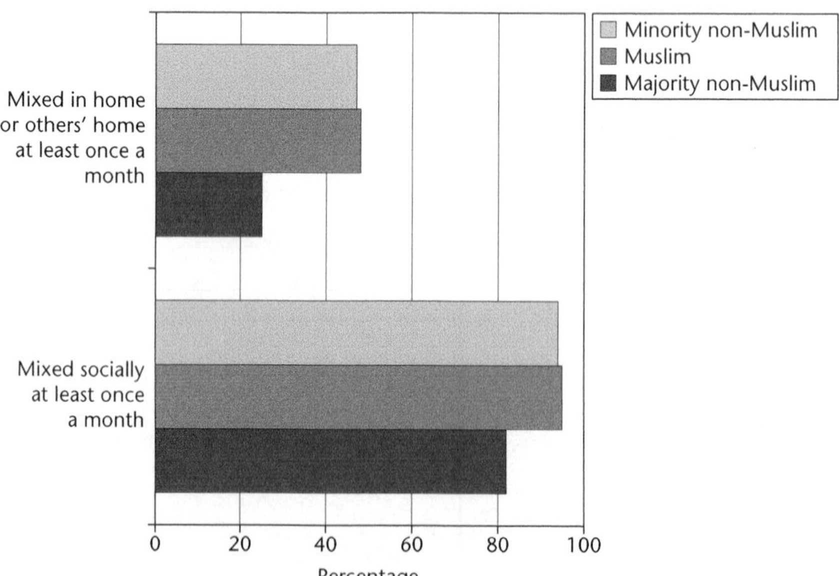

FIGURE 3.2 Predicted probabilities of social mixing among the majority, Muslims and non-Muslim minorities (source: Citizenship Survey 2008/2009)

Note
Probabilities are for UK-born men with average characteristics living in a couple. The predictions for non-Muslim minorities and for Muslims are not significantly different from each other, but they are significantly different from the majority for both groups.

TABLE 3.6 Numbers of close friends: percentages with different numbers of friends, 2008/2009

	Muslims					*Non-Muslims*			
	All	*Pakistani*	*Bangladeshi*	*Black African*	*Indian*	*Indian Sikhs*	*Indian Hindus*	*All*	*All minorities*
None	13	15	12	12	16	9	16	8	9
1–2	38	40	38	38	36	29	32	32	31
3–5	34	30	33	22	37	37	39	39	38
6–10	9	9	9	15	8	14	10	15	14
10+	6	6	8	13	4	11	3	5	8

Source: Citizenship Survey 2008/2009.

somewhat lower than among non-Muslims. These differences in friendship patterns between Muslims and non-Muslims (both groups) are statistically significantly different, and this is the case for both women and men, though for men the difference is only significant at the 10 per cent level. This gives some indication that, while only small proportions of British Muslims lack close friends altogether, they do so at a somewhat higher rate and have smaller numbers of close friends than the non-Muslim majority or other minorities.

Table 3.6 also suggests there are some differences among Muslims, particularly between black African and other Muslims. Black African Muslims appear to have more close friends on average, contrasting with their lower rates of social activities found in the 2001 survey. These differences across Muslim groups are, however, not statistically significant either for both sexes pooled or when broken down separately for men and women. Conversely, there *are* significant differences across the three religious affiliations among Indians: these are statistically significant among women, and significant at the 10 per cent level among men. Thus, both Muslim men and women seem to have lower rates of close friends than their Hindu and to a lesser extent Sikh counterparts from the same Indian ethnic group. Contrary to expectations, then, in patterns of sociability, ethnicity appears to provide a less strong distinction among Muslims than religion does within ethnicity, at least for describing patterns of friendship. The same caveats about these descriptions not implying causal relationships between either ethnicity or religious affiliation and social behaviour that were noted above clearly apply here as well.

From an initial inspection – that is, comparing Table 3.2 with Table 3.6, it might appear that close friendships form an alternative to communal sociality and that there are relatively specific patterns across different ethno-religious groups. Since the information comes from different sweeps, however, we cannot analyse it together. And, since we are talking about averages across population groups, it may well be that those who have an active social life also have more close friends. On initial inspection, then, opportunities for close friendship would appear to be lower among Muslims than among others. However, friendships are also susceptible to life-stage influences and family context. Moreover, comparison between men and women suggested that Muslim women tended to have fewer close friends than Muslim men. Models were therefore estimated to explore the association between Muslim, majority and non-Muslim minority groups and friendship probabilities, controlling for key characteristics. First, a binary logistic regression was estimated on the probability of having no close friends, as compared with some close friends. In addition, an ordered logit was estimated to explore the chances of having increasing numbers of friends according to the bands provided (see Table 3.6). Having 10 or more friends was combined with having 6–10 friends for these purposes. The results of the two models can be found in Table 3.7, models 1 and 2, and are consistent across the two ways of addressing the question of friendships. The specification for the models was reduced compared to that in Table 3.5, since country of birth was not found to be associated with friendship, and there was no evidence of a non-linear relationship between friendship and age. However, given the differences in close friendships that were observed between Muslim men and women in the data, sex was additionally interacted with group. A further model which controlled for employment status as a potential source of friendship was also estimated, and results are given in Table 3.7, model 1a. Given women's greater overall propensity to close friendships but lower average employment rates, it seems likely that the role of employment as a potential source of friendship may vary between men and women; and therefore employment status was further interacted with sex in this supplementary model.

From Table 3.7 we can see that most of the coefficients go in the expected direction. Younger people are more likely to have close friends, as are those in a couple (where their partner may be a close friend), and income is also positively associated with close friendships, showing once again the importance of opportunity structures. In general, women are less likely to lack close friends and tend to have more of them. However, the opposite is the case for Muslim women. While both Muslim and minority-group men have a higher probability than majority-group men of having no or fewer close friends, models 1 and 2 show that Muslim women have significantly higher chances than Muslim men of having no or fewer close friends.

It has often been pointed out that one of the key distinctive features of the profile of Muslim women is their relatively low employment rates. Given that employment can provide opportunities for social contacts, it may be influential on patterns of friendship over and above its economic contribution. Thus, in model 1a we see the results of the binary logistic regression on the chances of having no friends re-estimated, controlling for employment status. In addition, employment status and sex are interacted to allow its role in friendship formation to differ across men and women, given the distinctive patterns of close friendships observable by sex. From the results of model 1a we can see that being employed is negatively associated with having no close friends for both men and women, though the difference is in fact only statistically significant for women. Controlling for employment, however, has little effect on the majority of the coefficients in the model; and it certainly does not 'explain' the lower numbers of Muslim women claiming close friendships.

Again these results are most easily illustrated as predicted probabilities. Concentrating just on the probability of having no close friends, Figure 3.3 illustrates the differences for men and women across the three groups of majority non-Muslim, Muslim and non-Muslim minorities. The bottom panel illustrates the probability of having no close friends, controlling for a limited set of demographic and contextual variables, as found in Table 3.7, with the values set to the mean values for most characteristics. The top panel represents the model controlling additionally for employment status and is constrained to represent the probabilities for those employed only.

Looking first at the bottom panel of Figure 3.3, we see that the probability of having no close friends is higher for both Muslim and non-Muslim minority men than for majority-group non-Muslims. Majority and non-Muslim minority women

TABLE 3.7 Probabilities of having close friends: binary logistic and ordered logistic model estimates

	(1)	*(1a)*	*(2)*
	Probability of having no close friends	*No close friends, controlling for employment status*	*Probability of having increasing levels of close friends*
Sex: Men (reference)	0	0	0
Women	–0.525***	–0.323*	0.217***
	(0.120)	(0.142)	(0.0593)
Age	0.0342***	0.0288***	–0.0158***
	(0.00400)	(0.00433)	(0.00190)
Couple (reference)	0		0
Single	–0.314+	–0.339+	0.260***
	(0.179)	(0.177)	(0.0780)
Separated/widowed/divorced	–0.239+	–0.227	0.195*
	(0.142)	(0.143)	(0.0804)
Number of adults in household	–0.0297	–0.0196	0.0399
	(0.0731)	(0.0731)	(0.0342)
Number of children	0.0324	0.0127	–0.0415
	(0.0674)	(0.0673)	(0.0312)
Income	–0.0169***	–0.0137***	0.00710***
	(0.00397)	(0.00398)	(0.000969)
Non-Muslim majority (reference)	0		0
Muslims	0.493**	0.460**	–0.382***
	(0.174)	(0.172)	(0.113)
Non-Muslim minorities	0.503**	0.480**	–0.151
	(0.187)	(0.185)	(0.118)

Woman by Muslim	0.970***	0.882***	–0.406*
	(0.239)	(0.249)	(0.162)
Woman by non-Muslim	0.0238	0.0899	0.00786
	(0.242)	(0.246)	(0.153)
Employed		–0.176	
		(0.170)	
Women by employed		–0.656**	
		(0.222)	
Constant	–3.463***	–3.171***	
	(0.384)	(0.389)	
cut1			
Constant			–2.805***
			(0.157)
cut2			
Constant			–0.654***
			(0.153)
cut3			
Constant			1.165***
			(0.154)
Observations	9,511	9,511	9,511
Pseudo R^2	0.088	0.094	0.018
Log likelihood	–2,336.3	–2,320.8	–11,730.1
chi^2	224.7	257.0	239.2
df	11	13	11

Source: Citizenship Survey 2008/2009.

Notes
Standard errors in parentheses. $^+ p < 0.10$, $^* p < 0.05$, $^{**} p < 0.01$, $^{***} p < 0.001$.

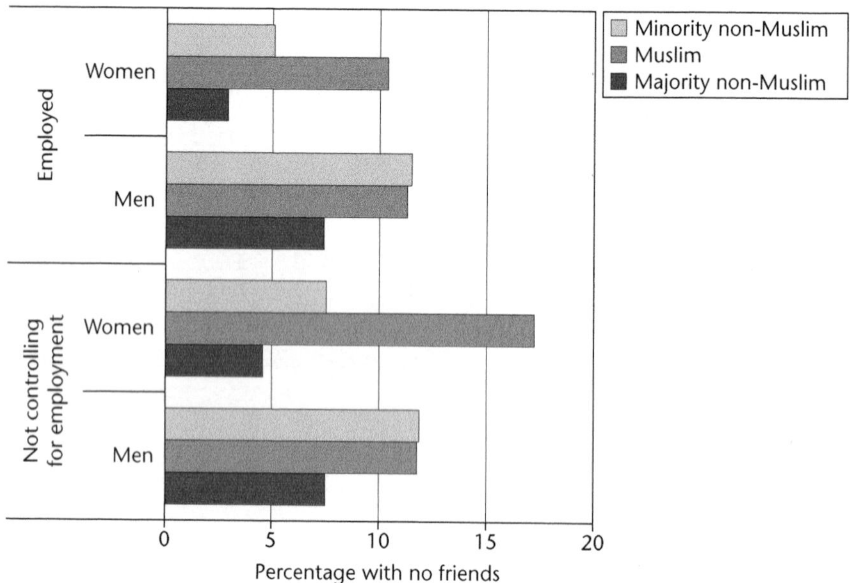

FIGURE 3.3 Predicted probabilities of having no close friends among Muslims and non-Muslims, by sex (source: Citizenship Survey 2008/2009)

Note
Probabilities are for those with average characteristics and living in a couple. The top panel is for those employed only. In the model not controlling for employment, predictions for non-Muslim minority men versus Muslim men do not differ significantly. The differences between Muslim women and majority and non-Muslim minority women and between Muslim men and majority men are significantly different. The probability for Muslim women is also significantly different to that for Muslim men. When controlling for employment and focusing only on those employed, the significant differences between groups are the same, except that the predications for employed Muslim women do not differ significantly from those for employed Muslim men.

are less likely to miss out on close friendships. However, Muslim women are more likely to have no close friends both compared to other women and compared to all groups of men. Thus, the gender association works in the opposite direction for these women. Turning to the top panel, which provides predictions for those in employment, Muslim and non-Muslim minority men remain significantly more likely than majority-group men to lack close friendships. Even though they are not as likely to lack close friends as Muslim women with average characteristics in the model without employment status, Muslim women in employment are nevertheless significantly more likely to have no close friends than employed majority-group women; and they are as likely as their employed male Muslim counterparts to miss out on such friendships.

Thus, despite the evidence throughout this discussion of relatively high levels of sociability and of different forms of social contact among Muslims, when it comes to the specific phenomenon of close friendships, Muslim women would appear to miss out relative to others, while Muslim and non-Muslim minority-group men are in a similarly less favourable position relative to majority-group men. Of course, both the interpretation of close friendship and the significance of it for overall well-being cannot be assumed to be the same across individuals. Nevertheless, if we accept that close friendship is a good in itself, then it would seem that minority men and Muslim women in particular have less of this good.

Conclusions

This chapter has explored various aspects of British Muslims' social spaces. It has explored the nature and intensity of social contact that British Muslims experience, as well as the extent to which social contact and friendships cross ethnic and religious boundaries. It has explored diversity among Muslims and the extent to which practices appear to be ethnically embedded rather than common across British Muslims. The analysis here is intended to open up the consideration of British Muslims' social activity and its nature. In the context of discussions about isolationism and separation, it is of interest to investigate the extent to which British Muslims' networks are large or small, heterogeneous or homogeneous, and to interrogate the factors that help to shape these aspects. The analysis is not intended to suggest any causal relationship between religious affiliation or identity and social practices (or indeed vice versa), but rather to map their nature and extent. Comparisons between Muslims and non-Muslims raise issues of the extent to which it is meaningful to speak of Muslim social spaces specifically, as does exploration of diversity among Muslims.

In this context the analysis can lead us to the following tentative conclusions. British Muslims appear to have somewhat distinctive patterns of sociality, with greater likelihood of participating in certain types of activities (such as visiting and being visited) and lower likelihood of participating in others (such as going out and participating in organized activities). A part of these differences is likely to stem from differential opportunities in terms of resources. While there appeared to be some differences across Muslim groups, there was not extensive evidence of significant differentiation among Muslims in these practices. The fact that Indian Muslims were the most likely to show these patterns and were significantly different from Indian Hindus and Sikhs additionally suggested that, contrary to expectations, patterns of social contact are not specifically ethnically embedded but differ across groups defined by religious affiliation as much as, or more than, those defined by ethnicity.

Patterns of sociality and friendship and heterophilic connections are clearly shaped by opportunity structures – not simply the opportunities related to the chances of interacting with a majority or minority group member, which are liable to make cross-group friendships and social mixing more common among minorities, but also opportunities related to resources. We saw that homophilic friendships on the basis of income and ethnicity were mutually reinforcing, and analysis of close friendships and cross-group mixing also revealed the role of income in creating opportunities.

Muslims shared with other minorities in increased chances of cross-group friendships and social 'mixing'. This extended to social mixing within the private and potentially exclusive environment of the home. British Muslims are thus distinctive in that they are more likely to have intergroup contacts than the majority population, and they are not distinctive, in that they share this propensity with non-Muslim minorities. These findings, even if not contrary to expectations, fly in the face of common claims that Muslims are different, exclusive or isolationist, as discussed in the introduction. Patterns of social contact are very much ones not of parallel existence but of sociability. Since social contact is often assumed to be fundamental to the development of shared understandings, this finding is important. Clearly, the interaction is two-way, even if the proportions of majority-group members that it can involve are constrained by very different population sizes.

It is only when we turn to propensity for close friends that the picture changes somewhat. Muslim men share with non-minority men a greater likelihood of lacking close friends, while among women, who in general are more likely to form close friendships, Muslim women are even more likely than Muslim men to lack close friends. Even when controlling for employment status, Muslim women's propensity to lack close friendships is greater than that of comparable non-Muslim women and is similar to that of Muslim men. In terms of personal well-being, then, minorities, and Muslim women in particular, face greater risks of lack of social support than the majority.

To some degree, then, British Muslims' social activities and opportunities are gendered. This was found in patterns of social activity and to a certain extent in terms of patterns of close friendship, although in the latter case employed Muslim women were more similar to employed Muslim men, while remaining distinct from other groups of women, who appeared to have greater social resources. Gendered differentiation among Muslims appears to be more pertinent – at least on some measures – than differentiation by ethnicity. Moreover, differentation along categorical axes of ethnicity or gender is likely to be compounded by the resource constraints on opportunities that have been noted. Giving more detailed attention to the intersection of income position and gender (Phoenix and Pattynama 2006) among British Muslims, and to the diversity of experiences across the income trajectory, is likely to be an important way of taking this exploratory outline forward. In addition, we need to examine more carefully whether forms of interaction complement or combine with each other in order to understand whether there are pockets of serious exclusion or isolation, or simply different contours to social engagement across Muslims. Such detailed foci are pertinent to further developing our understanding of British Muslims' social spaces, in their complexity as in their broader outlines.

Note

1 The estimates are similar if the models are estimated on Muslims relative to non-Muslim minorities, though here an equally good fit to the M + E + I + [IE] + [ME] is provided by the M + E + I + [IE] + [MI] model. In both cases, ethnic and income homophily would appear to reinforce each other. The comparable odds ratio to the 3.2 cited in the main text is 4.1 for the relationship between ethnicity and income similarity.

References

Ahmad, F. (2001) 'Modern traditions? British Muslim women and academic achievement', *Gender and Education* 13 (2): 137–152.

Ahmad, W. I. U. and Evergeti, V. (2010) 'The making and representation of Muslim identity in Britain: conversations with British Muslim "elites"', *Ethnic and Racial Studies* 33 (10): 1697–1717.

Alam, M. Y. and Husband, C. (2006) *British-Pakistani Men from Bradford: Linking Narratives to Policy*, York: Joseph Rowntree Foundation.

Ansari, H. (2002) *Muslims in Britain*, London: Minority Rights Group International.

Archer, L. (2009) 'Race, "face" and masculinity: the identities and local geographies of Muslim boys', in R. Gale and P. Hopkins (eds) *Muslims in Britain: Race, Place and Identities*, Edinburgh: Edinburgh University Press.

Battu, H. and Zenou, Y. (2010) 'Oppositional identities and employment for ethnic minorities: evidence from England', *Economic Journal* 120 (542): F52–F71.

Battu, H., McDonald, M. and Zenou, Y. (2007) 'Oppositional identities and the labor market', *Journal of Population Economics* 20: 643–667.

Bécares, L., Nazroo, J. and Stafford, M. (2009) 'The buffering effects of ethnic density on experienced racism and health', *Health and Place* 15 (3): 700–708.

Birt, J. (2009) 'Islamophobia in the construction of British Muslim identity politics', in R. Gale and P. Hopkins (eds) *Muslims in Britain: Race, Place and Identities*, Edinburgh: Edinburgh University Press.

Bisin, A., Pattacchini, E., Verdier, T. and Zenou, Y. (2008) 'Are Muslim immigrants different in terms of cultural integration?', *Journal of the European Economic Association* 6 (2–3): 445–456.

Blackaby, D. H., Drinkwater, S., Leslie, D. G. and Murphy, P. D. (1997) 'A picture of male and female unemployment among Britain's ethnic minorities', *Scottish Journal of Political Economy* 44 (2): 182–197.

Brown, M. S. (2000) 'Religion and economic activity in the South Asian population', *Ethnic and Racial Studies* 23 (6): 1035–1061.

Burchardt, T. (2002) 'Measuring social exclusion', in J. Hills, J. LeGrand and D. Piachaud (eds) *Making Social Policy Work*, Cambridge: Cambridge University Press.

Bush, H., Williams, R., Bradby, H., Anderson, A. and Lean, M. (1998) 'Family hospitality and ethnic tradition among South Asian, Italian and general population women in the West of Scotland', *Sociology of Health and Illness* 20 (3): 351–380.

Cheong, P. H., Edwards, R., Goulbourne, H. and Solomos, J. (2007) 'Immigration, social cohesion and social capital: a critical review', *Critical Social Policy* 27 (1): 24–49.

Community Cohesion Review Team (2001) *Community Cohesion: A Report of the Independent Review Team Chaired by Ted Cantle*, London: Home Office.

Department for Communities and Local Government and National Centre for Social Research (2010) Citizenship Survey, 2008–2009 [computer file]. Colchester: UK Data Archive [distributor], February. SN: 6388. Online, available at: http://dx.doi.org/10.5255/UKDA-SN-6388-1.

Dhindsa, K. S. (1998) *Indian Immigrants in United Kingdom: A Socio-economic Analysis*, New Delhi: Concept.

Diehl, C., Koenig, M. and Ruckdeschel, K. (2009) 'Religiosity and gender equality: comparing natives and Muslim migrants in Germany', *Ethnic and Racial Studies* 32 (2): 278–301.

Dwyer, C. (2000) 'Negotiating diasporic identities: young British South Asian Muslim women', *Women's Studies International Forum* 23 (4): 475–486.

Fieldhouse, E. and Cutts, D. (2007) 'Mobilisation or marginalisation? Neighbourhood effects on Muslim electoral registration in 2001', *Political Studies* 56 (2): 333–354.

Furbey, R., Dinham, A., Farnell, R., Finneron, D. and Wilkinson, G., with Howarth, C., Hussain, D. and Palmer, S. (2006) *Faith as Social Capital: Connecting or Dividing?* Bristol: Policy Press.

Georgiadis, A. and Manning, A. (2011) 'Change and continuity among minority communities in Britain', *Journal of Population Economics* 24 (2): 541–568.

Geys, B. and Murdoch, Z. (2010) 'Measuring the "bridging" versus "bonding" nature of social networks: a proposal for integrating existing measures', *Sociology* 44 (3): 523–540.

Home Office, Communities Group, and BMRB, Social Research (2003) Home Office Citizenship Survey, 2001 [computer file]. Colchester: UK Data Archive [distributor], November. SN: 4754. Online, available at: http://dx.doi.org/10.5255/UKDA-SN-4754-1.

Jacobson, J. (1997) 'Religion and ethnicity: dual and alternative sources of identity among young British Pakistanis', *Ethnic and Racial Studies* 20: 238–256.

Jayaweera, H. and Choudhury, T. (2008) *Immigration, Faith and Cohesion: Evidence from Local Areas with Significant Muslim Populations*, York: Joseph Rowntree Foundation.

Karlsen, S. and Nazroo, J. Y. (2010) 'Religious and ethnic differences in health: evidence from the Health Surveys for England 1999 and 2004', *Ethnicity and Health* 15 (6): 549–568.

Lawton, J., Ahmad, N., Douglas, M., Hanna, L., Bains, H. and Hallowell, N. (2008) '"We should change ourselves, but we can't": accounts of food and eating practices amongst British Pakistanis and Indians with type 2 diabetes', *Ethnicity and Health* 13: 305–319.

Letki, N. (2008) 'Does diversity erode social cohesion? Social capital and race in British neighbourhoods', *Political Studies* 56 (1): 99–126.

Levitas, R. (2006) 'The concept and measurement of social exclusion', in C. Pantazis, D. Gordon and R. Levitas (eds) *Poverty and Social Exclusion in Britain: The Millennium Survey*, Bristol: Policy Press.

Lin, N. (2001) *Social Capital: A Theory of Social Structure and Action*, Cambridge: Cambridge University Press.

Lindley, J. (2002) 'Race or religion? The impact of religion on the employment and earnings of Britain's ethnic communities', *Journal of Ethnic and Migration Studies* 28 (3): 427–442.

Longhi, S., Nicoletti, C. and Platt, L. (2009) *Decomposing Wage Gaps across the Pay Distribution: Investigating Inequalities of Ethno-religious groups and Disabled People*, report commissioned by the National Equality Panel, ISER Working Paper 2009-32, Colchester: Institute for Social and Economic Research, University of Essex.

McPherson, M., Smith-Lovin, L. and Cook, J. M. (2001) 'Birds of a feather: homophily in social networks', *Annual Review of Sociology* 27: 415–444.

Modood, T. (2009) 'Muslims and the politics of difference', in R. Gale and P. Hopkins (eds) *Muslims in Britain: Race, Place and Identities*, Edinburgh: Edinburgh University Press.

Nagel, C. and Staeheli, L. (2009) 'British Arab perspectives on religion, politics and "the public"', in P. Hopkins and R. Gale (eds) *Muslims in Britain: Race, Place and Identities*, Edinburgh: Edinburgh University Press.

Nazroo, J. Y. (2003) 'Patterns of and explanations for ethnic inequalities in health', in D. Mason (ed.) *Explaining Ethnic Differences: Changing Patterns of Disadvantage in Britain*, Bristol: Policy Press.

Open Society Institute EU Monitoring and Advocacy Program (2004) *Aspirations and Reality: British Muslims and the Labour Market*, Budapest: Open Society Institute.

Peach, C. (2006) 'Islam, ethnicity and South Asian Religions in the London 2001 census', *Transactions of the Institute of British Geographers* 31 (3): 353–370.

Phoenix, A. and Pattynama, P. (2006) 'Intersectionality', *European Journal of Women's Studies* 13 (3): 187–192.

Platt, L. (2005) *Migration and Social Mobility: The Life Chances of Britain's Minority Ethnic Communities*, Bristol: Policy Press.

Platt, L. (2009) 'Social participation, social isolation and ethnicity', *Sociological Review* 57 (4): 670–702.

Putnam, R. D. (2000) *Bowling Alone: The Collapse and Revival of American Community*, New York: Simon & Schuster.

Saeed, A. (2009) 'Muslims in the West and their attitudes to full participation in western societies: some reflections', in G. B. Levey and T. Modood (eds) *Secularism, Religion and Multicultural Citizenship*, Cambridge: Cambridge University Press.

Salway, S., Platt, L., Chowbey, P., Harriss, K. and Bayliss, E. (2007) *Long-Term Ill Health, Poverty and Ethnicity*, Bristol: Policy Press.

Thapar-Björkert, S. and Sanghera, G. (2010) 'Social capital, educational aspirations and young Pakistani Muslim men and women in Bradford, West Yorkshire', *Sociological Review* 58 (2): 244–264.

Townsend, P. (1979) *Poverty in the United Kingdom: A Survey of Household Resources and Standards of Living*, Harmondsworth: Penguin.

Verkuyten, M. (2007) 'Religious group identification and inter-religious relations: a study among Turkish-Dutch Muslims', *Group Processes and Intergroup Relations* 10 (3): 341–357.

Warde, A. (1997) *Consumption, Food and Taste*, London: Sage.

Werbner, P. (2005) 'The translocation of culture: "community cohesion" and the force of multiculturalism in history', *Sociological Review* 53 (4): 745–768.

Zetter, R., Griffiths, D., Sigona, N., Flynn, D., Pasha, T. and Beynon, R. (2006) *Immigration, Social Cohesion and Social Capital: What Are the Links?* York: Joseph Rowntree Foundation.

4

MUSLIM CHAPLAINS

Working at the interface of 'public' and 'private'

M. Mansur Ali and Sophie Gilliat-Ray

Introduction

Chaplaincy has a long history in British hospitals (Cox 1955: 7; Swift 2009), prisons (Priestley 1985), the military (Snape 2005) and industry (Fuller and Vaughan 1986; Johnston and McFarland 2010), as well as many other sectors (Legood 1999). The Christian churches have largely dominated this sphere of work, and in England the appointment of Anglican chaplains in particular, usually in the most senior post, has been an extension of the 'established' character of the Church of England (Davie 1994). The 1952 Prison Act stipulates the appointment of an Anglican chaplain, and fulfilling the requirements of the Patient's Charter of 1991 usually means the appointment of an Anglican chaplain in hospitals. These posts are funded through taxes, and though the 'sending churches' endorse the qualifications and competence of chaplains from Christian denominations, they are the employees of the institutions in which they work.

Over time, various Christian dominations, Jews and, more recently, members of other world religions – especially Muslims – have been drawn into the chaplaincy profession. The employment of Muslim chaplains has often been a pragmatic and necessary way of ensuring that the religious needs and rights of Muslim patients or prisoners are fulfilled. Other institutions might employ Muslim chaplains for more strategic reasons, such as the wish to attract overseas (Muslim) students in the case of higher education institutions, or to increase the representation and recruitment of ethnic minority personnel in the case of the military. These relatively new Muslim chaplaincy appointments have sometimes raised complex questions about the status of religion in the law and in public institutions (Beckford and Gilliat 1998). Thus, the work of Muslim chaplains provides an interesting lens through which to look at a particular dimension of the public accommodation of Islam in Britain and the relationships and synergies between Muslim communities,

Established churches, other faith communities, policy-makers and the managers of public institutions.

Since about 2000 there has been a dramatic increase in the number of employment opportunities for Muslims in publicly funded chaplaincy in Britain (Birt 2005; Gilliat-Ray 2008, 2010b). Throughout the United Kingdom, Muslim chaplains contribute to multi-faith chaplaincy teams in most large prisons and hospitals on either a full-time or a part-time basis, and in a small but growing number of cases they are acting as the senior coordinator for all chaplaincy and religious matters in their institution. A decade ago it would have been hard to predict the scale and rapidity of these developments. But after mosques and Islamic centres, the Ministry of Justice/Prison Service is now probably the largest single employer of Muslim religious professionals in Britain. Over 200 Muslim chaplains work in British prisons on either a full-time or a sessional basis, and this figure includes 12 women, mainly serving in all-female establishments.[1] Similarly, there has been a substantial increase in the number of Muslim chaplains in the National Health Service (NHS), and the emergence of these opportunities has provided a further avenue for women to take up professional religious roles in public institutions.

The political, social and religious dynamics underpinning the growth of Muslim involvement in chaplaincy during the late 1990s and 2000s have already been documented (Gilliat-Ray 2008), so these will not be rehearsed again here. Instead, this chapter reports on some initial findings from the first major study of Muslim chaplains in Britain (Gilliat-Ray *et al.* 2013). We begin by exploring the significance of the work that chaplains are undertaking, based on their location within public institutions. We argue that there are important consequences arising out of their work which have implications not only for Muslim scholars and jurists, but also for those interested in the accommodation of Islamic traditions within the operational and policy norms of public institutions. The development of Muslim chaplaincy roles reflects important realities about the institutionalization of Islam in Britain and can tell us a great deal about the changing practical, legal and structural place of Muslims in Britain more widely. We suggest that whereas Muslims have in previous generations been principally concerned to engage in 'bonding activities' that have strengthened the internal coherence and resources of Islamic organizations, Muslim chaplains are often engaged in 'bridging activities' (Fetzer and Soper 2004: 154) that are enabling Islamic traditions to make positive and practical contributions to public institutions and British society more widely. Their employment is also an important way of reversing the under-representation of Muslims in public office.

The Muslim Chaplaincy Project

The Muslim Chaplaincy Project, funded by the AHRC/ESRC 'Religion and Society' programme, is examining the work and personnel involved in Muslim chaplaincy in Britain.[2] Over a period of 28 months the research team has been seeking to establish answers to four main questions. The first of these relates to *people*, and to the educational and religious background of those who decide to become chaplains. We want to establish how and why Islamic scholars, both male and female, are drawn into chaplaincy work as a career. Our second set of research questions relate to *practice*. Because there is no formal tradition of institutionalized pastoral care in Islamic societies, the role 'Muslim chaplain' is a novel one. So what do Muslim chaplains actually do, and how and in what ways do they draw upon Islamic sources and traditions for their work? Third, we want to establish how Muslim chaplains navigate their way through the *politics* that shape their work, both within and outside their institutions, and in relation to the wider professional chaplaincy community. What are the enabling and constraining structures that impact on their role? Lastly, we have been keen to explore the short-, medium- and long-term *potential* of Muslim chaplaincy practice. How, if at all, is the work of Muslim chaplains shaping the role of other Islamic religious professionals (such as imams), or influencing debate about the kind of religious leadership that British Muslim communities now seem to expect (Gilliat-Ray 2010b)? Does the work of Muslims involved in 'community chaplaincy' help to reduce re-offending?

To begin answering these questions, we have interviewed over 65 Muslim chaplains working in prisons, hospitals, educational institutions, the courts, airports, shopping centres, the military and in 'community chaplaincy'.[3] Our sample has included chaplains from different schools of religious thought, men and women, and chaplains with varying levels of experience and Islamic knowledge. In addition, we have interviewed and observed some of those training to be Muslim chaplains, especially through the certificate course offered by Markfield Institute of Higher Education in Leicester. Another group of interviewees has included 'stakeholders', by which we mean those who have observed, or been directly involved in managing, the work of Muslim chaplains from a policy, training or institutional perspective; few of our stakeholders have been practitioners of chaplaincy. Finally, we have spent short periods of time 'shadowing' Muslim chaplains at work, typically for two or three days at a time (Gilliat-Ray 2010a, 2011). This has enabled us to have a more contextualized understanding of their role, while offering chaplains themselves an opportunity to comment on their work, in situ. In a small number of prisons and higher education institutions we have also conducted focus groups with the 'clients' of Muslim chaplaincy, and with key senior managers. In this way, we have been able to form impressions about the impact and significance of the work that chaplains are doing, from the perspective of 'consumers' and managers. Our focus groups in prisons have deliberately included diverse establishments, including a women's prison, a young offender institution and a local remand prison. The extensive interview and fieldwork data gathered through the project are being analysed using the qualitative data analysis program NVivo.

Working at the boundary of 'public' and 'private'

The established church has close links with politics and public policy in Britain, and over the past thirty or forty years, British Muslim activists have often referred to these links as part of their efforts to secure greater political recognition of Muslim needs and interests (Fetzer and Soper 2004). These efforts have included campaigns for such things as separate publicly funded Islamic schools, or the right to protection from religious discrimination (Modood 2003). Much of this activism has taken place through the efforts of so-called community leaders (Burlet and Reid 1998) or those engaged in independent Islamic welfare and social projects. However, as state employees in publicly funded institutions (in the case of prisons and hospitals), Muslim chaplains are uniquely and strategically well placed to lobby for the recognition of Muslim interests. Campaigns for particular rights, or adjustments to existing procedures or norms, can be made within the language of public service discourse, and Muslim chaplains often have the authority and know-how to question what has previously been taken for granted. But chaplains are no longer simply campaigning for rights and changes that benefit Muslim communities alone. Some of their efforts are directed towards the benefit of institutions and communities more generally, and the examples that form the second part of this chapter explore particular initiatives in detail.

All chaplains, Muslims included, usually work on the blurred spatial boundary of 'public' and 'private', and most usually in public spaces that have become transformed into 'private enclaves' (Adler and Adler 1994: 388). A good example might be a 'quiet room' on a hospital ward, where nursing staff or chaplains might gather family members together to discuss end-of-life palliative care, or burial arrangements following a death. An unused meeting room on a prison wing might be an opportunity for a chaplain to discuss private family matters with a prisoner, or support arrangements following his or her release. A busy concourse at a courthouse can nevertheless accommodate private discussion between a chaplain and a defendant or witness. In such spaces, 'conventional definitions of public and private may be inadequate' (ibid.), confirming Herbert's (2003) assessment that the boundary between 'public' and 'private' can be both contentious and somewhat artificial. However, it is precisely the blurred 'grey area' between public and private realms that has provided an opportunity for Muslim chaplains to develop their own roles and practices that draw simultaneously on Islamic religious teachings, traditional chaplaincy practices and the norms of professional working life in public institutions. Our research has been keen to investigate exactly what happens within this 'grey area', and to evaluate the significance of what we find.

Chaplaincy requires an ability to work within the policy and operational norms of a public institution, as well as the capacity to meet and manage the private needs of individuals and families. Consequently, chaplains have to engage in multiple forms of communication with a wide range of audiences, and they need the skills to embody and rapidly switch between different roles. Participation in the daily briefing meeting of senior managers in a prison, to leading an Islamic class for Muslim young offenders, may occur within the space of minutes. Likewise, leading a training programme for new nursing staff might quickly follow bereavement support for a grieving family. A single issue, such as the provision of halal food in a prison or hospital, requires an ability to negotiate between clients, catering managers, kitchen staff, financial managers and ward staff or prison officers. Shifting between these multiple roles and discourses requires the ability to form effective networks of cooperation, and the skill to communicate in a way that is calm, assertive and professional (Saint-Blancat and Perocco 2005). More than that, the task often involves a certain degree of 'translation' across the languages and worldviews of those who have very different perspectives – 'for without successful translation there is no prospect of the substantive content of religious voices being taken up in the agendas and negotiations within political bodies and in the broader political process' (Habermas 2006: 11). To be heard effectively, the discourse that Muslim chaplains use in their work must take account of the assumptions and organizational principles that shape working life in secular public institutions.

To the extent that Muslims in Britain self-consciously follow a particular 'school of thought', the tradition of Islamic law that nevertheless prevails in Britain is Hanafi. The predominance of the Hanafi 'school' is a direct reflection of the fact that many of the Muslims who arrived in Britain in the post-Second World War period were South Asian, and inevitably brought with them the legal interpretations and religious traditions that were most familiar to them.[4] A large majority of the chaplains interviewed for our project also followed this school, and many have been trained in *dar ul-uloom* (Islamic seminaries) that reflect the Deobandi tradition.[5] However, the diversity among professional Muslim chaplains in terms of their religious training or 'school of thought' is such that chaplaincy also provides a unique opportunity for some degree of intra-faith dialogue about the precise ways in which the religious needs of British Muslims should be delivered. Just how are the requirements of Shariah to be interpreted and implemented, given the constraints of hygiene and infection control in healthcare settings, security in prison settings, and the financial pressures in most areas of public service? Although there are contests among chaplains from different schools of thought around even apparently simple issues such as 'what counts' as halal, the very fact that the conversation is taking place, framed by the limits and assumptions that govern a public institution, is notable. Although the Hanafi school of law predominates, there are a sufficient number of Muslim chaplains who follow other legal schools to enable a process of intense debate.

> So, for example, we have the whole issue of dog searching. Now it's a big thing in the prison services. Certain prisons are investing in disposable aprons that they put on visitors so that the dog does not touch their clothing. In the prison cell, for example, if a dog comes into search for drugs and so on, they remove the bedding from the prisoner and they get a fresh load of clothes, and all this is there because the Hanafis believe that the saliva of dog is *najis* (impure), whereas the Malikis believe that they're OK, all animals are clean ... we have nice little juicy discussions. We have maybe about five or six very staunch Maliki scholars, so they'll debate on this issue, then you have the Shafi'i mix and the Hanafi mix, so it's quite good ... when we meet up in the evening we sit and we can discuss until early hours in the morning. And that I think I find it very exhilarating.
>
> *(Stakeholder, interviewed March 2010)*

The long-term impact and implications of these conversations are of course hard to predict, but it is possible that they will contribute to the development of a new generation of Muslim religious professionals who are capable of spanning the private world of families and faith communities, and the public world of institutions and policy-making, as well as the capacity to view issues from different Islamic legal perspectives.

The organization of the public sphere now takes increasing account of religious sensibilities and needs. According to Fetzer and Soper (2004), Modood (2003) and others, this is largely a consequence of the Muslim presence in Britain, and the way in which Muslims have rejected the assumption that secular worldviews should dominate in public life. Muslim chaplains often have an important role in actualizing this reversal of assumptions as they oversee the delivery of practical needs to their clients, or play an advisory role for their employing institutions. It has also become clear in our research that Muslim chaplains are often the first and only informed Islamic religious professional that many other staff (or clients) have ever met. As we have 'shadowed' chaplains within their institutions, it has become clear that many of them have done a great deal to improve knowledge and understanding of Islam and Muslims in Britain.

In the remainder of this chapter we explore some implications of Muslim chaplaincy practice, not only for Islamic religious and legal scholars in Britain but also for the wider public. How have Muslim chaplains been influenced by working at the interface between 'private' and 'public'? How do they manage to reconcile the potentially conflicting demands of the secular workplace, with Islamic practices and norms? And what are the religious and legal implications of the methods they are using to negotiate their role in public life? The reflections of a prison chaplain from Yorkshire provide some insightful perspectives on these issues and serve as an introduction to some case studies and examples of contextual Islamic leadership and pastoral care in Britain today.

Interpretive effort and theological reflection

> It's [chaplaincy] changed my view of the world, it's changed my view of the way people act and interact as well, I think it's changed me profoundly because what I've noticed, I've become a lot more liberal, *fiqh* [law] wise, it's sort of really opened my mind up. Because I'm always trying to help people, as long as there's *fiqh* [law] there to help the people.
>
> *(Prison chaplain, Yorkshire, interviewed January 2009)*

Chaplaincy appears to be stimulating the development of new theological reflection and interpretation of Islamic traditions. As chaplains become exposed to new people and communities, as well as the bureaucratic workings of public institutions, they are often confronted by situations that require an ability to think and act in new ways. A simple example of what this might mean in practice can be seen in relation to the differing norms surrounding gender relations within and outside Islamic communities. Most schools of Islamic law regard any physical contact between unrelated men and women (even a simple handshake) as sinful, and contrary to the teachings of Islam (Haneef 1979; Khuri 2001). Aisha, the Prophet Muhammad's wife, said, 'No, by God, the Prophet never touched the hand of a woman' (al-Bukhari). But the requirements of modesty and assumptions about the separation of unrelated men and women can pose particular challenges in the mixed-gender context of a British prison or hospital, where conventional norms of formal greeting are likely to include shaking hands. This issue became a challenge for one newly appointed hospital chaplain. He admitted to being reserved towards female non-Muslim colleagues, refusing to 'look them in the eye' or shake their hand. His behaviour was interpreted as discriminatory and misogynist, and formal disciplinary action was taken against him. Subsequent mentoring by a more experienced chaplain, however, offered him a new perspective on traditional assumptions about gender relations. Although he explained to the senior chaplain that his understanding of Islamic law did not permit contact with members of the opposite gender, even for professional reasons, his more experienced colleague rejected this narrow legal interpretation. He explained that in a public workplace a theology of pluralism should prevail. This is because chaplains at times have to encounter people with many different religious, philosophical and ideological beliefs which may be at odds with their personal worldviews. The more experienced chaplain explained how his own approach, developed over some years, involved a consideration of the different weight and significance of individual sin as against collective sin. He argued that if the newly appointed chaplain deemed shaking hands with the opposite gender as sinful, it would nevertheless only constitute an individual sin. In contrast, if the outcome of not shaking hands was the portrayal of a negative and bigoted picture of Islam, this would become a far more serious collective sin. He suggested that in such circumstances, preference must always be given to maintaining a positive impression of Islam and the avoidance of collective sin, even at the expense of worries about compromising personal piety. Clearly, those who feel unable to make such compromises rarely stay in chaplaincy.

It is evident from this example that chaplaincy is exposing Muslim religious professionals to new ideas and worldviews and enabling new theological reflection. The ability to engage a different hermeneutics that reconciles text and tradition with contemporary practice and reality arguably has significance both within and beyond Muslim communities. To what extent, however, does this constitute *ijtihad* (independent legal reasoning)? *Ijtihad* is a technical term in Islamic legal theory, which originally meant personal effort and struggle to find a solution to a legal problem (Hallaq 1995; Saeed 2006). By the beginning of the tenth century, Muslim jurists had reached a consensus that questions related to every aspect of Muslim life and practice had been exhausted, and no further *ijtihad* needed to be done (Ali-Karamali and Dunne 1994; Codd 1999). The 'closing of the gates of *ijtihad*' (Esposito 1988; Hallaq 1984; Saeed 2006) gave rise to the widespread practice of *taqlid*, which means imitation of those scholars (*mujtahids*) who had been engaged in *ijtihad* before the tenth century. Among classically trained Islamic scholars, this understanding of *ijtihad* and *taqlid* has generally prevailed into the twenty-first century. It came as no surprise when the chaplains in our research were reluctant to call their new interpretations of text and practice '*ijtihad*', on account of the weight and significance of the term, and the controversy that surrounds it.

Regardless of terminology, however, there seems little doubt that Muslim chaplains in Britain are involved in different levels and forms of *ijtihad* as they exercise interpretive effort to translate the principles of Shariah into the practice of chaplaincy. This might sometimes involve new interpretive judgement, as the example concerning handshakes demonstrates; in other cases it might entail the decision to search for alternative Islamic legal opinions on a particular issue, even if that means choosing interpretations derived from a different school of Islamic law. The legal tradition in Islam is far from homogeneous, and this is regarded by some chaplains as an enabling opportunity, not a difficulty.

By force of necessity and circumstance, some chaplains are sometimes availing themselves of the opportunity to 'pick and choose' between Hanafi, Maliki, Hanbali, Shafi'i and Ja'fari traditions. For example, in Hanafi legal thought it is not permitted to perform a funeral prayer (*janazah*) if the body of the deceased is not visibly present (Abidin 1994). This being the case, what happens when a prisoner loses a close relative through death and is refused an application (on the grounds of security) to attend the funeral prayer? This is exactly the scenario that one of the chaplains in our study encountered. He deemed that the best pastoral response for the grieving prisoner would be to allow him to read the *janazah* prayer in his cell, as far as possible at the same time as the funeral prayers were being read at the graveside, outside the prison. This decision was directly contrary to the school of law in which he had trained:

> Now the *fiqh* [legal tradition] that I follow ... I don't read *ghaib salat al-janazah* [absent funeral prayer], you know if somebody's not there you don't read the *janazah salat* [funeral prayer] but in the Hadith [teachings of the Prophet] and there are certain other *'ulama* [scholars] that follow that if the person's not there, you still read. And I said [to the prisoner], 'Look, fine, if you want to read it, this is the way you read it.' Now normally outside I would never have done that. But here I know I have to do that, I have to give him something and because it's based in Shariah. 'That's up to you', I said. 'At the end of the day it's up to you; if you're going to do it, that's fine; if you don't want to do it, that's fine as well, but I'm giving you an option.' Because he's in a difficult position, some of the people that I deal with, so you've got those kind of things ... so I think it's [chaplaincy] given me much more sort of openness and [made me] a lot more broad-minded as well and also it's made me much more stronger in my faith, and to tell you the truth I make *shukr* to Allah [thanksgiving to God].
>
> *(Prison chaplain, Yorkshire, interviewed January 2009)*

Not only is this an interesting example in its own right, but it highlights why a chaplain may be willing to adjust his own theological position for the benefit of others. In this particular case, the prisoner's grief and the restrictions of the prison setting provided the justification for his actions. It is ironic that the confines of a prison, both physically and bureaucratically, enabled the development of imaginative religious practice and thought, alongside the strengthening of personal faith. Alongside this, however, we must note the fact that the chaplain states explicitly that he would not have exercised such 'free-thinking' outside the prison. Our research shows that this is not unusual. It is hard to find evidence of sustained day-to-day 'interpretive legal effort' taking place *outside* chaplaincy settings to any significant degree.

This is likely to be a reflection of numerous factors, the most obvious of which is that the routine mosque-based work of most imams in Britain probably means that they rarely encounter, or actively involve themselves in, the kind of situations where significant 'interpretive effort' might be required. Even if they did engage with such situations, those who assume that the 'gates of *ijtihad* are closed' may be reluctant to look beyond their own school of thought, or may question their own scholarly capabilities to do so. A further disincentive, however, is the degree to which theological conformity is regarded as safer in relation to perceptions within religious peer networks and community-based congregations. Behind the closed doors of prisons, hospitals and higher education institutions, however, chaplains have greater freedom to explore the theological and legal traditions of Islam without fear of judgement and criticism. The traditions of research and scholarly inquiry that shape medical institutions and university life make these conducive settings in which to explore new ideas. Without realizing the fact, chaplains are engaged in *ijtihad* on many different levels, and asking themselves challenging questions that might have a direct bearing on the future of Islam in Britain.

> I felt that I wasn't using my full potential in the mosque, or the mosque wasn't allowing me to use my full potential. The mosque wasn't allowing me to be who I was … there was a set model that was there for [the] imamate, and that is the model you had to work in. If you worked beyond that model, you were doing something innovative and therefore you were challenging the established norm. Sometimes you were pressured by the management committee, sometimes you were pressured by your other peer imams. And … you were meeting the same static community all the time, so you were always speaking to the converted, if you know what I mean, in that sense; you were always speaking to people who are already comfortable, to people who are already confident to come to the mosque. What about the people who aren't comfortable and confident to come to the mosque? Who is reaching out to them? And I thought chaplaincy was one way you could go out. Who was teaching Islam to the local community? Who was talking to the people who were Islamic, who were faithful, but weren't coming to the mosque?
>
> *(Prison chaplain, London, interviewed March 2009)*

Teamwork

There are now a number of Muslim chaplains in Britain who have been working in their institutions for well over a decade, and they have in most cases fully absorbed the professional identity of 'chaplain'. This includes recognition of the need to work for the interests of the whole institution – all clients and staff of all faiths and none – not simply the needs of Muslim clients alone. Our research is interested in exploring the implications of such an outward-facing worldview.

> I'm not here to invite; in this place you're not here to give *da'wah* [preach], I'm not here to propagate the *deen* [religion], I'm here just to be human for anybody who has a need to talk about whatever and if that involves talking about Allah *subhanahu wa ta'ala* [He is glorified and exalted], then fine, we'll talk about Allah *subhanahu wa ta'ala*. So, being responsive to the human aspect, I think that is hundred per cent Islamic.
>
> *(Hospital chaplain, Yorkshire, interviewed January 2009)*

This kind of outward-facing, inclusive ethos involves an ability to work as part of a multi-faith chaplaincy team, where real 'teamwork' might involve supporting and substituting for other members as needs dictate. One chaplain saw no religious impediment to facilitating a Christian service one Sunday, owing to the sudden absence of a Christian colleague. Clearly, this didn't involve him in Christian worship per se, but it did entail the rapid creation of a framework to enable the corporate worship of others. Various chaplains in our study have recounted incidents where they have had to facilitate the private religious practice of prisoners or patients from other faiths, as the following quotation illustrates:

> I used to provide the Bible and I used to sit with the prisoner from the Christian faith, or from the other faith, to read with them and to guide them, to teach them what they need to read each day, to say their prayers.
>
> *(Prison chaplain, London, interviewed November 2008)*

While acting as 'duty chaplain', some Muslims have been called upon to 'pray with' (as opposed to 'pray for') prisoners and patients of other faiths. While there is a tradition of offering extemporaneous prayer within some Christian traditions, it is far less common within Islam, since praying for the welfare of another is usually done privately and silently as part of *salat*. Speaking about such requests, chaplains have had to develop a new understanding of what prayer might involve, not only in terms of their own practice but also in relation to what those from other faiths (or none) may find comforting and helpful at times of distress. In many cases this will involve moving away from Islamic supplications in Arabic and developing the ability to pray in English, 'otherwise the client won't understand, and what use is that?' (prison chaplain, south-west England, January 2011).

Some of the most inspiring chaplains in our study have demonstrated the value of being able to combine Islamic knowledge and teamwork with an awareness of the pressures and constraints of working in public institutions. Effective Muslim chaplains are well placed to act as 'troubleshooters' and to diffuse potentially difficult situations which often require quick thinking and keen observational skills. One (female) Anglican chaplain interviewed for our study told us about the way in which her Muslim colleague, Henna, had done this on a young offender wing of a woman's prison:

> First day she came here, I was taking her around, and it just so happened we had two prisoners in the juvenile unit. One was very cooperative, the other was being thoroughly bolshy and awkward, demanding things. She was sitting on the floor, and she didn't get up when Henna went in to see her – and this was the first day she'd been in the prison, and I was sort of sussing her out as much as she was sussing us out – and this girl sat there and said, 'I want a prayer scarf, for when I pray.' And Henna said, 'Oh, you've got a hoodie, haven't you, you can use that', and I thought, 'You'll do.' She didn't bite her head off or anything, she just gave a perfectly calm, sensible, straightforward response to which there was no answer. And I thought, 'Ah, right, we'll have you.' If she can sort that out, and she's completely new to the establishment, she's going to be fine.
>
> *(Anglican coordinating chaplain, Midlands, interviewed February 2011)*

The subject of gender and Muslim women's involvement in chaplaincy is clearly a subject in its own right. But even in the early stage of our data analysis there is evidence that, regardless of sector, Muslim women serving as chaplains often have unique access to the 'private' sphere of family life and relationships. When this is combined with effective professional teamwork practice alongside a male Muslim chaplain, there are often direct benefits for the institution concerned. For example, a major incident that brings large numbers of distressed relatives to a busy hospital accident and emergency unit is usually more effectively managed if males and females can be separated and comforted by a chaplain of the same gender. A female community chaplain working alongside a male prison chaplain may be able to negotiate more conducive resettlement arrangements for an offender if she has the chance to talk to mothers and sisters at home, prior to release. Thus, Muslim chaplains are engaging in teamwork both within and beyond their own faith community.

Innovating networks

The kind of work that Muslim chaplains in Britain are undertaking complicates our understanding of what counts as either 'private' or 'public', not only in terms of spatial and political boundaries, but also in relation to what counts as 'personal' or 'public' information. At one hospital the physiotherapy team were providing patient information leaflets on 'healthy exercise' in a city with a high percentage of Muslims. These leaflets advocated the health benefits of everyday activities, such a 'taking the dog for a walk'. In this case the institution-wide modus operandi of the Muslim chaplain provided him with an opportunity to intervene, and to facilitate the development of more culturally sensitive approaches to physiotherapy services within the hospital. He explained that most devout Muslims regard dogs (or, more precisely, the saliva of dogs) as 'unclean' (Roff 1983), and thus are unlikely to keep them as pets requiring exercise, along with their owners. Removing the recommendation of dog-walking from the leaflet, however, left the physiotherapists with the question as to how they might encourage simple, non-strenuous stretching exercises. His response was to suggest that leaflets might explain the health and physical benefits of the different postures for Islamic prayer (*salat*) on the basis that these would be likely to have far greater resonance for some Muslim service-users. While this seemed like a good idea in theory, the physiotherapists felt uncomfortable asking clients about their religious practice for fear that it was a 'private' matter that should not be discussed. He assured them that this was not the case.

> [N]o, from an Islamic point of view, for a Muslim, Islam is part of life. It tells you A to Z how to lead your life, so it's not a private question, it is a way of life for us, and therefore, for you to ask the question, they would not feel offended, but they would feel more relaxed that you are asking them a question about their faith that they can relate to.
>
> *(Muslim chaplain, Yorkshire, interviewed January 2009)*

Having convinced his physiotherapy colleagues of the opportunities to be derived from a new approach, they together devised a patient information leaflet that considered physiotherapy from an Islamic point of view, with prayer as a central dimension. The outcome was first prize in a national competition and a £1,000 award to do further research into anatomy and physiotherapy from an Islamic perspective. Arguably, interventions of this kind are valuable not only for the individuals who benefit most immediately, but also for public institutions more generally. This is because they prompt recognition and awareness of changing population demographics and new service-user needs, and this awareness can go on to stimulate innovative thinking about ways in which other services might be developed or improved.

Dealing with death and bereavement is hard for most families, but is often made more distressing when there is a legal requirement to carry out a post-mortem examination of the deceased. Post-mortem procedures are usually highly invasive and generally entail the pathological dissection of body parts in order to determine the cause of death. According to some Muslim scholars, such treatment of the body is contrary to Islamic law since it involves a violation of the sanctity and integrity of a body created by God. A Hadith of the Prophet claims that 'breaking a dead man's bone is like breaking it when he is alive' (Abu Dawood, Book 20, Hadith 3201).[6] The same teaching is put forward by Ibn Maajah (Hadith 1617): 'Breaking the bones of a dead person is like breaking his bones when he is alive, in terms of sin.' These Hadith accord with Qur'anic principles about the sanctity of the human body, and the respect and honour that should be offered to the dead. Invasive post-mortem examination further undermines the right of the deceased to return to the earth intact, in readiness for the Day of Judgement. A more practical complication associated with pathological examination, however, especially when histology samples need to be sent for analysis, is the delayed burial of the body, which under normal circumstances should be done within 24 hours of death in order to conform to Islamic law.

These kinds of concerns about the need for rapid burial and the sanctity of the body (both dead and alive) are equally the subject of ethical and religious concern for Jews, for many of the same kinds of reasons. Rabbinic opinion is that the body 'is not just a container which houses the holy soul, but the body itself has intrinsic holiness' (Steinberg 2003: 78). Not surprisingly, therefore, both Muslim and Jewish communities have been involved in two major coroner-led pilot projects in Bolton and Salford, and in Rochdale, Greater Manchester, over recent years. These projects have been examining the feasibility of non-invasive magnetic resonance imaging (MRI) of the deceased body, instead of invasive pathological post-mortems. Working the Bolton Council of Mosques, Her Majesty's Manchester West Coroner, Jennifer Leeming, has been developing the technique in order to address the concerns of both Jewish and Muslim communities. Using scanners at night, when they are less likely to be in use for the living, means that the cause of death can usually be ascertained quickly, and in some cases this can enable burial within the prescribed period.

Not surprisingly, Muslim chaplains in other parts of the United Kingdom are becoming aware of the legal, practical and medical implications of what has become known as the 'Bolton Protocol'. But the efficacy of their communication and networking abilities can often determine whether or not their hospital can offer a non-invasive post-mortem to Muslim families. One of the Muslim chaplains in our study recounted the effort involved in winning senior manager support for the procedure by providing evidence of demand, and clearly documenting what would be necessary to make MRI post-mortems practical. In his case, however, the situation was logistically complicated because his hospital could not guarantee the simultaneous availability of a specialist radiologist and an MRI scanner. Undeterred, and aware of the fact that deceased bodies remain the responsibility of the coroner at all times, he arranged for the secure transportation of bodies to a nearby private hospital, in order that the procedure could be carried out elsewhere. Since 2009 the grief and distress of at least eight Muslim families have been reduced on account of this initiative.

Not only is this a particularly striking example of the multifaceted role of Muslim chaplains in Britain today, and the necessity to interface with many different discursive communities and professional practices, but it also illustrates some of the ways in which Muslim chaplains span the 'private' and 'public' realms. But more than this, when the House of Commons Public Bill Committee discussed the implications of the Manchester pilot projects in February 2009,[7] its members advocated that the availability of the technique of MRI scanning should be extended to the 'whole community, not just the Jewish and Muslim communities' (Brian Iddon, Bolton South East, Labour). Examples were cited where this might be helpful to families of all faiths, and none. These include cases where a post-mortem may need to be carried out quickly – 'for example, if they are visiting a loved one in this country who dies, and they need to return quickly to their own country because of their occupation'.[8] Seen in this light, it is clear that some of the largely unrecorded and pioneering work of Muslim chaplains, underpinned by good relations with Jewish faith leaders, coroners and senior health service managers, is enabling the development of new initiatives that have wider public significance. This example is a fulfilment of a prediction about the ways in which Muslims are contributing to society as a whole: '[T]here is every reason to believe that Muslims will engage in such bridging activities to improve the communities [and institutions] in which they live' (Fetzer and Soper 2004: 154).

Emerging from the examples and case studies discussed in this chapter is a developing 'theology of pastoral care'. Many chaplains have argued that their theology of compassion and care is deeply and inherently Islamic, but has come to the fore as a result of the context in which they are now working:

> Imams are taught to be distant. The imam–congregation relationship in our communities is one that you don't befriend an imam. You ask [the] imam for [a] *fatwa*, he gives you a *fatwa* and then he leaves. In the prisons when you've got a Lifer Unit, you build relationships. So it's quite an interesting dynamic, it's different, pastoral care is totally different. You go and visit the health centre, 'how are you, are you OK?', 'do you want to say a prayer', 'how's family?' – you know, all that. So it's quite an interesting … and I think they're adjusting quite well.
>
> *(Stakeholder, London, interviewed March 2010)*

For many of the chaplains in our study, an articulate understanding has emerged about the opportunity that chaplaincy provides to bring a creative reconciliation of *deen* and *dunya*, by which they usually mean the skilful combination of their religious duties (with a view to the Hereafter) and the necessity of worldly economic activity.[9]

> It's given me satisfaction that I'm doing something in my life which is helping other people in their life; and that's the main objective for me because I know it's part of our religion, it's part of our duty to visit sick people. And to me that's filling part of my religious duties as well.
>
> *(Hospital chaplain, South Wales, interviewed September 2009)*

Conclusion

Muslim chaplains are a new and important category of social actor in British public life, and despite their relatively low numbers they are making a disproportionate impact on the institutions in which they work. Our research suggests that '[t]hey provide arguments for public debates on crucial morally-loaded issues' (Habermas 2006: 7), such as the respectful treatment of a corpse. A public service ethos that requires chaplains to meet institutional needs for staff and clients, whether they are Muslim or not, could help to foster more engaged, outward-looking forms of religious leadership that looks beyond the welfare of the immediate congregation.

Alongside the intrinsic social and religious benefits that can arise through the employment of Muslim chaplains for society as a whole, their experiences and skills have significant implications for Islam in British society more generally. 'In the differentiated architecture of modern societies, the religious certainties are in fact exposed to an increasing pressure for reflection', notes Habermas (2006: 9). Working as part of multi-faith chaplaincy teams, Muslims are to some extent forced to think about their faith *reflexively*. They are required to examine how their worldviews and religious truths relate to those of others, as well as to the principles of public life – especially the ideas of egalitarian individualism and the universalism of modern law and morality (Habermas 2006). A recognition that these principles need not contradict or endanger their own claims to truth, combined with an ability to make meaningful connections between their faith and the predominance of modern scientific expertise, reflects the 'arduous work of hermeneutic self-reflection' (ibid.: 14). Where this is occurring, there are likely to be important implications for Muslim communities and intellectuals, and the outcomes may bring many positive benefits for the structural position of Islam and Muslims in Britain in the future.

Acknowledgements

This chapter would not have been possible without the financial support of the AHRC/ESRC 'Religion and Society' programme. We acknowledge also the generosity of Muslim chaplains who have kindly allowed us to interview them and to observe their work. Thanks are due to Markfield Institute of Higher Education, Leicester, for enabling us to conduct research with past students of their 'Certificate in Training of Muslim Chaplains', and we especially appreciate the ongoing interest and involvement of Dr Ataullah Siddiqui. We have benefited from the feedback on an earlier draft of this chapter by our Co-investigator, Professor Stephen Pattison of Birmingham University, to whom we also offer our thanks.

Notes

1 I am grateful to Ahtsham Ali, the Muslim Adviser at the Prison Service Chaplaincy Headquarters for providing figures on the number of Muslim prison chaplains in the United Kingdom, accurate as of December 2010.

2 Award reference: AH/F008937/1: 'Leadership and Capacity Building in the British Muslim Community: The Case of Muslim Chaplains' (2008–11). The Principal Investigator is Gilliat-Ray; the Co-investigator is Professor Stephen Pattison at Birmingham University, and Dr Mansur Ali is the full-time Research Assistant.

3 Community chaplaincies are independent faith-based organizations that work alongside prisoners, ex-prisoners and their families, offering practical, social, relational and spiritual

support within prison, through the gates and out in the community. The work harnesses the extensive resources that are available within the faith communities, most particularly volunteers who give their time to support those who are seeking to make a fresh start after leaving prison. Community chaplaincies are multi-faith and work with offenders of all faiths and none (www.communitychaplaincy.org.uk).

4 The Hanafi school of thought was founded by Abu Hanifa (d. 767), a jurist of Persian origin. Being the preferred law school of many Muslim rulers during history, such as the Abbasids and Ottomans and the Mughals in India, it is now prevalent in many parts of the Muslim world, and especially the Indian subcontinent. About three-quarters of Britain's Muslim population are of South Asian origin.
5 This is discussed in more depth elsewhere (Gilliat-Ray 2008).
6 www.muslimaccess.com/sunnah/hadeeth/abudawud/020.html.
7 See www.publications.parliament.uk/pa/cm200809/cmpublic/coroners/090224/pm/90224s01.htm for a full transcript of the debate.
8 See note 7.
9 The distinction *deen* and *dunya* is culturally determined; the Qur'an contrasts *dunya* (this world) with *ahkirah* (the Hereafter).

References

Abidin, I. A. (1994) *Radd al-Muhtar Sharh Durr al-Mukhtar*, Beirut: Dar al-Kutub al-Ilmiyya.

Adler, P. A. and Adler, P. (1994) 'Observational techniques', in N. K. Denzin and Y. S. Lincoln (eds.) *Handbook of Qualitative Research*, London: Sage.

Ali-Karamali, S. P. and Dunne, F. (1994) 'The ijtihad controversy', *Arab Law Quarterly* 9 (3): 238–257.

Beckford, J. A. and Gilliat, S. (1998) *Religion in Prison: Equal Rites in a Multi-faith Society*, Cambridge: Cambridge University Press.

Birt, J. (2005) 'Locating the British *imam*: the Deobandi *'ulama* between contested authority and public policy post-9/11', in J. Cesari and S. McLoughlin (eds) *European Muslims and the Secular State*, Aldershot: Ashgate.

Burlet, S. and Reid, H. (1998) 'A gendered uprising: political representation and minority ethnic communities', *Ethnic and Racial Studies* 21 (2): 270–287.

Codd, R.A. (1999) 'A critical analysis of the role of *Ijtihad* in legal reforms in the Muslim world', *Arab Law Quarterly* 14 (2): 112–131.

Cox, J. G. (1955) *A Priest's Work in Hospital*, London: SPCK.

Davie, G. (1994) *Religion in Britain since 1945: Believing without Belonging*, Oxford: Blackwell.

Esposito, J. L. (1988) *Islam: The Straight Path*, Oxford: Oxford University Press.

Fetzer, J. and Soper, J. C. (2004) *Muslims and the State in Britain, France and Germany*, Cambridge: Cambridge University Press.

Fuller, J. and Vaughan, P. (eds) (1986) *Working for the Kingdom: The Story of Ministers in Secular Employment*, London: SPCK.

Gilliat-Ray, S. (2008) 'From "visiting minister" to "Muslim chaplain": the growth of Muslim chaplaincy in Britain, 1970–2007', in E. Barker (ed.) *The Centrality of Religion in Social Life: Essays in Honour of James A. Beckford*, Aldershot: Ashgate.

Gilliat-Ray, S. (2010a) 'Body-works and fieldwork: research with British Muslim chaplains', *Culture and Religion* 11 (4): 413–432.

Gilliat-Ray, S. (2010b) *Muslims in Britain: An Introduction*, Cambridge: Cambridge University Press.

Gilliat-Ray, S. (2011) '"Being there": the experience of shadowing a British Muslim hospital chaplain', *Qualitative Research* 11 (5): 469–486.

Gilliat-Ray, S., Pattison, S. and Ali, M. M. (2013) *Understanding Muslim Chaplaincy*, Aldershot: Ashgate.

Habermas, J. (2006) 'Religion in the public sphere', *European Journal of Philosophy* 14 (1): 1–25.

Hallaq, W. B. (1984) 'Was the gate of ijtihad closed?', *International Journal of Middle East Studies* 16 (1): 3–41.

Hallaq, W. B. (1995) 'Ijtihad', in J. Esposito (ed.) *The Oxford Encyclopedia of the Modern Islamic World*, vol. 2, Oxford: Oxford University Press.

Haneef, S. (1979) *What Everyone Should Know about Islam and Muslims*, Lahore: Kazi Publications.

Herbert, D. (2003) *Religion and Civil Society: Rethinking Public Religion in the Contemporary World*, Aldershot: Ashgate.

Johnston, R. and McFarland, E. (2010) ' "Out in the open in a threatening world": the Scottish churches' industrial mission, 1960–1980', *International Review of Social History* 55 (1): 1–27.

Khuri, F. I. (2001) *The Body in Islamic Culture*, London: Saqi Books.

Legood, G. (ed.) (1999) *Chaplaincy: The Church's Sector Ministries*, London: Cassell.

Modood, T. (2003) 'Muslims and the politics of difference', *Political Quarterly* 74 (1): 100–115.

Priestley, P. (1985) *Victorian Prison Lives*, London: Methuen.

Roff, W. R. (1983) 'Whence cometh the law? Dog saliva in Kelantan, 1937', *Comparative Studies in Society and History* 25 (2): 323–338.

Saeed, A. (2006) *Islamic Thought: An Introduction*, London: Routledge.

Saint-Blancat, C. and Perocco, F. (2005) 'New modes of social interaction in Italy: Muslim leaders and local society in Tuscany and Venetia', in S. McLoughlin and J. Cesari (eds) *European Muslims and the Secular State*, Aldershot: Ashgate.

Snape, M. (2005) *God and the British Soldier: Religion and the British Army in the First and Second World Wars*, London: Routledge.

Steinberg, A. (2003) *Encyclopedia of Jewish Medical Ethics: A Compilation of Jewish Medical Law*, Jerusalem: Feldheim Publishers.

Swift, C. (2009) *Hospital Chaplaincy in the Twenty-First Century: The Crisis of Spiritual Care in the NHS*, Aldershot: Ashgate.

5

YOUNG MUSLIMS IN LONDON

Gendered negotiations of local, national and transnational places

Louise Ryan

Introduction

MONA: Yeah, I was on the bus and this man looked up and saw me and he jumped.

RUKAYA: That is one advantage: you can always get a seat on the bus now, no one wants to sit near you.

ABDUL: That happened to my friend, he got on the train and people moved, like he was the Angel of Death.

(Focus group 3)

In this exchange, three young Muslims discuss the impact of terrorist events such as the bombing of the London transport system on 7 July 2005. Visibly identifiable Muslims such as these two young women, who both wear the hijab (headscarf), feel that they are regarded by fellow commuters as potential suicide bombers. Similar stories were told by participants throughout this study. Although the young people joke that they can always get a seat now on public transport because no one wants to sit near them, it is clear that such incidents mark out Muslims as potentially threatening. These encounters construct Muslims as dangerous outsiders who are not welcome in public places. This raises questions about how young Muslims are placed and position themselves in different social and geographical locations and how these processes shape identity formation.

Drawing on the complex and fluid concept of 'place', this chapter explores how young Muslims encounter, negotiate and shape place in different social and geographical locations. Young Muslims are often enmeshed in family relationships across national borders. In addition, they may embrace a diasporic identity, the international Muslim community, the Ummah, which is accessed, for example, through global cultural flows such as media and the internet. Nonetheless, that is not to suggest a simple, de-territorialized identity. Day-to-day experiences of place are mainly rooted in the local – the neighbourhood environments where people live, work, study, socialize and worship. This chapter suggests that the interconnections between the experiences of the local and the wider, national and international contexts are complex, multidimensional and shifting.

The research study took place in an area of north London and involved a diverse range of participants. Drawing in particular upon the focus group discussions involving young men and women, this chapter analyses the gendered ways in which specific places are navigated and understood. Crossing boundaries often revealed the contextual nature and meaning of gender performances in particular sites – for example, on a London street, on the train, in the mosque or on a family visit to the 'homeland'.

In exploring the dynamics between place and identity, the chapter argues that these young people both shape and are shaped by the places they encounter. This calls for a more nuanced understanding of how young Muslims in Britain actively encounter and navigate different places through the complex interplay of gender, religion and age.

Theorizing place

Over the past few decades there has been a fundamental shift in conceptualizing the interrelations between identity, space, place and material lives, with increasing emphasis on fluidity in contrast to fixity (Jackson and Penrose 1993; Keith and Pile 1993; Brah 1996; Massey 1998; Dwyer 2000). Identities, whether ethnic or religious or combinations of both, cannot be seen as given or fixed. Despite evocations of tradition rooted in the distant past, identities are dynamic and change both temporally and spatially (Alba 1990). Identities emerge in the dynamic interplay of self-ascription and ascription by others (Barth 1996) – in other words, as 'a product of both "other definition" and of "self definition"' (Castles and Miller 2003: 33). Hence, identity is regarded 'as a process that is always in progress and that is being made within particular contexts' (Dwyer 2000: 475).

As well as regarding identity as fluid and continually being constructed and renegotiated, there has also been a reappraisal of 'place'. It is no longer accepted as a bounded and enclosed site of authenticity, and there has been a questioning of place as 'fixed' in relation to 'spaces as flows' (Massey 1998: 5–7). As Appadurai (1990) has observed, under the conditions of global cultural flows there is increased fluidity of social formations. Under the influence of globalization, the time–space compression brought about by new technology (see Harvey 1989), and growing geographical mobility leading to disembedding (Giddens 1991), people are now thought to live less localized lives (Albrow 1997).

This is a theme taken up by Relph (2008) in the preface to his reissued classic work *Place and Placelessness*, originally published in 1976. Relph reflects on how conceptualizations of place have changed during the intervening decades: 'The recognition of what might be called the boundlessness of place is, I think, the most important recent contribution to understanding place' (ibid.: vii). He argues that place is simultaneously grounded and boundless. In other words, 'place' is rooted in the particular and familiar, yet also connected to the wider world:

> Place, both as a concept and as phenomenon of experience has a remarkable capacity to make connections between self, community and earth, between what is local and particular and what is regional and worldwide ... sense of place has the potential to serve as a pragmatic foundation for addressing the profound local and global challenges.... Indeed, effective resolution of these challenges may be possible only through a firm grasp of their simultaneously grounded and yet boundless characteristics, which is the very quintessence of understanding place.
>
> *(ibid.: vii)*

The interconnections between the local and the translocal are particularly apparent within migration studies, where research reveals how migrants' daily experiences, relationships and communications may simultaneously occur in far-flung places. The result has been a focus on diasporic identities which 'cross cut and displace national boundaries, creating new forms of belonging' (Dwyer 2000: 475). This perspective has led some to argue that 'locality has a much less absolute salience for individuals and social relations than older paradigms of research allow' (Albrow 1997: 43).

But that is not to suggest that people are living de-territorialized lives, uprooted and disconnected from the localities in which they reside. The recent focus on transnationalism has perhaps led to a relative neglect of the ways in which migrant communities experience their day-to-day lives at a local level (Ryan 2010). For example, some migration scholars have challenged the dichotomous construction that presents local and transnational ties as mutually exclusive. Ehrkamp, for instance, argues that 'such dichotomies are problematic because they overly simplify complex processes of identity construction, assimilation and adaptation' (2005: 348). Instead, she argues for an analytical engagement with the ways that migrants construct their identities in relation to both their new and their old homes. She goes on to suggest that 'the geographical concept of place allows for an understanding of how immigrants' transnational practices create new places of belonging that allow them to engage the receiving society on their own terms' (ibid.: 346). She examines how Turkish migrants in Germany use their transnational practices not to disconnect from German society but, on the contrary, to build meaningful lives within local neighbourhoods that combine aspects of Turkish and German cultures.

While transnational relationships are a key element in migration stories, it is important not to overlook the role of local sources of support in combating loneliness and isolation as well as providing practical assistance. As I have argued elsewhere (Ryan 2007), locality remains significant; migrants do not live their lives only in transnational spaces. They negotiate their daily lives; their access to jobs;

their commute to work; social interactions with colleagues, friends and neighbours; involvement in schools; and experience of discrimination, harassment or abuse in localized spaces. In addition, their involvement in clubs, faith groups or community associations, which may have transnational dimensions, is also organized and experienced through local districts, regions and neighbourhoods (Archer 2009). The employment rights, pay and conditions, immigration status, access to housing, and entitlement to health care of migrants and their families are shaped by local authorities or national policies (notwithstanding the influence of global economic forces or wider intergovernmental agreements). While migrants and their families may access global cultural flows such as satellite television and the internet, these are experienced, shared, discussed and debated with friends or relations within specific local sites: in each other's homes, the workplace, place of worship, school or college. The interactions and interconnections between the local, national and transnational are complex, multifaceted and shifting. Migrant communities may not be entirely bounded by the local but neither are they entirely free and unfettered within transnational spaces (Ryan 2010).

Of course, it is important to acknowledge the great diversity of migrants' experiences. As Albrow (1997) notes in his study of Tooting, south London, people's engagement with the global varies enormously. Access to resources may root people in localized environments (ibid.). Similarly, in her work on Bengali elders in Tower Hamlets, east London, Gardner (1999) found limited levels of geographical mobility, especially among older women. They were connected to Bangladesh through family communication, satellite television and occasional visits. Nonetheless, the majority of their day-to-day experiences rarely extended beyond a specific block of flats, community centre or local shopping district. The Bengali community has visibly shaped the landscape of the area. However, the lifestyles, expectations and experiences of Bengalis have also been shaped by living in Tower Hamlets. Indeed, many stated that it would be impossible to live in Bangladesh because they had become so accustomed to British standards of living (ibid.). Hence, their attitudes towards Bangladesh are shaped through their lives in London, and vice versa.

Thus, identities are experienced and expressed within a complex mix of interconnected local and translocal spaces. As Doreen Massey (1998) argues, identity is not rooted in a fixed and bounded place. Identities are constructed through a web of social relations within overlapping spaces and places. Far from being natural, neutral or given entities, spaces and places are constructed and politically charged arenas. As Keith and Pile have argued, 'space cannot be dealt with as if it were merely a passive, abstract arena on which things happen' (1993: 2). Following the work of Soja, they state that 'space is not an innocent backdrop to position, it is itself filled with politics and ideology' (ibid.: 4). Similarly, Jackson and Penrose suggest that 'the constructedness of place is revealed through its capacity to be moulded' according to different social influences (1993: 13).

Focusing on the dynamic relationship between place and identity, this chapter considers how young Muslims shape and are shaped by the places in which they live, socialize and study, and places that they visit. While exploring these different places the chapter also highlights the interconnections between them: the local neighbourhood, London as a global city; the 'homelands' where they, or their parents, were born; and the transnational Muslim Ummah. The chapter argues for a more nuanced understanding of how young Muslims in Britain actively navigate 'place' through the complex interplay of gender, religion and age.

Methods

The research was carried out in north London between 2007 and 2009. Overall, 37 young people, aged between 17 and 29 years, took part in the study. We conducted three focus groups involving a total of 17 participants. In addition, 20 individual interviews were carried out with the assistance of two community researchers (Ryan *et al.* 2011). The participants were drawn from a range of socio-economic groups, but because two of the focus groups took place in educational settings (a further education college and a university) there were a large number of third-level students among the participants.

Although there was a gender balance in one-to-one interviews (10 male, 10 female), the focus groups tended to attract more female than male participants. Thus, overall there were 15 men and 22 women in the study. One focus group was women-only while the other two were mixed. Hence, unlike many previous studies which have interviewed young Muslim males and females separately, this research presented an opportunity to explore lively exchanges and debates between young men and women.

Focus-group participants were recruited through personal networks, community associations and college tutors. Participants were also recruited by the community researchers. To increase diversity among our participants, we deliberately chose community researchers of different genders, age and ethnicity. One was an Afghani man in his late twenties, the other a Somali woman in her early twenties. Both succeeded in recruiting a diverse range of participants in terms not only of age and gender but also of ethnicity. Unlike many previous studies of young Muslims which have focused on people of South Asian origin, our study draws from a wide range of ethnic backgrounds (for more details, see Ryan *et al.* 2009).

The topic guide explored issues such as home, belonging, identity, intergenerational relations, gender and the importance of religion and ethnicity for the young people. This discussion begins by exploring the complex meanings of home.

The multiple scales of home

In answering a question about where she is from, Hanan, who came to Britain as a child from Somalia, replied, 'It depends on how people ask me the question. If they ask me, "What is your ethnicity?", I say I am from Somalia and I am a Muslim, but if they say, "Where are you from?", I say, "From London."' As I have argued at length elsewhere, the young people had quite ambivalent attitudes about their belonging in and attachment to Britain. While Britain was often perceived as not inclusive of their identities, London was regarded much more positively as a place of possibilities (see Ryan *et al.* 2009).

In response to the question 'Where is home?', Safia gave the following answer:

> I describe Somalia as home. When people ask, "Where are you from?", I would automatically say Somalia ... there is still that connection ... but also [the] UK, I have lived here all my life, I really don't know any different, you know. I haven't lived away from here. Like, this is my home as well; if I go away on holidays I am dying to come back. This is home, this is what I know. You are attached to where you know and I know this place best. It is where I feel comfortable.

Although Safia had only visited Somalia once, as a young child, she began by asserting that Somalia is 'home'. Nonetheless, she then went on to qualify her response by saying that actually the United Kingdom is 'home as well', and in fact as her answer develops, it is apparent that she has lived in the United Kingdom all her life; it is the place she knows best and where she feels comfortable. However, later on, in an exchange with another participant, she qualified her notion of home, specifying that London is where she actually feels most at home.

SAFIA: It is London, I could be anywhere but as long as I am in London.
KARIMA: As soon as you land in London Heathrow – oh, I am back home.
SAFIA: Yeah, I am happy to be home. If I landed in Scotland I would feel, 'Oh God, where am I?' But as long as I am in London. If I am in Bristol, I have family there, but after a few days, I need to come back.

(Focus group 1)

Safia demonstrates the multiple scales of home. As Blunt and Dowling (2006) have argued, the concept of home can range from the household, to the city, to the nation and beyond. While Safia uses the term 'home' to apply to London, the United Kingdom and Somalia, she also suggests some of the complexities and ambivalences of belonging.

Although London may be home, it is apparent that specific areas within the city are regarded very differently. Safia and her family used to live in Tower Hamlets, east London, before moving to the north of the city. Despite being very positive about London, Safia refers to isolated experiences of verbal abuse: 'We got called names in Tower Hamlets you know when the BNP started, you know Black-this and Nigger-that.' By locating and containing abuse within an extremist minority, the BNP (British National Party), within a specific locality (Tower Hamlets), Safia is able to go on asserting that London is a safe, good and inclusive place to live.

Several participants suggested that racism happened somewhere else, not 'around here', not in the specific neighbourhoods where they currently resided. For example, Aishe said, 'But I don't think we really feel racism around here because it is so mixed, isn't it? But maybe other places, like in the countryside, and places like that.'

This point was taken up by Rukaya, who had lived somewhere else before moving to north London:

> It depends on the area you live in as well. London is very multicultural. That is why we appreciate here ... I used to live in Essex. They didn't know what Islam was: 'What is that on your head, do you have hair, are you bald?' It is so ridiculous that you have to laugh. In Essex they didn't know anything about Islam.

The phrase 'it depends on the area' was repeatedly used by participants, and calls attention to the role of place. It suggests that racism is experienced in specific places rather than being a general experience. As Keith and Pile (1993) have argued, identities are constructed through a web of social relations within spaces and places. However, far from being a neutral backdrop to this process, spaces and places become constructed as ethnic sites. Jackson and Penrose (1993) illustrate the various ways in which specific places can become racialized. A number of studies have examined how dominant groups construct and organize difference and regulate 'others' within multi-ethnic sites (see, for example, Grillo 2000; Cross and Keith 1993). Thus, in the example given above we can see that Essex was experienced as a racialized site, where being Muslim was very difficult and uncomfortable. By contrast, London is regarded as a city of possibilities where Muslims can construct spaces of belonging.

Nonetheless, as was noted at the beginning of this chapter, many focus group participants described incidents of hostility encountered in public places, especially on London's public transport. Some young women also described specific incidents of racist abuse:

NAHLA: Van drivers ... they have a reputation for making racist comments. I had that experience. They shout 'rag head' at me when they are driving by.

RUKAYA: I know someone who was spat on as well.

MONA: My next-door neighbours used to call my mum a 'cup head'.

(Focus group 3)

Thus, another way in which the young people made sense of racism was by associating it with an isolated minority, for example a rude neighbour or an ignorant van driver. As Sultana stated, 'but that is people who are ignorant and not educated, I think it is [a] minority who do that. When I go to other schools, or academic places, I find I am treated normally, I am not treated any differently'. Hence, Sultana suggests that while an ignorant minority are prejudiced, most educated people she meets in her day-to-day life as a student teacher in London treat her normally.

London is depicted as an open, inclusive city, a place where they enjoy religious freedom and can freely express their Muslim identities. Mona asserted, 'I wear my headscarf and I never have any hassle in London.' To which Rukaya responded, 'We do have a lot of freedom in London and I do appreciate that.'

As a diverse and multicultural city, London does not belong to any one particular group but can accommodate notions of 'home' for a wide range of people. 'In the case of London, the narrative of the multicultural, cosmopolitan city reflects a powerful imaginary ... diversity and multiculture emerge as aspects of the city's identity' (Hatziprokopiou 2009: 24).

In the discussions above, London emerges not as a fixed, bounded place but rather as a fluid and shifting web of interconnected locales which is greater than the sum of its parts (see also Gill 2010). London can be seen as an imaginary, cosmopolitan idea that floats above the particular pockets of racism or hostility. As we will see in the sections that follow, London provides a medium through which attachments to different local and translocal places can be negotiated and articulated, for example enabling a critical reflection on specific cultural practices, lifestyles and standards of other locations.

Transnational belonging

As was noted in the previous section, several participants referred to their (or their parents') country of origin as 'home'. However, connections to that homeland could be quite complex and ambiguous, as illustrated by the following focus group discussion:

ABDUL: When we go back to Bangladesh we are not seen as Bengalis; they will always look at you and say, 'You are not from here, you are from the UK.' Then you get a sense that here you are not looked at as a UK citizen; you are looked at like you are Bengali. You have two frames of mind and which one would you like to pick? Pick which is the best. But even if we wanted to be Bengali we couldn't, because if we had to manage our lives there we would probably struggle. It is different to the UK.

RUKAYA: Different standards.

NAHLA: We are too spoilt here.

ABDUL: Exactly, we are more used to the lifestyle here. In that sense we are probably more British than Bengali.

(Focus group 3)

Abdul's story clearly illustrates how his sense of identity is differently positioned in specific places. In Britain he is 'looked at' as Bengali, while in Bangladesh he is told, 'You are not from here.' He constructs his sense of himself against these conflicting influences. However, he emphasizes that his choice of identity is constrained by life experiences. Even if he wanted to be Bengali, he could not, because he would not cope with life in Bangladesh. Thus, he concludes that it is easier just to be British. Similarly, Nahla discussed how she felt on her return visit to the country of her birth:

NAHLA: I would say I am Somali. I feel I am Somali.
LOUISE: When you went to Somalia, how did you feel?
NAHLA: You feel more British, because you are not used to the standards there, but here we are used to it.

(Focus group 3)

Nahla's experiences chime with those of the young Somalis interviewed by Valentine and Sporton in Sheffield. Although the journey back to Somalia was 'imagined as a homecoming', 'on arrival many were shocked by the poverty they encountered as well as struggling to adjust to the heat, food, sanitation and lifestyle' (2009: 743). This observation suggests not only the relevance of spatial context but also the complexities of diasporic identities across different locales. As was argued earlier in this chapter, identity is a dynamic process of self-definition and ascription by others. We are not free to choose any identity we wish. The meaning and recognition of identities change in different places. In some places, particular identities may be denied legitimacy: 'spatial norms regulate the subject positions individuals are able to occupy – defining who is out of place' (ibid.: 747). This suggests some of the limits of diasporic identities based on ethnicity, be they Bengali or Somali, especially when individuals are placed or position themselves as not belonging in the 'homeland'.

In the focus-group discussions it became apparent that religious identity can change meaning and salience in different places. For example, Rukaya is a young British-born woman who wears the hijab and jilbab and strongly prioritizes her Islamic identity. Nonetheless, she notes that during family visits back 'home' to Morocco her religious identity marks her out as different:

> But then sometimes when you go back home they are like, 'Why are [you] so religious?' when you are just normal ... and they say to me, 'Are you wearing the scarf, seriously? You live in London, why are you doing that?' I get funny comments from my family, honestly they make me laugh.

In the same focus group, another young woman, Mona, picked up the theme:

> When I went to Dubai, I was wearing this headscarf, but still they realized I was from London, somehow they did know that. They were like, 'Do you go out on the street like that, do you work like that?' I was like 'yeah', they said, 'Oh, really?'

It is noteworthy that despite, or perhaps because of, their hijabs, both of these women were firmly placed as 'outsiders' by their family and friends overseas.

In a different focus group, Sultana observed that when she went on family visits to India she felt very conscious of wearing the hijab. In India she and her sister stood out as being different from other young women and attracted a considerable amount of attention (see also Ahmad, Chapter 9 of this volume). In an individual interview, Nazia remarked that her hijab marks her out as different when she visits her fashionable young cousins in a large Pakistani city. When visiting other countries, including Muslim countries, all of these young women have to explain and justify their choice of clothing. Their overtly religious identity is regarded as surprising and unexpected. Hence, these young women position themselves and are positioned by others as 'out of place'. These stories are interesting in revealing the young people's transnational mobility; their local and translocal connections. However, these anecdotes also raise questions about how an Islamic identity can be seen as boundless and deterritorialized when it is confronted, created and contested within specific places or construction sites (Ryan 2011).

It has been suggested in the literature that instead of ethnically based identities, young Muslims living in Britain are increasingly adopting a diasporic Islamic identity (see, for example, Dwyer 2000; Abbas 2007; Hopkins and Gales 2009). Line Nyhagen Predelli (2008) notes that first-generation migrants are more likely to relate to the national diaspora of country of origin, but for the second generation the country of origin may be less influential and instead the Muslim diaspora and/ or the country of birth become stronger influences. They may feel 'out of place' in their ancestral homeland where ethnic or national identities are experienced as somewhat unstable and shifting across time and space. By contrast, a Muslim identity may be affirmed as stable, fixed and continuous (Valentine and Sporton 2009). Prioritizing religious identity over ethnic, cultural or national affiliation may enable the young people to negotiate belonging in an imagined, de-terroritorialized umma (Werbner 2007).

Several participants spoke about feeling connected to the global Muslim brotherhood and sisterhood through their sense of injustice about the oppression of Muslims in Gaza and the wars in Iraq and Afghanistan (for more detail, see Ryan *et al.* 2009). One interviewee, Farid, expressed this view quite forcefully: 'I follow the news on what's happening around the world, e.g. the situation in Gaza right now, and how the whole world is watching but nobody is doing anything to stop the ethnic cleaning/genocide on the Palestinian people.' Similarly, Hamid spoke about the Muslim victims of the war in Iraq: 'Yeah, it gets to us as well. We feel their pain. A sense of injustice.'

In addition, as Dwyer notes, 'new Muslim identifications, which draw upon links with a pan-Islamic diaspora, may offer ways of reworking gender identities' (2000: 481). Young women are challenging dominant 'discourses in the community and are engaged in a form of social criticism that entails decoupling culture and religion' (Sanghera and Thaper-Bjorkert 2007: 175; see also Ahmad and Mirza, Chapters 9 and 6 respectively of this volume). This was particularly apparent in the comments made by Zara, who had recently moved to London from Somalia:

> I would say I am Muslim first and then Somali ... I would not do certain Somali cultural things which are against the Islamic religion. If I say I am Muslim first, then that means I am living my life in that way ... there are

> things that a Somali person will do because of their culture, like a father will force his daughter to marry, and in Islam it is not actually allowed to force someone to marry unless she agrees to marry that person.

From her new position as a Muslim living in London, Zara has adopted a more critical stance on Somali culture. As Tiilikainen has observed, 'If Somalia carries an image of continuous war, refugees and misery, Islam as a global religion, instead represents dignity, respect and morality. If Somalia is no longer a home to return to, Islam may provide a new basis for establishing a home' (2003: 65).

Indeed, several participants used their religion as a way of distancing themselves from their parents' cultural traditions (see also Ahmad, Chapter 9 of this volume). Like Zara, several people also spoke out against cultural practices such as forced marriages which had been erroneously attributed to religion:

SULTANA: Yeah, it is the cultural practices, like if you look at Pakistan you see that they also practise some things like in India, but that is not about religion but culture.

KARIMA: It happens, like FGM [female genital mutilation] in Africa, people who are not even Muslim. People say it is Islamic; well, it is not. But people think it is.

FATIMA: People don't know what is actually in the Qur'an.

(Focus group 1)

In many instances the research participants referred to the Qur'an as the source of their knowledge and understanding of Islam, undiluted by cultural practices. In another focus group, Abdul elaborated on the tensions between ethnic culture and religious identity:

> If you are just surrounded by Bengalis and they just talk about being Bengali, then all you are going to know about is being Bengali, unless someone comes along and tells you about Islam. Then you think, OK, there is a difference between being Bengali and being a Muslim.... Islam gives you the bigger picture. If you are only in your own culture, then you are only going to be looking out for your own people ... Islam is more universal, not just keeping within your own culture.

For Abdul, Islam is universal; it enables one to become part of something bigger, beyond narrow ethnic communities. Several participants in the research study suggested that religion was more important to them than culture. Tahir went so far as to suggest that 'there is no such thing as culture, no, it is just about religion. I heard in Islam, you are not supposed to believe in culture, it is about religion. What do we mean by culture, anyway?'

It was apparent that the tensions between ethnic culture and religion impacted on some young people's negotiations with the older generation:

AHMAD: Like, the youth, we were not invited into the mosques, by our own people, the Asian old men, are not so nice, they like to go to the front.

ABDUL: One of the first times I went to the mosque, these old guys just looked at me, like 'Are you lost, this is a mosque not a club.' It is a shame. The younger generation is now getting the real Islam and hopefully we can spread the real Islam, the right one.

(Focus group 3)

The 'Asian old men' assert their authority within the mosque, which is a place they apparently like to keep for themselves. However, by claiming knowledge of the 'real Islam', these two young men felt able to negotiate space for themselves within the mosque despite the hostility they had encountered from older men. Knowledge of the 'real Islam' can also impact on the young people's negotiations with their parents:

> But like your parents too, you go to your parents and tell them something about the religion and they say, 'What makes you think you are better than me, I am your parent' ... because they are more interested in their culture, they don't practise the religion so much.
>
> *(Mona)*

The possible tensions between ethnic cultural traditions and religious teaching were further discussed by Rukaya in the same focus group:

> Sometimes culture contradicts religion. Like, for example, music: some Muslims say you can't listen to music, some say you can. So at weddings you can have a clash within families – some want music, some don't. That is a problem because people don't want to let go of their culture, but it is just a culture, forget it. Of course there might be some good things in culture, but if it contradicts Islam then you should just leave it.

After she had finished speaking, Ahmad simply added, 'I hate culture.' Among the young people in this particular focus group there seemed to be a shared view that cultural practices were often too insular and divisive, while Islam was a global, unifying influence (see also Modood and Ahmad 2007). This was clearly illustrated by Abdul: 'Islam is very beautiful. Like with marriages, it should not come down to colour. It is about the faith. Islam breaks boundaries. When you see all the mixing in marriages, it makes you realize that Islam is very beautiful' (see also Ahmad, Chapter 9 of this volume).

Thus, Islam offers a way of challenging the confines of narrow ethnic categories and enables young people to resist cultural traditions such as forced marriages. Being part of a global Islamic Ummah opens up a world of possibilities in relation to potential marriage partners, for example. Nonetheless, it is also apparent from the discussions above that despite claiming an unbounded, de-territorialized diasporic Muslim identity, the young people experienced, negotiated and constructed their identities in specific places and spaces, for example in the local mosque, at family gatherings such as weddings, and on visits back to the country of origin (see also Archer 2009). Thus, although being Muslim may be embraced as a universal, de-territorial identity, as is discussed at length in the next section, it is grounded in localized encounters.

Gendered negotiations of place

While a diasporic Islamic identity may be assumed as a way of asserting a stable, fixed and continuous identity, it is apparent that this identity also has to be continually negotiated and explained in different places. What it means to be a Muslim, and to adopt a particular style of dress and behaviour, changes in different social and geographical locations.

This is particularly clear in the case of Zara, who, having arrived in London quite recently, only then started to wear the hijab and jilbab:

> When you come here, you actually feel that you need to show your identity, to show that you are a Muslim ... you need to show them that you are a Muslim person, that you are not like them, you are not like a non-Muslim person. You have to practise. You can get more satisfaction like when you stop wearing those short skirts or whatever.

In this statement, Zara clearly illustrates how moving to London changed her sense of herself. She now felt that she has 'to show' she is a Muslim. She feels the need to emphasize her difference from 'them', i.e. non-Muslims. Changing her style of attire thus reflects her changing sense of identity in this new place. The trend among Somali women to adopt more conservative styles of attire after migration has been noted by other researchers (see Tiilikainen 2003; Ajrouch and Kusow 2007).

However, it would be misleading to suggest that all the young people who took part in this research shared a similar worldview (see Ryan *et al.* 2009). Not all the women wore the hijab, and in fact it proved to be quite a controversial issue. Zara, wearing jilbab and hijab, was sitting beside Miriam, who was unveiled and casually dressed in jeans and a T-shirt. There was a palpable tension between these two young women. Soon after Zara had spoken about her decision to wear the hijab in London, Miriam made the following remark: 'If I am dressed like this on the road I would get less attention than someone who is wearing the full hijab.'

Her comment was greeted by a chorus of voices, mostly male: 'No, no, that is not true.' Despite this, Miriam carried on making her point:

MIRIAM: People like me, yeah, just normal dress, you wouldn't get that much attention than someone wearing the full hijab ... Women wearing the hijab, they still get lots of looks from English people or any other races, than a person who is just dressed normal...

TAHIR: It depends on the area...
AISHE: You don't attract any attention around here ... but maybe in other areas they might be suspicious.
MIRIAM: Well, in central London you would.

(Focus group 2)

It is significant that Miriam uses the word 'normal' to describe casual dress – that is, jeans and a T-shirt – whereas in a previous focus group Rukaya described the hijab as 'just normal'. This suggests the relative and contextual nature of what is considered 'normal' dress for young Muslim women.

It is also interesting to note Tahir's remark that 'it depends on the area'. This phrase once again draws attention to the role of place and suggests that reactions may be experienced differently in specific places. While Aishe points out that women wearing the hijab do not attract attention 'around here', meaning the neighbourhood where the focus group was taking place, Miriam argues that reactions differ in 'central London'. This echoes the comments made in another focus group about how Muslims are regarded with suspicion on public transport – that is, travelling between areas. However, it quickly became apparent that the discussion of the hijab was also embedded in debates about women's clothing and morality:

TAHIR: I have three sisters, they all wear headscarves, well, the eldest one takes it off sometimes, but then she definitely gets more attention from the boys. If I saw a girl wearing the scarf I would not go up and talk to her, but if a girl isn't wearing a scarf...
MIRIAM: Well, that is just sexist.
HAMID: If you saw a pretty girl on the road, you would want to approach her; you don't look at a girl wearing a scarf out of respect.

(Focus group 2)

There are several points to highlight in this exchange. Miriam's remarks are regarded as highly controversial in the group and are greeted with a heated response, especially from the young men. While she asserts that wearing 'normal' clothes results in less unwanted attention and stares from passers-by, the young men suggest the opposite: that being veiled protects women from unwanted attention. They would respect a young woman who is veiled. The young men feel that a 'girl' who is not veiled is inviting their attention. As has been noted by other researchers, some young Muslim men may perceive unveiled women as 'fair game', morally 'loose' and inviting sexual attention which can lead to harassment (Ramji 2007).

As the discussion continued, Miriam changed strategy: 'In my area you get so many men staring at you, because their women are all covered up.' Having said that she attracted less attention from 'English people', especially in central London, by not wearing the hijab, she now acknowledges that she gets stared at by Muslim men in her local area because 'their women' are covered up. Thus, she differentiates between the reactions she encounters from different types of people in different places. Miriam asserts that men who stare at women are 'sexist'. Thus, she firmly puts the responsibility onto men. The young men in the focus group resist this strategy and once again try to shift the blame back on to Miriam. Tahir argues that men stare 'because of how you dress', while Hamid says that 'you shouldn't dress the way you dress if you don't want attention'. To which Miriam retorts, 'But those men are sinning by staring at me.' In suggesting that men who stare at her are 'sinning', Miriam is invoking an argument that other Muslim women have also used. As a woman in Tiilikainen's study argued, 'if you don't want to see me you should control your eyes' (2003: 62). This argument shifts the responsibility for maintaining modesty on to men as well as women. However, it was clear that the young men in the focus group did not accept this argument and insisted that Miriam deserved all the unwanted attention she received. In the face of such personal criticism, Miriam felt under pressure to assert her moral worth: 'You can't judge someone by how they dress.... I know right from wrong, I know not to be rude, not to steal, but the way I dress that is just appearance, it doesn't really matter.'

Another interesting dimension to this exchange was when some young women turned the attention back on the young men. Hanan, also unveiled, intervened to assist Miriam:

HANAN: Well, you guys are not meant to be wearing what you are wearing right now, there are actually certain things, like you should not be wearing earrings, Tahir, there is an image that you are meant to look up to.

TAHIR: OK, yeah, the earrings ... we up dress for special days like Eid day, Ramadan...

HAMID: Yeah, there are times when we have to dress in a particular way to go to the mosque or something ... well, guys can wear what they like but women have to hide their bodies for self-respect.

(Focus group 2)

The young men accepted that they had to dress in specific ways at particular times and places. But in the main, they argued that men can dress in any way they like, though the question of whether or not it is acceptable for Muslim men to wear earrings was not fully resolved. This discussion chimes with observations by other researchers in the field. As Werbner notes, clothing is 'a symbolically laden vehicle' (2007: 163). Young Muslim men are less constrained in their social interaction, dress and leisure pursuits, while young women are often expected to conform to traditional cultural norms and practices (Sanghera and Thapar-Björkert 2007; Werbner 2007; Ramji 2007). Wearing a headscarf can be regarded as liberating, a means through which women can safely negotiate public places free of harassment (Ramji 2007). However, as the focus group exchanges clearly illustrate, young women may come under pressure from their male peers to adopt the hijab or risk being regarded as immoral, immodest and sexually available. Hence, as Dwyer argues, the hijab has become 'an over-determined signifier against which individual women must negotiate their own identities in relation to a complex of different meanings' (1999: 8).

The role of place is clearly significant in this heated focus-group exchange. The staring and unwanted attention takes place in public spaces, for example 'on the road' or in 'central London'. Doreen Massey points out that gender relations are also 'strongly implicated in the debates over the conceptualization of place' (1998: 7). Women's mobility within the city streets can be seen as a threat to a patriarchal gendering of space and place (ibid.: 11). In analysing female mobility, Parsons (2000) argues that women's negotiation of urban spaces continues to be framed by issues of safety and respectability. As well as the fear of being harassed or even attacked, powerful images of 'the deviant woman', 'the street walker', 'the woman of the streets', the sexually available woman, serve to curtail 'respectable' women's freedom of movement within the city.

In addition, women and girls from ethnic minority backgrounds confront the city in ways that are both gendered and racialized (Ryan 2003). The young women in this study were sensitive to the complex ways in which the hijab was perceived and how its meaning changed in different social and geographical contexts. In some places it warranted respect, while in other places it attracted suspicion and even harassment. The heated exchanges described above clearly illustrate the gendered navigation and construction of place.

Conclusion

This chapter has explored how young Muslims are placed and position themselves in different social and geographical locations and how these processes inform identity formation. The participants in this study were enmeshed in family relationships across national borders. In addition, they also had a sense of diasporic identity within the international Muslim community, the Ummah. Nonetheless, they lived their lives within quite localized places: specific neighbourhoods, colleges and social spaces. The complex interconnections between the local and the transnational or translocal were experienced and negotiated in varied ways, for example through family visits back to the country of origin. The chapter has used the concept of place to make sense of young Muslims' situated identities. As Relph (2008) argues, place is simultaneously grounded and boundless. In other words, 'place' is rooted in the particular and familiar yet also connected to the wider world.

I have argued that London is a space in and through which these young people can express diverse Muslim identities. Their diasporic identity is constructed from the perspective and positionality of living in London. This impacts on how they perceive ethnic culture, their ancestral homeland and also their sense of religious identity. London gives them the freedom to forge Muslim identities. But that is not to imply that London is entirely open and free of prejudice and hostility. Space should not be regarded as an innocent backdrop to position, but rather is filled with politics and ideology (Keith and Pile 1993). This research has also found that negative experiences are usually explained in terms of an ignorant minority who are contained within specific pockets of the city – or outside of the city, in the case of Essex. London can thus remain a place of possibilities, an imaginary space where belonging can be negotiated and proclaimed.

In line with what other academic scholars have found, the findings from this research also suggest that religious identity may give these young people a space within which to reflect upon and critique specific ethnic cultural practices. For young women, in particular, Islam provides a lens through which to challenge practices such as forced marriages or FGM. For both young men and young women, proclaiming knowledge of the 'real Islam' based on their studies of the Qur'an enables them to question the authority of the older generation (a debate picked up by Ahmad and Mirza in their chapters in this book).

But that is not to suggest that all the participants expressed their Muslim identities in the same way. There were a range of attitudes, for example, about whether or not women should wear the hijab. While some women proclaimed the liberating power of 'covering up', it was clear that refusal to adopt the hijab could also result in harassment and criticism. The heated debates about the hijab highlight the relevance of place. Contrary to what some other observers have maintained, this chapter argues that despite a paradigmatic shift towards the transnational, diasporic and global within the literature, the local still has salience. Reactions to the hijab were shaped by gendered and racialized discourses within local sites such as the street, on the Underground, in central London or in specific neighbourhoods. Of course, these reactions to the hijab may be influenced in part by wider debates and images circulated through global media, for example. Nonetheless, the reactions were experienced and resisted in local places. This suggests the interconnectedness of the local and transnational. Thus, while ostensibly a boundless, de-territorialized religious identity, Muslimness is also grounded in particular experiences in particular places.

The complex interconnections between the local and the translocal were often articulated in terms of visits to the country of origin. Here their religious identity, far from denoting belonging, may have heightened the young people's sense of being 'out of place'. Hence, this chapter concludes that Muslimness is simultaneously boundless and grounded, universal but also particular, transcendent as well as situated.

Acknowledgements

This study was funded by the Department for Communities and Local Government and was commissioned by the Barnet Muslim Engagement Partnership. The researchers working on this project were Louise Ryan, Eleonore Kofman and Ludovica Banfi. The author would like to thank the various community organizations that facilitated this research: Ayesha Community Education, the Paiwand Afghan Association and the Somali Family Support Group. The two community researchers who assisted with fieldwork were Mustafa Mansury and Faiza Bashe.

References

Abbas, T. (ed.) (2007) *Islamic Political Radicalism: A European Perspective*, Edinburgh: Edinburgh University Press.

Alba, R. D. (1990) *Ethnic Identity: The Transformation of White America*, New Haven, CT: Yale University Press.

Albrow, M. (1997) 'Travelling beyond local cultures: socioscapes in a global city', in J. Eade (ed.) *Living the Global City*, London: Routledge.

Ajrouch, K. and Kusow, A. M. (2007) 'Racial and religious contexts: situational identities among Lebanese and Somali Muslim immigrants', *Ethnic and Racial Studies* 30 (1): 72–94.

Appadurai, A. (1991) 'Global ethnoscapes: notes and queries for a transnational anthropology', in R. G. Fox (ed.) *Interventions: Anthropologies of the Present*, Santa Fe, NM: School of American Research.

Archer, L. (2009) 'Race, "face" and masculinity: the identities and local geographies of Muslim boys', in P. Hopkins and R. Gale (eds) *Muslims in Britain: Race, Place and Identities*, Edinburgh: Edinburgh University Press.

Barth, F. (1996) 'Ethnic groups and boundaries', in J. Hutchinson and A. D. Smith (eds) *Ethnicity*, Oxford: Oxford University Press.

Blunt, A. and Dowling, R. (2006) *Home: Key Ideas in Geography*, London: Routledge.

Brah, A. (1996) *Cartographies of Diaspora*, London: Routledge.

Castles, S. and Miller, M. J. (2003) *The Age of Migration: International Population Movements in the Modern World*, Basingstoke: Palgrave Macmillan.

Cross, M. and Keith M. (1993) *Racism, the City and the State*, London: Routledge.

Dwyer, C. (1999) 'Veiled meanings: young British Muslim women and the negotiation of difference', *Gender, Place and Culture* 6 (1): 5–26.

Dwyer, C. (2000) 'Negotiating diasporic identities: young British South Asian Muslim women', *Women's Studies International Forum* 23 (4): 475–486.

Ehrkamp, P. (2005) 'Placing identities: transnational practice and local attachment', *Journal of Ethnic and Migration Studies* 31 (2): 345–364.

Gardner, K. (1999) 'Narrating location: space, age and gender among Bengali elders in east London', *Oral History* 27 (1): 65–74.

Giddens, A. (1991) *Modernity and Self-Identity: Self and Society in the Late Modern Age*, Stanford, CA: Stanford University Press.

Gill, N. (2010) 'Pathologies of migrant place-making: the case of Polish migrants to the UK', *Environment and Planning A* 42 (5): 1157–1173.

Grillo, R. D. (2000) 'Plural cities in comparative perspective', *Ethnic and Racial Studies* 23 (6): 957–981.

Harvey, D. (1989) *The Condition of Postmodernity*, Oxford: Oxford University Press.

Hatziprokopiou, P. (2009) 'Strangers as neighbors in the cosmopolis: new migrants in London', in S. Hemelryk Donald, E. Kofman and C. Kevin (eds) *Branding Cities: Cosmopolitanism, Parochialism, and Social Change*, New York: Routledge.

Hopkins, P. and Gale, R. (eds) (2009) *Muslims in Britain: Race, Place and Identities*, Edinburgh: University of Edinburgh Press.

Jackson, P. and Penrose, J. (1993) *Constructions of Race, Place and Nation*, London: UCL Press.

Keith, M. and Pile, S. (1993) *Place and the Politics of Identity*, London: Routledge.

Massey, D. (1998) *Space, Place and Gender*, Cambridge: Polity Press.

Modood, T. and Ahmad, F. (2007) 'British Muslim perspectives on multiculturalism', *Theory, Culture and Society* 24 (2): 187–213.

Nyhagen Predelli, L. (2008) 'Religion, citizenship and participation: a case study of immigrant Muslim women in Norwegian mosques', *European Journal of Women's Studies* 15 (3): 241–260.

Parsons, D. L. (2000) *Streetwalking the Metropolis: Women, the City and Modernity*, Cambridge: Cambridge University Press.

Ramji, H. (2007) 'Dynamics of religion and gender among young British Muslims', *Sociology* 41 (6): 1171–1189.

Relph, E. (2008) *Place and Placelessness*, London: Pion.

Ryan, L. (2003) 'Moving spaces and changing places: Irish women's memories of London in the 1930s', *Journal of Ethnic and Migration Studies* 29 (1): 67–82.

Ryan, L. (2007) 'Migrant women, social networks and motherhood: the experiences of Irish nurses in Britain', *Sociology* 41 (2): 295–312.

Ryan, L. (2010) 'Transnational relations: family migration among recent Polish migrants in London', *International Migration* 49 (2): 80–103.

Ryan, L. (2011) 'Muslim women negotiating collective stigmatisation: we're just normal people', *Sociology* 45 (6): 1045–1060.

Ryan, L., Kofman, E. and Banfi, L. (2009) *Muslim Youth in Barnet: Exploring Identity, Citizenship and Belonging Locally and in the Wider Context*, research report, Middlesex University.

Ryan, L., Kofman, E. and Aaron, P. (2011) 'Insiders and outsiders: working with peer researchers in researching Muslim communities', *International Journal of Social Research Methodology* 14 (1): 49–60.

Sanghera, G. and Thaper-Björkert, S. (2007) 'Gendering political radicalism', in T. Abbas (ed.) *Islamic Political Radicalism: A European Perspective*, Edinburgh: Edinburgh University Press.

Tiilikainen, M. (2003) 'Somali women and daily Islam in the Diaspora', *Social Compass* 50 (1): 59–69.

Valentine, G. and Sporton, D. (2009) '"How other people see you, it's like nothing that's inside": the impact of processes of disidentification and disavowal on young people's subjectivities', *Sociology* 43 (4): 735–751.

Werbner, P. (2007) 'Veiled interventions in pure space: honour, shame and embodied struggles among Muslims in Britain and France', *Theory, Culture and Society* 24 (2): 161–186.

6

MULTICULTURALISM AND THE GENDER GAP

The visibility and invisibility of Muslim women in Britain

Heidi Safia Mirza

Introduction

In this chapter I argue that Muslim women occupy a unique space of visibility and invisibility within the multicultural discourse in Britain. On one hand they 'fall between the cracks' of liberal multiculturalism, which, in its many shifting manifestations, has consistently functioned to privilege 'race', religion and ethnicity over gender. A gender-blind multicultural discourse means that Muslim women, who are located at the intersectionality of race, class, gender, sexuality, religion and patriarchy, remain largely invisible, locked into the private space of the home and family, where oppressive gendered cultural and religious practices are still played out. For example, Muslim women who are subject to culturally specific forms of violence against women, such as honour crimes and forced marriage, are caught up in the contradictions of the cultural relativism of British faith-based multiculturalism as well as the private–public divide of the family which characterizes mainstream approaches to violence against women more generally. On the other hand, since 11 September 2001 and, more recently, the 7 July 2005 bombings by young British Muslim men in the United Kingdom, there has been an overwhelming preoccupation with the 'embodied' Muslim women in our public spaces. In particular, the spotlight on Muslim women wearing the veil has preoccupied our western media (see also Ahmad and Ryan, Chapters 9 and 6 respectively of this volume). In the West's ideological 'war on terror' the 'Muslim woman' has come to symbolize the 'barbaric Muslim other' in our midst. In the ensuing discourse of Islamophobia, produced by the global threat to security from Islamic extremism, Muslim women have become pathologized as voiceless victims of their 'backward' communities in need of 'saving' by the enlightened 'West' (Abu-Lughod 2002).

My argument in this chapter is there are real consequences arising from the way in which Muslim women are constructed in the contested multicultural space occupied by the post-colonial Muslim diaspora in Britain. Caught up in the 'collision of discourses', the concerns of Muslim women can easily 'slip through the cracks' of everyday policy and politics. At one and the same time, Muslim women are highly visible and pathologized as victims in the discourse of Islamophobia, yet they are largely absent and invisible in the normative (white) discourse on familial and communal domestic violence. In the discourse of multiculturalism they are ultimately at risk of not being fully protected by the state as equal citizens. Often, professionals, such as teachers, social workers or doctors find themselves 'walking on eggshells' – that is, in a state of paralysis, not wanting to offend the community's sensibilities, afraid of accusations of racism, or feeling a lack of cultural expertise and knowledge about Islam (Mirza 2010). In this gendered post-modern multicultural malaise, Muslim women can suffer a lack of protection, or inaction, from individuals and organizations charged with their well-being. Understanding the tensions between recognizing gender oppression within Muslim communities and preserving the important but contested space of multicultural difference in Britain is at the heart of my concern in this chapter. It is a fine but important line to walk.

Throughout this chapter I use the collective term 'Muslim women' to encompass black and other ethnic minority women from Asian, African, South American, Mediterranean, European, Arabic and Middle Eastern Islamic cultures who now live and work in Britain. While there are women of different faiths and cultures, such as Sikh, Hindu, Jewish, Buddhist and Christian women, who also suffer from the collision of multiculturalism and violence against women, it is the effects the Islamophobic discourse and the construction of ethnicized or racially objectified 'Muslim woman' within this context that I am interested in exploring here. The post-colonial Muslim feminist anthropologist Lila Abu-Lughod argues that, while we need to be specific about the history, politics and development of different Islamic societies and cultures, we must also be vigilant concerning the West's reifying tendency 'to plaster neat cultural icons like "the Muslim woman" over messy historical and political dynamics' (2002: 784).

Multiculturalism and the marginalization of Muslim women

Yuval-Davis (1997) argues that women are the 'bearers of races' and 'guardians of culture', and, as such, central to the ideological construction and reproduction of national identity and hence the (multicultural) state. However, the British national story writes out the complexities of Muslim women's struggle for a place in the post-colonial national picture. The journey towards twenty-first-century multicultural Britain began in the post-war era of the 1940s when migrants came from the British colonies of India, Africa and the Caribbean as well as what later became Bangladesh and Pakistan to work in the 'motherland' (Hall 2004). Britons' response to the post-colonial 'dark stranger' in their midst was marked by racism and hostility which have continued to the present day, marked by high-profile masculine racist clashes on the streets between white and Muslim young men and the underperformance of Pakistani, Bangladeshi and Turkish boys in the classroom (Bhavnani *et al.* 2005; Tomlinson 2008). The story of Muslim women's struggle for recognition and rights within their own communities and the wider British context is a lesser tale told.

In the 60 years since post-war migration began, British national identity has been transformed by the irresistible rise of multicultural Britain (Gilroy 2004; Hall 2004). There are now three generations of British-born young ethnic minority men and women who are claiming the new hyphenated (but contested) identities of Black-British, Asian-British and Muslim-British (Nandi and Platt 2009). According to Office for National Statistics data, ethnic minority groups make up 7.9 per cent of the British population and are on the whole younger on average than the white population (ONS 2006). It is claimed that Muslims, who make up 4.2 per cent of the British population, are the fastest-growing group, increasing in number from 1,870,000 in 2004 to 2,422,000 in 2008 (BRIN 2010). Pakistanis, originating mainly from the Azard Kashmir region, are the most dominant group and make up 43 per cent of Muslims in Britain. Other established and significant South Asian migrant Muslim communities come from Bangladesh and India. The majority of white Muslims in Britain are classified as 'other white' and come from Turkey, Kurdistan, Cyprus, North Africa, Albania, Bosnia and Kosovo. Smaller black African Muslim communities come from Central and West African countries, mainly Nigeria. However, the Muslim population has grown in recent years with refugees and asylum seekers from Afghanistan, Iran, Iraq, Somalia and the former Yugoslavia (Abbas 2010). With Muslims having a growth rate purportedly ten times faster than the rest of British society, this increase generated a hysterical reaction in the press about Muslims overrunning Britain. As the *Daily Mail* headline screams, 'Mohammed has become the most popular name for newborn boys in Britain' (Doyle 2010)! If high rates of childbirth among ethnic minority communities are indeed the case, then women, it would seem, and particularly ethnicized Muslim women of Asian, African, South American, Mediterranean, European, Arabic and Middle Eastern origin, are central to reproduction of the British multicultural state.

There have been different state responses to post-colonial immigration, from assimilation and integration in the 1960s, to multicultural pluralism in the 1980s, to the celebration of difference and diversity in the 1990s (Mirza 2009). Multiculturalism in the British context has been hard-won and has evolved from a liberal notion of coexistence based on respecting diversity and valuing cultural difference in the context of core shared values in society (Hall 2000; Runnymede Trust 2000; Parekh 2005). *The Parekh Report: The Future of Multi-ethnic Britain* called Britain a 'community of communities', describing it as a multicultural post-nation in which there are shared values, but also the autonomy of cultural expression to wear the Muslim hijab or eat halal meat (Runnymede Trust 2000). This negotiated coexistence is predicated upon what Stuart Hall (2000) has called 'multicultural drift'. Here Hall describes state intervention, policy and professional discourse as developing in a loose and historically haphazard way. Indeed, multicultural policies in Britain have been piecemeal, based on concessions, extensions and exemptions such as scheduling exams to avoid key festivals for religious groups, or Sikhs being exempt from wearing helmets, or slaughterhouses for Jews and Muslims (Harris 2001). Such concessions have been won or lost through the struggles of post-war migrant communities living in Britain. However, the struggle for an inclusive multiculturalism in the British context has been deeply racialized (Hesse 2000). As Goldberg (2004) explains, 'multiculturalism' is what happens to nations when their essential national purity is challenged by the influx of racial others. For example when the Commission on the Future of Multi-ethnic Britain suggested that 'Britishness' as a national identity had unspoken racial connotations linked to Empire, the report was met with a hostile media backlash (McLaughlin and Neal 2003). The notion of a racially inclusive multicultural national identity was seen to challenge the homogeneity of an exclusive imaginary 'white' Britishness (see also Sales, Chapter 2 of this volume).

In the face of growing racist political rhetoric, Islamophobia and anti-asylum and immigration policies in Britain, we are witnessing a retreat from multiculturalism and a move towards civic integration. In a multicultural 'post-nation', integration and active citizenship are now seen as the solution to economic inequality, political under-representation and structural segregation in housing and education in the ethnic enclaves that serve our cities (Wetherell *et al.* 2007). As part of the civic integration agenda, newcomers have to swear an oath of allegiance at citizenship ceremonies; there is also an English language requirement when acquiring British citizenship, and mandatory citizenship education in schools (Joppke 2004). In the context of the racial unrest and ethnic segregation among Muslim youth in towns in northern England in 2001 and the 7 July bombings by British-born Muslim youth in 2005, 'community cohesion' through civic integration has become the new official discourse on multiculturalism. Community cohesion emphasizes the building of bridges between faith-based communities, in particular targeting what are seen as segregated Muslim communities whose members are deemed to live 'parallel lives' (Wetherell *et al.* 2007). The focus on interfaith and cultural understanding in the context of civic integration legitimates the link between citizenship and nationhood as essential for multicultural coexistence. These themes are further explored by Sales in Chapter 2.

However, the shift to a faith-based approach within the multicultural discourse has many implications for equality and the human rights of Muslim women in their communities. Pragna Patel and Hannana Siddiqui (2010) argue that since the Rushdie affair in the 1980s, the overarching aim of the British multicultural state has been to isolate religious extremists by creating a space for religious moderates to take up key leadership positions in their communities. This move to multi-faithism has resulted in what Patel and Siddiqui call 'the shrinking of secular spaces' for black and ethnic minority women to struggle autonomously for their human rights. The rise in power of unelected and unaccountable Muslim community leaders means those who are able 'to shout the loudest' establish a platform and the authority to impose conservative patriarchal religious interpretations which traditionally discriminate against women. An example of this is the establishment of Muslim arbitration tribunals and Shariah councils affiliated to mosques (Bano 2010). Both act as an alternative to dispute resolution in Muslim communities, using Islamic law in family matters, including domestic violence and forced marriage. These unofficial quasi-legal bodies which are sanctioned within the multicultural state draw on the knowledge of unelected male elders in their conservative interpretation of Islamic law (Patel and Siddiqui 2010).

Clearly, liberal multiculturalism in Britain in its many shifting manifestations, including the most recent form, community cohesion, has consistently functioned to privilege 'race' and ethnicity, and now religion, over gender (Samantrai 2002; Phillips 2007). It fails to recognize the gendered power divisions within ethnic groups when dealing with problems *between* communities, and turns a blind eye to problems *within* communities. A gender-blind multiculturalism has consequences for Muslim women, who remain largely invisible, locked in the private sphere of the home, where, despite state recognition of the human rights abuses of forced marriage and honour violence, gender-oppressive cultural and religious practices are still played out (Patel and Siddiqui 2010). Beckett and Macey highlight the contradictions of gendered multiculturalism which invisibilizes women. They write:

> Multiculturalism does not cause domestic violence, but it does facilitate its continuation through its creed of respect for cultural differences, its emphasis on non-interference in minority lifestyles and its insistence on community consultation (with male self-defined community leaders). This has resulted in women being invisibilized, their needs ignored and their voices silenced.
>
> *(2001: 311)*

While liberal multiculturalism is popularly and politically conceived as celebrating diversity and 'tolerating' different cultural and religious values between groups, the notion of mutual tolerance is fragile. It could be argued that one way in which multiculturalism negotiates this fragility is by maintaining a laissez-faire approach to gendered cultural difference (Okin 1999; Phillips 2007). Multiculturalism in this sense is 'skin-deep', and it works only if the demands of visible and distinct ethnic groups are not too 'different' and not too rejecting of the welcoming embrace or 'gift' of the 'host' society (Ahmed 2004). The figure of the veiled Muslim woman challenges the values that are crucial to the nation, such as values of freedom and culture. As Sara Ahmed explains, 'She becomes a symbol of what the nation must give up to be itself, a discourse that would require her unveiling in order to fulfil its promise of freedom' (ibid.: 132)

To understand the social construction of gender and violence within multiculturalism, we need to look at the way ethnicity has been reified and fixed among ethnic minority groups. This process of reification, whereby ethnic group identity becomes defensive, and cultural and religious practices are constructed within imagined but rigid boundaries, leads to a form of 'ethnic fundamentalism' (Yuval-Davis 1997). Migration, whether forced or planned, often leads to the breakdown of traditional certainties and structures, thereby heightening anxieties of loss and belonging. Patriarchal practices can be amplified for migrant Muslim women, who are seen as upholding traditional values when they are estranged from their homelands (Abbas 2010). Under threat, certain aspects of culture may be preserved, ossified or romanticized – what I call 'pickled in aspic'. When this happens, as in the context of the discourse on Islamophobia, we witness a resurgence and persistence of fixed and regressive notions of ethnicity and nationalism underpinned by traditional beliefs (Elliott 2002).

Halima Begum (2008) demonstrates how this plays out in the secular yet religious and ethnically inscribed multicultural space of 'Banglatown' in the East End of London. She argues the streets of 'Banglatown' have become nationalistic, male-dominated Bengali public spaces, from which Bangladeshi women feel excluded and often unsafe. Second-generation young Bengali women, whose bodies are still inscribed with conservative cultural values, in turn prefer to express their 'Muslimness' as an inner private belief and transcendental identity. Thus, it would seem in the secular British multicultural national context, where, according to Werbner (2007), religious practice, though valorized, is still located in the unregulated private sphere of civil society, Islam can be mobilized as a power resource in the construction of an unfettered hegemonic masculine Muslim identity (Balzani 2010). Hasmita Ramji (2007) discusses the way in which young working-class Asian Muslim men in Britain exercise patriarchal power by invoking common-sense, and often contradictory, readings of the Qur'an which they use to legitimate the regulation and surveillance of women through policing their 'modesty'. To be a 'proper' Muslim man means being a provider for and protector of women, whose freedom of movement, including the right to work, must ultimately be curtailed.

However, Islamic feminist scholars argue that patriarchy and gendered oppressive practices are not foundational to Islam (Wadud 1999). Leila Ahmed's detailed scholarly history of women in Islam finds egalitarianism to be a constant element of the ethical utterances of the Qur'an and states that 'nowhere is veiling explicitly prescribed' (1992: 55). The Qur'an provides women with explicit rights to inheritance, independent property, divorce and the right to testify in a court of law. It also prohibits violence towards women and duress in marriage and community affairs (Wadud 2002: 202). Fatima Mernissi (1996) points to the progressive role of women in Islam, including the Prophet's third wife, Aisha, who led troops into battle, suggesting that the lowly image attributed to women in Islamic societies is due not to the absence of traditional memory or historical evidence, but rather to conservative forces shaping the image-making in the Muslim world which discriminates against women. The rise of Islamic fundamentalism has had much to do with this negative gendered representation. Haidah Moghissi argues that, as with the rise of western capitalism, the control of women and the authority of the patriarchical family are central to the Islamic fundamentalist utopia. To this end, she explains, 'Islamic fundamentalists dig up medieval Islamic texts, prescribe moral codes or invent rules of conduct when the need arises' (1999: 73). For Asma Barlas (2002), the solution to the disputes on gender equality in Islam lies in what she sees as understanding the liberatory hermeneutics of the Qur'an. She writes, '[A]s long as Muslims continue to read gender inequalities into the Qur'an, we will not be able to ensure gender equality in Muslim societies' (Barlas 2008).

It could be argued that it is controversial to focus on culturally specific forms of gender oppression and violence against women (Dustin and Phillips 2008; Gill and Mitra-Kahn 2010). By highlighting issues of communal and familial violence in Muslim communities, are we perpetuating the stereotype of these communities as backward and barbaric? Similarly, it could be asked whether by distinguishing these forms of gendered violence as special cultural phenomena we are placing an undue emphasis on the 'Muslim woman' and in effect racializing her. The debate centres on highlighting gendered sexualized practices in particular Islamic cultures, such as female genital mutilation, forced marriages and honour killings, where the sanctity of (male) community rights is privileged over the bodily rights of individual (female) victims. However, violence against women is not just an issue of religious, racial or ethnic differences; it is a question of economic, political and social development and of levels of democracy and the devolution of power within communities (Gill 2003).

To develop a truly multicultural, multi-agency policy framework in our education, health, criminal justice and social services that uncompromisingly responds to cultural forms of domestic violence, we need a 'mature multiculturalism' (Patel and Siddiqui 2010). Such an approach would address the tensions between recognizing gender oppression and valuing multicultural difference by challenging cultural and social attitudes through public education and informed anti-racist professional practice (Mirza 2010).

Islamophobia: Muslim women, honour and the veil

Reading sensationalized press reports of fathers and other close relatives, including women, who inflict violence and brutality on their own children in the name of honour or *izzat*, we are incredulous. How could they harm their own? As I write, on the front pages of our newspapers is the outcome of the case of Banaz Mahmod, a 20-year-old Kurdish woman who was sexually brutalized and murdered by her father and uncles and cousins because her boyfriend was not a strict Muslim from their community. She was strangled with a shoelace and her body stuffed in a suitcase buried under a patio (BBC 2010). Hannana Siddiqui, of Southall Black Sisters, argues that the use of the term 'honour' in such a context is a misnomer. She argues, 'The crimes themselves are dishonourable: they are merely justified by the perpetrator, and wider community, in the name of honour' (RWA, 2003: 6). Honour crimes are acts of violence against women where 'honour' is invoked to justify male violence. However, it is only in relation to religious and ethnic communities that the concept of honour is misappropriated in this way, preventing women from escaping domestic violence or justice as victims of domestic violence (Phillips 2003). As Maleiha Malik argues (2006a) the legal 'right to exit' a marriage or familial relationship is not a realistic option for women in traditional cultural and religious communities where as individuals they are subject to internal inequalities of power with little or no control over their own bodies or those of their children.

Acts of violence against women for breaking an honour code constitute an abuse of human rights and must be named as such. As Salim (2003) argues, the killing of women must never be seen as a cultural matter but always as a human rights issue. It is estimated that there may be as many as 17,000 female victims of honour-based crimes in Britain (Brady 2008). Following a police review of 22 domestic homicides in Britain in 2005, 18 cases were reclassified as 'murder in the name of so-called honour' (Meetoo and Mirza 2007). The Forced Marriage Unit (FMU) deals with approximately 300 cases annually of marriage conducted without freely given consent (FCO 2006). Though many of these reported crimes do not concern Muslims, since the 11 September attacks, risks associated with gender-based violence in Muslim communities have been high on the public and political agenda. This was highlighted when hostilities against Afghanistan began, as a response to the attacks. Cherie Blair and Laura Bush, the then wives of the UK prime minister and US president, took up the issue of the 'Taliban oppression of women and children in Afghanistan' (Ward 2001). Holding special meetings in 10 Downing Street to 'give back a voice' to Afghani women, Cherie Blair chose to spotlight the 'shocking and inspiring stories' of the women and raise charitable funds for the cause. In response to the 2003 illegal war on Iraq, Maleiha Malik pinpoints the truly awful two-faced reality behind this heightened concern for the Muslim female 'other' among female politicians in Blair's cabinet. She writes (2006b):

> There is a risk that their powerful female voices will inadvertently sustain another political discourse: the words and actions of an illustrious line of men who continue to justify their imperial ambitions on the bodies, often dead bodies, of Muslim women.

This heightened attention raises the question, 'What is behind this growing concern for the hitherto invisible and marginalized "Muslim woman"?' Gayatri Spivak writes, 'the postcolonial woman intellectual asks the question … "What does this mean?" – and begins to plot a history' (1988: 297). To chart this story we need to begin by looking at the consequence of the increased focus on 'honour'-based crimes within the current climate of Islamophobia. Since the 'war on terror', reports on honour crimes are often sensationalized and engage in a 'pornography of violence' focusing on the individual family and their barbarity and senselessness. As the CIMEL/Interights (2001: 31) report concludes, 'The combination of sex and violence involved in honour crimes lends itself readily to lurid images and, in the case of the Western media, cultural stereotyping, which can result in a backlash on the issue at a national level.'

Sensationalist images and analysis are in frequent use in the media, as are generalized and simplified explanations of honour crimes. Patriarchal atrocities, acts of violence and backward cultural practices in any society should be challenged in no uncertain terms. Honour-based crimes are real in *effect*: women *are* brutally murdered in many societies, by no means all of them Muslim societies, across the globe. However, honour-based crimes are constructed as ethnicized, often Islamic phenomena within the racialized multicultural discourse in Britain. As such they are also an *affect*, or emotive manifestation of the anti-Islamic discourse. In this regard the media reports have a real consequence. They contribute to putting women at risk through sensationalizing these crimes through their style and content of reporting, which results in voyeuristic spectacle, such as cries of 'how dreadful', followed by multicultural paralysis and inaction – that is, 'It is nothing to do with us! It is part of their culture and religion.'

Why has violence against women, and in particular honour crimes, become associated with Islam and the risk of terrorism in our midst? Mary Douglas (1992) suggests that particular risks are selected at particular times, and constructed and legitimated for public attention. Risks are chosen for their usefulness to the social system, and constructed through particular forms of social organization and their interaction in the wider political culture. Describing the climate of supposed global threat to security from Islamic extremism, Fekete (2004) argues that we are living in a time of fear not only of 'outsiders' but of Muslims within the United Kingdom. The heightened focus on honour-based crimes must be seen within this climate of Islamophobia. While the focus on honour-based crimes has opened up the issue of individual human rights for ethnicized Muslim women, it has also exacerbated Islamophobia and fear of the 'other'. Sara Ahmed argues that discourses of fear and anxiety which have circulated since 11 September, work by securing what is the 'truth' about 'the other'. She states:

> [F]ear operates as an affective economy of truth: fear slides between signs and sticks to some bodies and not others. For example the judgment that somebody 'could be' a terrorist draws on past and affective associations that stick various signs (such as Muslim, fundamentalist, terrorist) together. At the same time, fear is reproduced precisely by the threat that such bodies 'may pass (us) by'. Such bodies become constructed as fearsome and as a threat to the very truths that are reified as 'life itself'.
>
> *(2003: 377)*

Press reports of honour-based crimes put the gaze on the racialized 'other' (Majid and Hanif 2003). A pathological pattern of visibility characterizes the popular representation of the 'Muslim woman'. This pattern is underpinned, on the one hand, by a Eurocentric universalism that reduces the complexity and individuality of these women's lives to a single objectified category – in this case, the ubiquitous, stereotypical 'Muslim woman'. On the other hand, the women are also characterized by a particular form of cultural relativism that highlights specific barbaric cultural practices. In these media narratives the young woman is constructed as either romantic heroine, struggling for the benefits of the 'West' against her cruel and inhuman father and family, or victim, succumbing to her backward and traditional 'Eastern' culture (Puwar 2003; Ahmed 2003).

Parallels can be drawn to colonial times where women's bodies were part of the debate over the civilizing mission. Franz Fanon argues that the veil and the woman become interchangeable as scopic signifiers of colonized Algeria. Unveiling the 'Muslim woman' is a metaphor for the colonial unveiling and hence subjugation of the Algerian state. Fanon writes, 'The European faced with an Algerian woman wants to see ... unveiling equals revealing ... baring ... breaking her resistance ... making her available' (quoted in Kanneh 1995: 347). Leila Ahmed (1992) argues that the history of western patriarchal colonial endeavour was to point to the inferiority and barbarism of pre-colonial Islamic societies as a rationale for superiority and subjugation. For example, it has been argued that the British abolition of *sati*, the practice of widow-burning in India, was a case of the heroic white male colonists 'saving brown women from brown men' (Spivak 1988: 296). However, in the current discourse the gaze, as ever, is on the woman, as the heated public debate triggered by Labour minister Jack Straw on the matter of Muslim women wearing the face veil demonstrates.

In 2006, Jack Straw announced to the press that, after 25 years in office, he felt uncomfortable with Muslim women wearing the face veil (niqab) in his constituency surgery in Blackburn (Bunting 2006). As media hysteria grew over several weeks, stories of the ubiquitous 'Muslim woman' appeared regularly on newspaper front pages. They still do. Five years later, in 2011, Sayeeda Warsi, co-chair of the Conservative Party and the first Muslim woman to serve in the British Cabinet, caused a media outcry with her lecture on Islamophobia and anti-Muslim sentiment in Britain. As she observes, Islamophobia has 'passed the dinner-table test', suggesting that it has become socially acceptable in the United Kingdom to be Islamophobic. This, she argues, is exemplified by the racialized representation of the veiled Muslim women in the national unconscious. She writes, '[I]n the road, as a woman walks past wearing a Burkha, the passers-by think: "that woman's either oppressed or making a political statement"' (Gardner 2011).

Clearly, as the Islamic feminist Haleh Afshar points out, a woman's right to wear the veil is a matter of choice, whether it be a personal, religious or political one (2008). Nevertheless, the Muslim woman's vulnerable yet over-determined body has become symbolic in the battle against Islam, the barbaric 'other' and the Muslim 'enemy within'. Her complex dress has been given symbolic meaning greater than its religious and social status (Dwyer 1999; Werbner 2007). As Kanneh writes, 'Ethnic dress becomes interchangeable with tradition and essentialism and the female body enters the unstable arena of scrutiny and meaning' (1995: 347). Her private reasons for wearing the niqab become public property, a 'weapon' used by many different competing interests, from male politicians in France to white feminists in Belgium, to argue their cases for and against assimilation, multiculturalism, secularism and human rights (Coene and Longman 2008; Scott 2007; Killian 2003). But unlike in colonial times the Muslim woman is not being 'saved' within the concurrent competing discourses of Islamophobia and multiculturalism in Britain. The visibility of patriarchal community and group cultural practices conveniently contribute to the western 'Orientalist' construction of the racialized 'other's' barbaric customs and cultures (Said 1985; Afshar 2008). It could be argued that what Muslim women are experiencing now is not so much a concern with their human rights and social conditions, but rather a post-modern reworking of the heroic colonial stance of 'being saved', as in the past. Only now, in a new era of post-colonial appropriation, we have, as in the case of Jack Straw and Cherie Blair, 'white men and women saving Muslim women from Muslim men'!

In what Chandra Talpade Mohanty (2003) has called the 'latent ethnocentrism' of the West, Muslim women are presented as voiceless, stereotyped, racialized victims rather than active agents working to determine and engage their rights as individuals (and see Ahmad, Chapter 9 of this volume, on Muslim women as active agents). Articulate Muslim women are hardly heard in the cacophony of competing interests for their 'veiled' agenda (Fawcett Society 2006); those who show self-determination and speak out on their freedom to wear the veil have been vilified, as in the case of the Muslim teacher who refused to remove her niqab (BBC 2006). As Phillips (2007) argues, culture is widely employed in the discourse on multiculturalism to deny the human agency of minority or non-western groups, who (unlike their western counterparts) are seen to be 'driven' by cultural traditions and practices that compel them to behave in particular ways. Thus, while South Asian and Muslim women are seen to suffer 'death by culture', white British or North American women (with their societies characterized by freedom, democracy and mobility) are deemed to be immune from culture, even when they become victims of culturally specific forms of patriarchal violence such as gun crime, date rape or domestic violence.

Islamic feminists have taken issue with the cultural superiority of simplistic, sensationalized cultural constructions of Muslim women in the media, constructions that negate Muslim female identity and agency, and depoliticize their (embodied) struggles for self-determination (Abu-Lughod 2002; Mernissi 1996). This tendency is not just preserved for Muslim women. Since the post-Second World War migration to the United Kingdom there has been a continuous post-colonial preoccupation with the ethnicized woman's victimhood and sexuality (Mama 1989). Black and post-colonial feminists have shown how African and Asian migrant women have been represented in Britain (Mirza and Joseph 2010: Reynolds 1997). If they have agency, they are often depicted as manipulative, scrounging refugees and asylum seekers or overbearing black female matriarchs who marginalize and emasculate their menfolk. If they are victims, they are portrayed as disempowered, sexually exploited mail order brides or sold into sexual trafficking.

Clearly, the social and economic realities of sexual exploitation and oppression need to be addressed. However, my point here is, how do Muslim women escape the racialized and gendered stereotypes that mainstream western society have of them? Stereotypes are powerful forms of knowledge that construct a repertoire of possible identities and hence subjectivities which, through powerful systems of representation, shape the lived experience of the ethnicized Muslim women.

Spaces of recognition: Muslim women, activism and the 'third space'

The power struggle between male Muslim community leaders and women's groups within a British multicultural policy framework needs to be openly addressed. As the Muslim Women's Network report 'She Who Disputes' records, 'We can't pussy foot around community leaders and not address issues for fear of getting their backs up. By not addressing controversial issues our communities are destroying themselves' (WNC 2006: 9). British Muslim women's activism across all communities has been local, grassroots and in response to immediate concerns such as their own and their children's education and health, as well as public and communal violence against women. Building basic capacity among Muslim women and finding a safe space for them to express their concerns has been a priority for Muslim women activists, but one achieved largely without much access to 'hard-to-get' government funding or support from male community leaders (WNC 2006). Projects such as the Muslim Women's Helpline, and refuges and care centres that cater to the specific needs of Muslim women, have struggled to survive under the new, blunt, racist Community Cohesion funding regimes, which, in response to fears about Muslim segregation and national security, have withdrawn specialist funding for specific ethnic communities (Wilson 2010).

In Britain, while there are successful Muslim women's organizations campaigning against human rights abuses, such as the Iranian and Kurdish Women's Rights Organisation (IKWRO) and Women Living Under Muslim Laws (WLUML), it has been secular activist coalitions of black and minority ethnic women such as Southall Black Sisters (SBS), Women Against Fundamentalism (WAF), the Newham Asian Women's Project (NAWP) and the Foundation for Women's Health Research and Development (FORWARD), among many others, that since the 1970s have also been central in placing Muslim women's issues on the public policy agenda. They have made many gains in the law and services as well as tackling the thorny issue of cultural and religious conservatism within minority ethnic and Muslim communities (Dustin and Phillips 2008; Patel and Siddiqui 2010; Wilson 2010).

With the setting up of the Home Office Working Group on Forced Marriage, Southall Black Sisters with others, including Muslim women activists, secured a major watershed victory in 1999 when they secured state recognition of gender-based violence in ethnic minority communities. This led to the Forced Marriage Civil Protection Act (2007), which gave statutory footing to the work of the Forced Marriage Unit in the Foreign and Commonwealth Office. Other gains have been made in relation to marriage-related immigration rules, such as amendments to the discriminatory Primary Purpose Rule and the One-Year (now Two-Year) Rule, which states that immigrant women must stay with their husbands for a minimum period or face deportation (Shama and Gill 2010). This rule effectively trapped women experiencing domestic violence, as they would lose their right to stay in the United Kingdom if they left their violent spouse. Another recent cruel and devastating rule is the No Recourse to Public Funds rule, which leaves women with insecure immigration status unable to claim welfare and thus forces them to remain destitute or to stay in abusive relationships. Patel and Siddiqui (2010) document the contradictory actions of the state with regard to black and ethnic minority women. On the one hand, the state supports progressive human rights-based legislation, with its action on forced marriage, but it also regulates ethnic minority communities through using cultural issues to tighten immigration controls.

Such human rights victories by women's groups can irrevocably shift the image and identity of the state as it is forced to make adjustments that embrace broader concepts of gendered rights which challenge hegemonic notions of British citizenship, British justice and the underpinning principle of British 'fair play'. Muslim and black and other ethnic minority activists have had a significant impact on the multicultural state by slowly instigating state behavioural change with regard to gendered human rights issues for women. Ranu Samantrai (2002) argues that black and ethnic minority feminist activism has been more than just about accessing rights and services. It is a contingent and politically destabilizing force, in a constant state of flux, where neither allies nor enemies are readily identifiable and where even its own campaigns and activists may become obsolete when gains are made. But more importantly, she argues, it plays a central role in challenging the fundamental core of British identity. It could be argued that by challenging the racial subtext of British majority and minority identities, black and ethnic minority feminists, including Muslim women activists, are engaged in the very radical project of refining the '*We*' of the nation – in effect, 'who are the British'. Muslim, black and ethnic minority women are writing themselves into the British multicultural national story (see also Sales in Chapter 2 of this volume).

Muslim and black and ethnic minority women's grassroots and human rights activism sheds new light on traditional conceptualizations of citizenship. In the classical political and social discourse on citizenship and belonging that underpins the current debates on multiculturalism and community cohesion, little space is given to 'gendered acts of citizenship' which require 'other ways of knowing'. In their gendered and/or racialized version of citizenship, Muslim and black and ethnic minority women activists use international and domestic law to challenge the patriarchal alliance between white and ethnic minority male leaders – an alliance that, despite state racism, remains secure and at the heart of the liberal democratic state in Britain. Muslim and black and ethnic minority women collectively combine their social and emotional capital, skills of resourcefulness and networking that enable them to carve out new spaces of contestation as radical collective transformative agents (Mirza 2009). It could be argued that their activism offers up a form of 'experiential socio-analysis' which opens up a 'third space' of strategic engagement. Such a discursive 'third space' has largely remained invisible in the traditional public (male) and private (female) dichotomy in current citizenship theorizing, which, as in the government's current vision of the 'Big Society', obscures 'other ways of knowing' and thus 'other ways of being' a British citizen.

For Muslim and black and ethnic minority women activists, raising difficult issues of sexism and domestic violence brings to the fore issues of power and patriarchy in their own communities (Crenshaw 1994). In vulnerable and racialized Muslim communities there are tensions between protecting men from the racism of state agencies and negative media representation on the one hand, and the need to raise the issue of gendered violence and protect women's rights in these communities on the other. As Salim (2003) explains, in the Kurdish community there is a fear among some that putting honour crimes on the public agenda might cause a dangerous backlash in the immigration debate and heighten xenophobic sentiments against asylum seekers. However, Muslim women scholars and Islamic feminists must and do raise difficult issues of sexism and violence against women within their communities. The call to 'a return to Shariah' by Islamist political ideologues in Iran in the 1970s had devastating consequences for Muslim women globally, with the return to outdated models of feudal social relations, gendered segregation, compulsory dress codes and the revival of cruel medieval punishments. The Islamic feminist Ziba Mir-Hosseini (2011) argues that the setting up of the United Nations General Assembly for the Convention on the Elimination of All Forms of Discrimination against Women (CEDAW) in 1979 was the watershed that gave Muslim women the language and tools to resist Islamist patriarchy by giving gender equality a clear international human rights mandate. Women's NGOs in Muslim countries, together with the transnational women's movement, made visible various forms of fundamentalist gender-based discrimination and violence rooted in regressive patriarchal, tribal cultural traditions and religious practices.

However, the relationship between feminist activism and Islam has not been easy, as Amina Wadud (2002) explains:

> Today Muslim women are striving for greater inclusiveness in many diverse ways, not all of them in agreement with each other. At the Beijing Global Women's Conference in 1995, nightly attempts to form a Muslim women's caucus at the NGO forum became screaming sessions. The many different strategies and perspectives just could not be brought to a consensus.

Wadud suggests there are three main stands of thinking within Islamic feminism. First, on the left are the Marxist-informed secular feminists and activists who, though Muslim themselves, see Islam in terms of its oppressive cultural manifestations in the western national post-colonial context. On the far right are the Muslim male authorities and their female representatives, known as Islamists, who identify an ideal Islam as the one lived by the Prophet. They take a reactionary, neo-conservative approach, adopting an unquestioned Shariah state imposed onto modern complexity. Between the secular Muslim feminists and the Islamists is Islamic feminism, which gained currency in the 1990s. Its adherents are Muslim women scholars who keep their allegiance to Islam as an essential part of their identity but strongly and empathically critique patriarchal control over the male Islamic worldview, including the feminist theological interpretation of Shariah compared to 'man-made' *fiqh* (Islamic jurisprudence) (Mir-Hosseini 1999).

Muslim women scholars, Islamic feminists and black and post-colonial feminists have been in the front line of opposing the post-colonial racist assertion that black, Asian and Muslim men are more barbaric. If we take a global perspective, honour killings and forced marriage are part of a wider patriarchal phenomenon of violence against women (Gupta 2003; Balzani 2010). Women are beaten and murdered across the globe for similar reasons. Violence against women cuts across race, class, religion and age. Violence is not particular to one culture or religious group or community. Patriarchal structures use violence extensively to subjugate women in relation to class, race, religion and ethnicity. While the intersectionality of race, religion, class, patriarchy and gender power dynamics produces culturally specific manifestations of violence against women, which are important to acknowledge and address in local service delivery, the responses and funding should be mainstreamed into informing domestic violence interventions more generally (Dustin and Phillips 2008). In evidence to the Working Party on Forced Marriage, Southall Black Sisters highlighted the failure of service providers to address the cultural needs of women and girls at risk of forced marriages and honour killings (Siddiqui 2003). Service providers cited cultural grounds for this failure, the assumption being that minority communities are self-policing and services do not need to intervene on behalf of women (Burman *et al.* 2004; Sanghera 2006). However, policies such as not putting non-English-speaking women into white-run refuges because of a perceived lack of 'cultural fit' can also leave desperate women without care or shelter (Wilson 2010). At the same time, it is important for Muslim and ethnic minority women's sense of empowerment to be in a refuge that enables their equal participation and values their decision-making (Gill and Rehman 2004).

Clearly, Muslim women are involved in new and strategic forms of engagement. In this sense they offer up a challenging vision. Though largely defined and excluded through their marginal status as women on the one hand and Muslims on the other, they adjust their strategies to accommodate a changing variety of racially contested public and private spaces.

Conclusion: moving beyond the gender gap

The intersectionality of race, class, gender, sexuality, religion and patriarchy frames the unique experience of Muslim women in Britain. Caught up in a collision of discourses, Muslim women are visible and yet pathologized as victims in relation to the negative media representation in the current discourse of Islamophobia. However, these women at the same time are largely absent in the normative discourse on domestic violence and violence against women in the West. Within the faith-based community cohesion discourse of British multiculturalism, race, ethnicity and religion are prioritized and gender differences and inequalities marginalized. Despite high-profile remedial consultative events in Downing Street to 'engage' Muslim women (DCLG 2006) and the much-publicized elitist Muslim Women's Power List – which includes three Muslim women life peers (Rose 2009) – everyday working-class, refugee and migrant women still 'slip through the cracks' of politics and policy and are constantly at risk of not being fully protected by the state as equal citizens.

While we need to be vigilant about the post-9/11 Islamophobic media discourse and its preoccupation and purpose with highlighting Muslim barbarism against women, we must accept that domestic violence is a reality in our ethnicized Muslim communities. When we are immersed in the multicultural context of respecting and accommodating cultural difference, we often do not see cultural forms of domestic violence in our British ethnicized Muslim communities as part of the bigger picture of endemic universal violence against women, which must be challenged. For professionals working in health, education and welfare who are tasked with delivering multicultural services to ethnically diverse populations, this can mean 'walking on eggshells' – that is, engaging in the accommodating of gendered cultural practices for fear of offending Muslim communities and inviting accusations of racism (Mirza 2010).

If we are to develop a more equitable and culturally neutral perspective where Muslim women's human rights are ensured and privileged over Islamic patriarchal cultural practices, we need a pragmatic and contingent dual approach to moving forward the debate on violence against women in Britain. Such a dual approach includes both religious Islamic feminist perspectives and secular Muslim and black and ethnic minority women's human rights activism in a multi-pronged 'transversal' (Yuval-Davis 1999) coalition in the campaign for state action to combat violence against women.

Islamic feminist scholarship, which powerfully explores the complex intersecting relationship between human rights, theology and gender equality, undermines the claims of male Muslim religious authority, which is at the heart of violence against women. As Amina Wadud (2002) writes,

> By going back to primary sources and interpreting them afresh, women scholars are endeavoring to remove the fetters imposed by centuries of patriarchal interpretation and practice. By questioning underlying presumptions and conclusions they are creating a space in which to think about gender.

However, as Haleh Afshar (1998) demonstrates in the case of Iran, Islamic feminist struggles are necessarily fraught with inherent contradictions and strategic compromises, such as the necessary collaboration with fundamentalist Islamic male authority, an alliance that, as Sahgal and Yuval-Davis (1992) point out, has never served women well.

In the absence of global social and political reform of violent patriarchal cultures where masculinity and honour are linked to female control, we ultimately need to draw on secular international human rights law-based challenges to protect the most vulnerable in our society (Gill and Mitra-Kahn 2010). At the 1995 UN World Congress on Women, the Beijing Platform for Action declared that culture, tradition and religion could not be used by the state to avoid its obligation to protect women (Kelly 2005). Walby (2002) suggests that in the United Kingdom, rather than relying on women's own resources in civil society, feminist activists have tended to draw on the wider political resources of the transnational movement against male violence in their engagement with the British state. While taking into account a country's own national concerns about sexuality, patriarchy and sexual autonomy, the Centre for Islamic and Middle Eastern Law (CIMEL) and Interights (2001) argue that it is important to raise honour crimes as a human rights violation before as many UN human rights bodies as possible, including the Human Rights Committee, the Committee on the Elimination of Racial Discrimination, the Committee on Economic, Social and Cultural Rights, the Committee against Torture and the Committee on the Rights of the Child. Only by using all available resources at our disposal in an alliance between secular feminist human rights activism and Islamic feminist scholarship can a 'third space of Muslim women's activism' effectively evolve to challenge the endemic shameful and heinous crime of violence against women in our Muslim communities in Britain.

References

Abbas, T. (2010) 'Honour-related violence towards South Asian Muslim women in the UK: a crisis of masculinity and cultural relativism in the context of Islamophobia and the "war on terror"', in M. M. Idriss and T. Abbas (eds) *Honour, Violence, Women and Islam*, London: Routledge.

Abu-Lughod, L. (2002) 'Do Muslim women really need saving? Anthropological reflections on cultural relativism and its others', *American Anthropologist* 104 (3): 783–790.

Afshar, H. (1998) *Islam and Feminism: An Iranian Case-Study*, Basingstoke: Macmillan.

Afshar, H. (2008) ' "Can I see your hair"? Choice, agency and attitudes: the dilemma of faith and feminism for Muslim women who cover', *Ethnic and Racial Studies* 31 (2): 411–427.

Ahmed, L. (1992) *Women and Gender in Islam: Historical Roots of a Modern Debate*, New Haven, CT: Yale University Press.

Ahmed, S. (2004) *The Cultural Politics of Emotions*, Edinburgh: Edinburgh University Press.

Ahmed, S. (2003) 'The politics of fear in the making of worlds', *International Journal of Qualitative Studies in Education* 16 (3): 377–398.

Balzani, M. (2010) 'Masculinities and violence against women in South Asian Communities: transnational perspective', in R. K. Thiara and A. K. Gill (eds) *Violence against Women in South Asian Communities: Issues for Policy and Practice*, London: Jessica Kingsley.

Bano, S. (2010) 'Shariah councils and the resolution of matrimonial disputes: gender justice and the shadow of the law', in R. K. Thiara and A. K. Gill (eds) *Violence against Women in South Asian Communities: Issues for Policy and Practice*, London: Jessica Kingsley.

Barlas, A. (2002) *'Believing Women' in Islam: Unreading Patriarchal Interpretations of the Qur'an*, Austin: University of Texas Press.

Barlas, A. (2008) 'Toward a feminist view of Islam', *Guardian* (London), 31 October.

BBC (2010) 'Banaz Mahmod "honour" killing cousins jailed for life', BBC News, London, 20 November. Online, available at: www.bbc.co.uk/news/uk-england-london-11716272 (accessed 16 November 2010).

BBC (2006) 'Veil teacher "should be sacked" ', BBC News Channel, 15 October. Online, available at: http://news.bbc.co.uk/1/hi/england/bradford/6050392.stm.

Beckett, C. and Macey, M. (2001) 'Race, gender and sexuality: the oppression of multiculturalism', *Women's Studies International Forum* 24 (3/4): 309–319.

Begum, H. (2008) 'Geographies of inclusion/exclusion: British Muslim women in the East End of London', *Sociological Research online* 13 (5). Online, available at: http://www.socresonline.org.uk/13/5/10.html.

Bhavnani, R., Mirza, H. S. and Meetoo, V. (2005) *Tackling the Roots of Racism: Lessons for Success*, Bristol: Policy Press.

Brady, B. (2008) 'A question of honour: police say 17,000 women are victims every year', *Independent* (London), 10 February.

BRIN (2010) 'How many Muslims?' Online, available at: www.brin.ac.uk/news/?p=598.

Bunting, M. (2006) 'Straw's storm of prejudice', *Guardian Unlimited Weekly*, 13 October.

Burman, E., Smailes, S. L. and Chantler, K. (2004) ' "Culture" as a barrier to service provision and delivery: domestic violence services for minoritized women', *Critical Social Policy* 24 (3): 332–357.

Centre for Islamic and Middle Eastern Law (CIMEL) and Interights (2001) *Roundtable on Strategies to Address 'Crimes of Honour': Summary Report*, Women Living under Muslim Laws Occasional Paper 12, November, London: CIMEL/Interights.

Coene, G. and Longman, C. (2008) 'Gendering the diversification of diversity: the Belgian hijab (in) question', *Ethnicities* 8 (3): 302–321.

Crenshaw, K. (1994) 'Mapping the margins: intersectionality, identity politics, and violence against women of color', in M. Albertson Fineman and R. Mykitiuk (eds) *The Public Nature of Private Violence: The Discovery of Domestic Abuse*, New York: Routledge.

DCLG (2006) 'Engaging with Muslim women: a report from the prime minister's event on 10 May 2006', 20 September, Department for Communities and Local Government: Women and Equality Unit (WEU). Online, available at: www.communities.gov.uk/publications/corporate/engagingwithmuslim.

Douglas, M. (1992) *Risk and Blame: Essays in Cultural Theory*, London: Routledge.

Doyle, J. (2010) 'Mohammed is now the most popular name for baby boys ahead of Jack and Harry', *Daily Mail* (London), 28 October. Online, available at: www.dailymail.co.uk/news/article-1324194/Mohammed-popular-baby-boys-ahead-Jack-Harry.html.

Dustin, M. and Phillips, A. (2008) 'Whose agenda is it? Abuses of women and abuses of "culture" in Britain', *Ethnicities* 8 (3): 405–424.

Dwyer, C. (1999) 'Veiled meanings: young British Muslim women and the negotiation of difference', *Gender, Place and Culture* 6 (1): 5–26.

Elliott, A. (2002) 'Beck's sociology of risk: a critical assessment', *Sociology* 36 (2): 293–315.

Fawcett Society (2006) 'The veil, feminism and Muslim women: a debate', 14 December. Online, available at: www.fawcettsociety.org.uk/index.asp?PageID=378.

Fekete, L. (2004) 'Anti-Muslim racism and the European security state', *Race and Class* 46 (1): 3–29.

Foreign and Commonwealth Office (FCO) (2006) *Forced Marriage: A Wrong not a Right – Consultation Report*, London: The Stationery Office.

Gardner, N. (2011) 'Britain is no nation of bigots, Baroness Warsi', *Telegraph* (London), 20 January.

Gill, A. (2003) 'A question of honour', *Community Care*, 27 March.

Gill, A. K. and Mitra-Kahn, T. (2010) 'Moving toward a "multiculturalism without culture": constructing a victim-friendly human rights approach to forced marriage in the UK', in R. K. Thiara and A. K. Gill (eds) *Violence against Women in South Asian Communities: Issues for Policy and Practice*, London: Jessica Kingsley.

Gill, A. and Rehman, G. (2004) 'Empowerment through activism: responding to domestic violence in the South Asian community in London', *Gender and Development* 12 (1): 75–82.

Gilroy, P. (2004) *After Empire: Melancholia or Convivial Culture?* London: Routledge.

Goldberg, D. T. (2004) 'The space of multiculturalism', *Open Democracy*, 15 September. Online, available at: www.opendemocracy.net/arts-multiculturalism/article_2097.jsp.

Gupta, R. (2003) 'Some recurring themes: Southall Black Sisters 1979–2003 – and still going strong', in R. Gupta (ed.) *From Homemakers to Jailbreakers: Southall Black Sisters*, London: Zed Books.

Hall, S. (2000) 'The multi-cultural question', in B. Hesse (ed.) *Un/settled Multiculturalisms: Diasporas, Entanglements, 'Transruptions'*, London: Zed Books.

Hall, S. (2004) 'Divided city: the crisis of London', *Open Democracy*, 28 October. Online, available at: www.opendemocracy.net/arts-multiculturalism/article_2191.jsp.

Harris, C. (2001) 'Beyond multiculturalism? Difference, recognition and social justice', *Patterns of Prejudice* 35 (1): 13–34.

Hesse, B. (ed.) (2000) *Un/Settled Multiculturalisms: Diasporas, Entanglements, 'Transruptions'*, London: Zed Books.

Joppke, C. (2004) 'The retreat of multiculturalism in the liberal state: theory and policy', *British Journal of Sociology* 55 (2): 237–257.

Kanneh, K. (1995) 'Feminism and the colonial body', in B. Ashcroft, G. Griffiths and H. Tiffin (eds) *The Post-colonial Studies Reader*, London: Routledge.

Kelly, L. (2005) 'Inside outsiders: mainstreaming violence against women into human rights discourse and practice', *International Feminist Journal of Politics* 7 (4): 471–495.

Killian, C. (2003) 'The other side of the veil: North African women in France respond to the headscarf affair', *Gender and Society* 17 (4): 567–590.

McLaughlin, E. and Neal, S. (2004) 'Misrepresenting the multicultural nation: the policy-making process, news media management and the Parekh Report', *Policy Studies* 25 (3): 155–74.

Majid, R. and Hanif, S. (2003) *Language, Power and Honour: Using Murder to Demonise Muslims*, October, Wembley: Islamic Human Rights Commission.

Malik, M. (2006a) ' "The branch on which we sit": multiculturalism, minority women and family law', in A. Diduck and K. O'Donovan (eds) *Feminist Perspectives on Family Law*, London: Routledge.

Malik, M. (2006b) 'This veil fixation is doing Muslim women no favours', *Guardian* (London), 19 October.

Mama, A. (1989) 'Violence against black women: gender, race and state responses', *Feminist Review*, 32 (Summer): 30–48.

Meetoo, V. and Mirza, H. S. (2007) 'There is nothing honourable about honour killings: gender, violence and the limits of multiculturalism', *Women's Studies International Forum* 30 (3): 187–200.

Mernissi, F. (1996) *Women's Rebellion and Islamic Memory*, London: Zed Books.

Mir-Hosseini, Z. (1999) *Islam and Gender: The Religious Debate in Contemporary Iran*, Princeton, NJ: Princeton University Press.

Mir-Hosseini, Z. (2011) 'Beyond "Islam" vs "feminism" ', *IDS Bulletin* 42 (1): 67–77.

Mirza, H. S. (2009) *Race, Gender and Educational Desire: Why Black Women Succeed and Fail*, London: Routledge.

Mirza, H. S. (2010) 'Walking on egg shells: multiculturalism, gender and domestic violence', in M. Robb and R. Thomson (eds) *Critical Practice with Children and Young People*, Bristol: Policy Press.

Mirza, H. and Joseph, C. (eds) (2010) *Black and Postcolonial Feminisms in New Times: Researching Educational Inequalities*, London: Routledge.

Moghissi, H. (1999) *Feminism and Islamic Fundamentalism: The Limits of Postmodern Analysis*, London: Zed Books.

Mohanty, C. T. (2003) *Feminism without Borders: Decolonizing Theory, Practicing Solidarity*, Durham, NC: Duke University Press.

Nandi, A. and Platt, P. (2009) 'Developing ethnic identity questions for Understanding Society, the UK Household Longitudinal Study', Understanding Society Working Paper Series no. 2009-03, ISER, University of Essex.

Office for National Statistics (ONS) (2006) Focus on Ethnicity and Religion: Ethnicity and Identity http://www.ons.gov.uk/ons/search/index.html?newquery=Focus+on+ethnicity+and+religion (accessed 20 February 2012).

Okin, S. M. (1999) 'Is multiculturalism bad for women?', in J. Cohen, M. Howard and M. C. Nussbaum (eds) *Is Multiculturalism Bad for Women? Susan Moller Okin with Respondents*, Princeton, NJ: Princeton University Press.

Parekh, B. (2005) *Rethinking Multiculturalism: Cultural Diversity and Political Theory*, Basingstoke: Palgrave Macmillan.

Patel, P. and Siddiqui, H. (2010) 'Shrinking secular spaces: Asian women at the intersect of race, religion and gender', in R. K. Thiara and A. K. Gill (eds) *Violence against Women in South Asian Communities: Issues for Policy and Practice*, London: Jessica Kingsley.

Phillips, A. (2003) 'When culture means gender: issues of cultural defence in English courts', *Modern Law Review* 66 (4): 510–531.

Phillips, A. (2007) *Multiculturalism without Culture*, Princeton, NJ: Princeton University Press.

Puwar, N. (2003) 'Melodramatic postures and constructions', in N. Puwar and P. Raghuram (eds) *South Asian Women in the Diaspora*, Oxford: Berg.

Ramji, H. (2007) 'Dynamics of religion and gender amongst British Muslims', *Sociology* 41 (6): 1171–1189.

Refugee Women's Association (RWA) (2003) *Refugee Women's News*, June and July, issue 23.

Reynolds, T. (1997) '(Mis)representing the black (super)woman', in H. S. Mirza (ed.) *Black British Feminism*, London: Routledge.

Rose, H. (2009) 'Meet the 13 most powerful Muslim women in Britain', *Sunday Times* (London), 21 March.

Runnymede Trust (2000) *The Parekh Report: The Future of Multi-ethnic Britain*, London: Profile Books.

Sahgal, G. and Yuval-Davis, N. (eds) (1992) *Refusing Holy Orders: Women and Fundamentalism in Britain*, London: Verso.

Said, E. (1985) *Orientalism: Western Concepts of the Orient*, Harmondsworth: Penguin.

Salim, S. (2003) 'It's about women's rights and women's rights are human rights', interview with Sawsan Salim, Coordinator of Kurdistan Refugee Women's Organisation (KRWO) 'Stop Violence against Women Honour Killing' Conference, 28 October 2005, London.

Samantrai, R. (2002) *AlterNatives: Black Feminism in the Postimperial Nation*, Stanford, CA: Stanford University Press.

Sanghera, J. (2006) 'Honour abuse: the victims' story', Karma Nirvana, Amnesty International 'Honour Killings' Conference, London.

Scott, J. W. (2007) *The Politics of the Veil*, Princeton, NJ: Princeton University Press.

Shama, K. and Gill, A. K. (2010) Protection for all? The failures of the Domestic Violence Rule for (im)migrant women', in R. K. Thiara and A. K. Gill (eds) *Violence against Women in South Asian Communities: Issues for Policy and Practice*, London: Jessica Kingsley.

Siddiqui, H. (2003) '"It was written in her kismet": forced marriage', in R. Gupta (ed.) *From Homebreakers to Jailbreakers*, London: Zed Books.

Spivak, G. C. (1988) 'Can the subaltern speak?', in C. Nelson and L. Grossberg (eds) *Marxism and the Interpretation of Culture*, London: Macmillan Education.

Tomlinson, S. (2008) *Race and Education: Policy and Politics in Britain*, Maidenhead: Open University Press.

Wadud, A. (1999) *Qur'an and Woman: Rereading the Sacred Text from a Woman's Perspective*, Oxford: Oxford University Press.

Wadud, A. (2002) 'A'ishah's Legacy', *New Internationalist*, issue 345, 5 May. Online, available at: www.newint.org/features/2002/05/01/aishahs-legacy/.

Wadud, A. (2006) 'Aishah's legacy: the struggle for women's rights within Islam', in M. Kamrava (ed.) *The New Voices of Islam: Rethinking Politics and Modernity*, Berkeley: University of California Press.

Walby, S. (2002) 'Feminism in a global era', *Economy and Society* 31 (4): 533–557.

Ward, L. (2001) 'Cherie Blair pleads for Afghan women', *Guardian* (London), 20 November. Online, available at: www.guardian.co.uk/politics/2001/nov/20/uk.september11.

Werbner, P. (2007) 'Veiled interventions in pure space: honour, shame and embodied struggles among Muslims in Britain and France', *Theory, Culture and Society* 24 (2): 161–186.

Wetherell, M., Laflèche, M. and Berkeley, R. (eds) (2007) *Identity, Ethnic Diversity and Community Cohesion*, London: Sage.

Wilson, A. (2010) 'Charting South Asian women's struggles against gender-based violence', in R. K. Thiara and A. K. Gill (eds) *Violence against Women in South Asian Communities: Issues for Policy and Practice*, London: Jessica Kingsley.

Women's National Commission (WNC) (2006) 'She who disputes: Muslim women shape the debate', Muslim Women's Network (MWN) and Women's National Commission, November. Online, available at: www.mwnuk.co.uk/go_files/downloads/992754-shewhodisputesnov06.pdf.

Yuval-Davis, N. (1997) *Gender and Nation*, London: Sage.

Yuval-Davis, N. (1999) 'What is "transversal politics"?', *Soundings*, issue 12 (Summer): 94–98.

7

EVERYDAY MAKING AND CIVIC ENGAGEMENT AMONG MUSLIM WOMEN IN SCOTLAND

Rahielah Ali and Peter Hopkins

Introduction

There is a tendency within popular discourse to see Muslim women as 'passive victims of oppressive cultures' and as the 'embodiment of a repressive and fundamentalist religion' (Dwyer 1998: 53). Muslim women are assumed to be the victims of a sexist and patriarchal culture, marginalized by their partners and forced to commit themselves to a life of housework and family care. Recognizing the ways in which gendered identities are constructed relationally, these problematic representations of Muslim women are often reinforced by stereotypes about Muslim men which see them 'constructed as militant and aggressive, intrinsically fundamentalist "ultimate Others"' (Archer 2001: 81; see also Phoenix 1997). As such, the stereotype of aggressive and domineering Muslim men reinforces the stereotype that Muslim women are marginalized and oppressed. Few representations acknowledge the complex and everyday experiences of 'ordinary' Muslim women, some of whom work to support their families, carry out community work and make conscious decisions to engage in the public sphere throughout their lives. Indeed, such women often engage with problematic gendered assumptions about their identities in sophisticated ways, challenging the representation of their faith communities and engaging politically on an everyday basis.

The Muslim women consulted in this research chose to participate more fully in community-based organizations and support networks in response to how they felt they were being portrayed negatively in the media. In this chapter we contribute to debates that have sought to problematize assumptions about the gendered identities and representations of Muslims in the UK (Dwyer *et al.* 2008; Hopkins 2008). In order to do so, we focus on the ways in which Muslim women in Scotland engage with the public sphere daily and participate in what Bang (2003) refers to as 'everyday making', whereby citizens engage subtly with political issues and processes on a daily basis without necessarily being directly connected to government or political structures. Muslim women in Scotland participate in everyday making through their political activism, community work and employment patterns. These activisms are not political protests or direct action as such but are instead responses to an overarching debate around responsibility within and for Muslim communities, making them subtler than general depictions of community activism as a reaction to social struggles or injustice (see Naples 1998; Kobayashi 1994).

Islamophobia and negative media representations

Negative media representations of Islam and Muslims are one of the reasons why the women involved in this research mobilized themselves to engage more actively in their local communities. In particular, these women are looking to resist powerful media representations that reinforce anti-Islamic and anti-Muslim sentiment worldwide. The events of 11 September 2001 resulted in Muslim communities that had previously been invisible being thrust into the 'political spectrum' (Pritchett 2005), and the change was reinforced in Britain with the London bombings of July 2005, resulting in the heightening of signifiers of Muslim identities and the extension of the already problematic demonization of what it means to be a Muslim (Hopkins 2004). The greater visibility of Muslims has been accompanied by a sense, among some, that they have a responsibility to stand up and (re)present their religious values, beliefs and practices in order to avoid being classified as a threat to the moral order of society. Gale and Hopkins point out that this response has challenged the 'homogeneity of Islamic identity and faith', which is now problematically seen to 'vary on the plane of their intensity between less and rather more "extreme" expressions' (2009: 2). Related to this, Modood highlights the intense and somewhat undeserved attention given to Muslim groups when discussing matters of 'immigration, and cultural diversity' (2009: 193), and argues that the shift from ethnic to religious identity has also focused acutely on Muslims rather than any other religious group, thus again bringing the matter of responsibility to the fore, questioning what roles Muslims are playing to prevent further attacks in secular and non-secular societies and countries. Such issues have also problematically fed through to government policy in the United Kingdom, which has arguably resulted in the subsequent alienation of the very communities needed and expected to aid counter-terrorism efforts (Spalek and McDonald 2009: 124).

Alongside these negative discourses about what it means to be Muslim, Islamophobia[1] – a 'form of cultural racism' – has led to a silencing of the majority Muslim voice (Werbner 1997: 237), and although Islamophobic behaviour existed prior to 11 September 2001, the events of that day, together with the bombings in London in July 2005 and the incident at Glasgow Airport in 2007, have led to the recognition of such events as not only national tragedies but globally and locally significant issues as well, impacting on spaces occupied by individuals, neighbourhoods and communities. Research in various countries and cities in the United Kingdom and the United States shows that the events of 11 September 2001, the subsequent 'war on terror' in Afghanistan and the invasion of Iraq have demonized and criminalized Muslims across the world (Peek 2003). Noble (2005) argues that subtle forms of Islamophobia and cultural racism are often overlooked by the authorities and so are unreported.

In England the violent outbreaks in the northern mill towns in 2001 (Phillips 2006; Hussain and Bagguley 2003) also became important sources of media representations of Muslims, and in particular those who were young and male were represented as violent, erratic, out of control and troublesome (Hopkins 2009). Hopkins (ibid.) argues that few depictions connect Muslims with everyday contributions that they make, economically, socially and, more recently, politically. The discourse of absence around this issue raises significant questions about the everyday lives, socio-economic contributions and political engagements of Muslims living and working in British cities. These realities – of which we see very little – are further examined in this chapter as we explore the ways in which Muslim women participate in the wider public sphere. Capturing themes from a larger doctoral study, the chapter focuses upon everyday making and civic engagement of Muslim women to illustrate the different ways in which they are responding to negative media coverage by creating spaces outside of the family home that are constructive and engaging, and demonstrate their political agency.

Muslim women and everyday making

Until recently, religion has received little attention as a marker of identity, with race, class, gender and age being given precedence (Kong 2001). It is only with developments made within the past two decades that geography and other social science disciplines have begun to examine closely the role that religion plays in debates surrounding belonging, inclusion and exclusion, citizenship, integration and everyday interactions. Further, Aftab (2005) notes that male historians have too often negated the issue of gender relations within a dominant patriarchal South Asian Muslim community.[2] In her work, Aftab argues that there are a number of reasons for women wanting to gain education, with Islam giving them this right as Muslimahs to edification, and that they are simply appealing for what is rightfully and morally theirs (ibid.: 89; see also Ahmad, Chapter 9 of this volume). Other examples of feminist Islamic activism include Arat's (1998) work on political discourse in Turkey. There, women's movements and organizations have been closely linked to geopolitical and worldwide developments (Moghadam 2008: 63) with the banning of Islamic clothing in both secular and Islamic states, and we are beginning to experience an increase in the number of feminist groups within Muslim communities (Wilson *et al.* 2005: 3) as an outcome of this. Wilson *et al.* (ibid.: 6) consider the divergence in the everyday realities faced by current and previous generations and argue that lessons have been learned as a result of earlier efforts. The lack of accurate accounts of Muslim women's lives reinforces representations of Muslim women as marginalized, oppressed and silent. As a result, Pritchett (2005: 11) argues, not only have women suffered, but feminism as a whole has been 'divided by unnecessary political compartmentalization'.

In her work with young Muslim schoolgirls, Dwyer argued that complex dynamics of what it means to be female and Muslim are relentlessly refigured, reproduced and represented by ongoing transformations within organizational practice and the media (1998: 53). It is in particular those women who present an image separate from the norm – women who choose to cover in a non-hijab-wearing society, or those who choose not to cover in a Muslim community – who are stereotyped, socially criminalized and victimized, as what they offer is different and therefore risky. In Hopkins' study (2009: 83) of Muslim men in Scotland, he identifies a 'patronising tone' among the young men as they discuss the roles of Muslim women, domestically and socially. More precisely, the men argue that Muslim women self-segregate through lack of interaction outside of the personal space of the home, therefore the women are ultimately responsible for the challenges they face (Hopkins 2009). While these conversations were context-specific, it is apparent that the young men were more than likely speaking of their own experiences in their families and friendship circles, and thus are unaware of the contributions and activisms taking place outside of the home and in civic spaces (see Ahmad, Chapter 9 of this volume). Furthermore, the patronizing tone they adopt about their female contemporaries may reflect sexism among Muslim youth.

While Muslim women may choose to enter sites of everyday politics, such responsibilities also carry with them expectations about appropriate gendered and religious modes of dress, practice and social modesty. Muslim women, when stepping outside of the boundaries of the home, enter the public sphere and are often subject to scrutiny by the local community, their friends and family and the non-Muslim community. Therefore, their movements are heavily observed, with political meanings with regard to their selection of dress, work lives and social choices. As a result of this heavy surveillance, a number of Muslim women who have successfully entered the public domain are still victims of much criticism from within Muslim communities, as they are often seen as moderate, liberal and essentially not of the 'right sort of Islam' (Glynn 2009: 183). An example is the attack upon Baroness Warsi, the Conservative Party chair, by a group of men who condemned her for not being 'a proper Muslim'.[3] Nevertheless, this has not deterred women from stepping onto the political platform. In contrast, a number of Muslim women were among MPs successful in the 2010 British general election.[4]

In other political campaigns, Muslim women have been at the forefront as organizers and demonstrators (Tarlo 2010). In her work on the practice of veiling and covering, Emma Tarlo presents uniquely understood meanings and interpretations drawn from the hijab and niqab which are simultaneously rooted in cosmopolitan, neo-liberal environments. In her book *Visibly Muslim: Fashion, Politics, Faith*, Tarlo brings together an innovative set of ideas surrounding the concept of the hijab, and with it the role of activism and Muslim femininities. She notes that the practice of hijab-wearing is not simply religious but one which has been informed by past and current political debate, global events and contemporary discourse, and argues that hijab campaigns are not just a matter of freedom, 'politics and human rights' (ibid.: 4) but also a movement by women for other women across the world, noting especially the banning of religious symbols in French schools and the Palestine and Gaza incursions. Calling this 'hijab activism', Muslim women have sought the responsibility of leading demonstrations against actions that are identified as threatening their religious independence and freedom of religious expression. These politico-religious movements place women within a space of matriarchal authority, countering many of the perceptions depicted within negative media discourse that sees the niqab as isolationist, separating its wearer from society and causing her to miss vital opportunities to engage and network. Here, Tarlo argues that by dressing in the hijab or niqab, women become executives of their interactions, choosing whom they want to interact with and at what stage, deciding for themselves the level of appropriate contact. This argument diverts attention away from Muslim women being stereotyped as dominated and oppressed, with problematic assumptions being made about their religious practice, gendered interactions and cultural backgrounds. Many women wear the hijab not only as a result of the increase in Islamic knowledge and closeness to their faith, but also as a political response to the images portrayed by the media. It is in this sense that some Muslim women are bearing the responsibility of facing hostile media, lack of support from wider institutions and, more crucially, the responsibility for Islam and Muslim action worldwide.

The project

This chapter draws upon doctoral fieldwork carried out between December 2009 and June 2010 for an ESRC- and Scottish government-funded study about Muslim women in Scotland. The wider aims of the study include the exploration of the everyday practices of Muslim women, spatial exchanges and experiences, the variations of choices that are made concerning their daily routines for their social, work and family lives, and ways in which they position themselves within Scottish society, a position that is informed through global processes, national policies and local interactions. The analysis here focuses upon 37 interviews and 5 focus groups. All names have been altered to respect the confidentiality of participants. A small number of the interviews were carried out with volunteers from various community organizations in Glasgow, Edinburgh and Dundee alongside a specific focus on the work done by the volunteers and workers of a Muslim women's group in Glasgow. These interviews were carried out and transcribed into English by the first author. Among other discussion topics, participants deliberated over issues of national identity, home and belonging, faith and practice, and media representations. This particular chapter focuses upon the issue of media representations and seeks to draw out the ways in which Muslim women participate in civic life.

Scotland's relationship with Islam and Muslims extends as far back as the seventh century (Maan 2008), although arguably its Muslim population was not to become noticeable until well into the nineteenth century and after the Second World War with the increase of labour demands and economic opportunities. Muslims also have a strong association with political parties, and there are a number of Scottish

Muslims who are heavily involved in formal politics,[5] although very few of these are female. Records from the 2001 National Census for Scotland find at least 42,000 Muslims living in Scotland, and it is likely that this figure has increased with larger numbers of asylum seeker and refugee communities coming from Islamic states, and also the rise in numbers of international students and their accompanying spouses. Muslims make up less than 1 per cent of the overall population of Scotland. Around 75 per cent of Scotland's Muslims are from Pakistani backgrounds (Marranci 2007). The largest proportion (42 per cent) reside in areas of Glasgow, with 16 per cent in Edinburgh and 7 per cent in Dundee (Scottish Executive 2005).

There are a number of organizations in Scotland that work with, and have been constituted by, Muslim communities. The following are a few of them:

- the Muslim Council of Scotland, whose focus includes integration, community cohesion and Muslim engagement with socio-political issues;
- Al-Meezan, an Islamic learning centre in Glasgow;
- Pakeezah, an umbrella organization providing support for smaller groups and sister establishments whose focus is often the female Muslim community located in Edinburgh;
- the Muslim Women's Association of Edinburgh (MWAE), specifically set up by and for Muslim women in Edinburgh and the Lothian areas; the group was set up to stimulate social activities for Muslim women to further engagement with the general population;
- Saheliya, a government-funded organization set up to specialize in mental care issues and to promote good health among ethnic minority women in Edinburgh and the Lothian areas, offering befriending services, domestic abuse counselling and complementary therapy to aid recovery;
- Shakti, a similar organization in the form of a charity that receives National Lottery funding to run its services as a women's aid group; a large number of its clients are Muslim and/or from South Asian backgrounds, and the group also offers culturally sensitive training to volunteers and staff;
- AMINA, the Muslim Women's Resource Centre, based in Glasgow but with offices in Dundee and with sister organizations in Edinburgh and across rural parts of Scotland.[6]

The doctoral study specifically worked with AMINA, the Muslim Women's Resource Centre (MWRC), and a number of interviews were carried out with staff and volunteers based in the centre. Their services range from befriending, capacity-building, the provision of a helpline for domestic abuse victims (which is a large part of their remit within the Muslim community), counsellor training and counselling services. They often also provide training for public and private organizations such as local schools, police and prison services to help deal with issues distinctively concerning Muslim clients and inmates. It is crucial to note that a large number of the organizations are government funded and others are community led, funded through national charitable schemes or receive private funding. The government-funded projects are increasingly more resourceful and nationally led too, as they are able to provide larger marketing schemes. This is evident within the work completed by AMINA, which has enabled projects to be completed within and around rural parts of Scotland. That said, the current economic downturn has severely affected organizations that are government funded, and a number of these are under the threat of funding cuts and even dissolution, which will inevitably weaken community resources and activities.

Responses to negative media representations

It was generally agreed by all participants that the media in general – including the print media – played a significant role in promoting negative depictions of Muslim communities. Kalsoom, who is 54 years old and living in Glasgow, describes how she feels that the media have failed to address the variation of religious belief among Muslims and have thus supplemented the already prevalent harm caused by some uninformed statements in newspaper articles:

KALSOOM: [W]ell, there's a new one adding because we're terrorists as well now but generally that we are oppressed, we are, you know, hard done by, by our religion, you know people, they don't just distinguish between the way people behave in their culture, they consider it's the religion.

(18 January 2010)

Kalsoom identifies that representations of Muslim women have been continually negative, although a 'new' depiction has arisen as a result of terrorist activities. Nagel and Staeheli's study found that British Arab activists felt this way too, and a number of participants commented that public suspicion had increased since 11 September 2001 (2008: 88). Similarly, Peek's study of Muslims in New York University campuses following 11 September 2001 also highlighted how participants felt anger and distrust towards the media (2003: 280). Kalsoom also recognizes that this representation is critically damaging for Muslim women as they access services (in this case, attempting to seek advice about domestic abuse counselling):

KALSOOM: Islam is going to be portrayed wrong or potentially is, so do we want to take that risk, and individual women also have to take that thought of 'If I go to the mainstream services and talk about my husband, they're not gonna understand my situation and are they just going to act on these stereotypes?'

(18 January 2010)

As previous literature also suggests, derogatory depictions within particular media have affected the integration of already isolated communities, making grass-roots work all the harder to perform (Haw 2009: 370). Kalsoom goes on to argue that the negative stereotypes only work to further segregate and silence already hard-to-reach women:

KALSOOM: Actually, instead of helping women it is counter-productive, it does the opposite, it actually forces women to stay quiet.

(18 January 2010)

On the other hand, Kalsoom also identifies that these media perceptions of Muslim women, aside from being defined as detrimental, are attempting to recognize the plight of women across the world and contextualize it in a secular British society. This effort has ultimately had the opposite effect for Muslim women in the West, furthering negative stereotypes and resulting in exclusion from public services (see also Mirza, Chapter 6 of this volume). Khadijah also senses this and, while unhappy to be stereotyped, she acknowledges some of the meanings behind such labels:

KHADIJAH: Islam is just seen horrendously, I think ... any article you read, there is seventy to seventy-five per cent that will always be against, or something negative will always be put across about Islam ... I think they see women are being repressed and they're being forced. And I think they are in certain countries and even maybe here in the UK, you do hear stories, it does happen unfortunately.

(15 December 2009)

Another participant, Aisha, a 35-year-old mother-of-two who lives in Dundee, addresses the problems of sensational media stories, noting that this sensationalism draws attention away from the 'real issues' experienced by Muslims in Scotland and across Great Britain (see also Mirza, Chapter 6 of this volume). These issues include everyday access to service provision and entering social spaces, which becomes a more difficult task:

AISHA: [T]hey never seem to get to the real issues and hit the nail on the head, they just seem to skirt around that side with things like that, you know, or the extreme views, of course, which are always coming to the forefront.

(29 January 2010)

Increasingly, Muslim women in Scotland and throughout Britain are becoming 'risk-aware' (Haw 2009: 365) and are acutely alert to the media portrayals surrounding Islam, Muslims and how this can impact on their social and political lives, together with having a detrimental effect upon their religious and gendered identities. The women are highly conscious of the perceptions being created about them within the media and often want to disassociate themselves from those perceptions. At the same time, however, through the use of words such as 'they' (non-Muslims) and 'the media', and 'my' (the wider Muslim community), they also indicate their position within the Muslim communities being stereotyped. The women are equally aware of how these media depictions can affect their lifestyle and use of mainstream services, as highlighted by Kalsoom above. The damaging images publicized by particular media, then, extend further than solidifying public perceptions.

They can also lead to a decline in quality of services that are vital to community integration and anti-segregation debates. Here, Shazia, a 25-year-old trainee solicitor from Glasgow, feels particularly angry about the events of 11 September 2001, describing how she is not responsible for other people's actions, only for her own, but feels that she was the victim of a lot of scrutiny at the time:

SHAZIA: I just think it's stupid, just stupid. It's anger, it's more like annoyance because of their actions we're gonna have to suffer and I'm gonna have to justify myself because I'm not gonna let anyone judge me by who I am, so I'm gonna have to justify myself now and I'm gonna have to put myself across more.

(14 December 2009)

Shazia feels that she now has to work much harder to gain social credibility, but also blames the media intrusion for the difficulties she has faced:

SHAZIA: Because Islam is not what is shown in the media, it's not that at all, it doesn't take a genius to dig behind those headlines, look at what Islam really is about and feel connected to it. Islam is not about bombing people, it's not about what the media makes it out to be at all. I mean, if you're thick as mince, then you're gonna believe that 'oh, I'm not gonna talk to a Muslim in case they're ticking'.

(14 December 2009)

Shazia is particularly upset about the negative media effects upon her own life, as she has worked hard to reach her career stage. In a later stage of the interview she talks about how she feels her career opportunities have suffered as a result of the negative media attention. While she is unable to prove any effects, she suspects that a number of applications were rejected on the basis of her Muslim name and background, echoing findings by Zine (2006). Hajra, who is 33 and from Glasgow, also discussed the sense of responsibility she felt had been forced upon her and others in the Muslim community as an unfair and unjust response to the events of 11 September 2001:

HAJRA: I think it's, it's the perception that just because this group of people did it and they were Muslims, then other Muslims, they have to make up, they have to compensate for what happened. Just as I wouldn't expect the British people, you know, or white people or, erm, the British government to compensate for the slave trade that happened thousands of years ago because it wasn't themselves that did it you know and it doesn't matter that they're the same colour or the same religion, they weren't the culprits.

(7 January 2010)

The participants in this research could be said to be experiencing a form of 'gendered Islamophobia' that 'operates socially, politically, and discursively to deny material advantages to Muslim women' (Zine 2006: 240). As a result of their marginalization as Muslims and as women, the negative media coverage is particularly challenging for these women, which is the reason why many of them responded to this discussion with such passion and disgust. Here, then, we see that Muslim women in Scotland are very aware of the persistently negative coverage of their religious identities and are therefore overturning simplistic stereotypes that see them as politically disengaged or at best neutral. As Gale and Hopkins (2009) note, Muslim communities throughout Britain have sought to challenge negative representations of their communities through public engagement. This has created spaces of community-level or personal activism, and it is to these that we now turn.

Everyday making and civic engagement

Referring to formal political participation, O'Toole and Gale (2010: 132) note that lower levels of electoral engagement among ethnic minority groups 'should not then be interpreted as evidence of political apathy'. Instead, they observe that 'ethnic minority groups are much more likely to be engaged in alternative rather than conventional forms of participation, and within social movements, as a consequence of exclusionary norms and practices within mainstream political arenas' (ibid.: 132). In line with this, we now focus upon the everyday engagements of Muslim women involved in this research, and in doing so demonstrate the subtle ways in which they engage with political issues on a daily basis and participate in complex forms of everyday activism. Following the work of Bang (2003), we are interested in the 'everyday making' of Muslim women in Scotland and the ways in which their everyday actions and engagements constitute an important set of engagements with political processes.

Here we use two case studies to highlight the everyday making activisms taking place within community-led and community-based organizations. A number of women participating in the study formed a network of volunteers working for charities in and around Scotland. Begum, who is 44 and from Glasgow, feels that civic duties are part and parcel of Islamic values and that political activity is crucial for integration. This integration, however, must be mutual for it to work, and Begum argues that Muslim women are failing in their task to become members of Scottish civic communities:

BEGUM: I do feel that Muslim women need to speak up and be heard and have a voice. They need to be proactive and, erm, I really feel that they need to get, I mean like I said to you, see because there's so few of us who get to work in the community, we have to double, triple work for others you see. So if everybody was like them, then it would be so much easier.

(27 January 2010)

For those women involved in community charities or women's groups, the study found that there are a number of reasons for participation within community-based organizations, and the decision-making processes involved various social, political and economic considerations. When asked to think about why she decided to begin working in the voluntary sector, Noreen, a 42-year-old paid worker, describes how she came to work for AMINA after having worked for a similar organization:

NOREEN: To be honest, I saw it's a place where I can have, erm, a good impact on the clients and, erm, something I feel is rewarding for me. I feel that I'm helping my community and I'm helping the people I understand more than others.

(13 April 2010)

For Shamaila, a 39-year-old volunteer who commutes daily from a small town located between Glasgow and Edinburgh, her own personal experiences led her to seek out women's groups as she felt there was a lack of social and political engagement in her town and, through various contacts and meetings, was informed of the work of AMINA and began working for it soon after:

SHAMAILA: I have been working with Muslim women for quite a while but not in this area so, erm, I do have a passion for, erm, to work with minority ethnic Muslim women and that passion to, led me to come here.

(13 April 2010)

A number of participants situated themselves in a role that gave them the responsibility of utilizing their cultural and religious backgrounds to facilitate and develop service provision and community integration. Together with exercising agency (Haw 2009: 364), the women in the study were able to contextualize their skills and create spaces of micro-level activism to support the wider local female Muslim community:

NOREEN: Because we understand those barriers, we understand those needs and this is why I feel that this is the place where you can make a difference because you know how you can go about it and stuff like that, but definitely there are many issues which will be well understandable for BME [black and ethnic minority] people more than others.

(13 April 2010)

Shamaila agreed with Noreen when discussing issues in her home town, from where she commutes:

SHAMAILA: We are a [very small] minority there so I feel there are many barriers, challenges that we face as a community and that kind of led me to get involved with AMINA.

(13 April, 2010)

The aftermath of 11 September 2001 and also 7 July 2005 led to an awakening in previously dormant feminist social circles, and previous studies have also identified ways in which Muslims have reintroduced themselves to communities and social spaces through a distancing from terrorist activities (Peek 2003; see also Ahmad, Chapter 9 of this volume), creating a positive space for everyday making and engagement with the public sphere. For a group in Edinburgh called Beyond the Veil, the preliminary initiative to set up the group came from the after-effects of events such as those of 11 September, as Humera remembers:

> HUMERA: When the 9/11 and the July bombings happened, then afterwards we decided we wanted to do something, you know, so we made a booklet called 'Pride and Prejudice' which we wanted to give or show to people or present to people to show this is what we actually are like, we're not like that, so we kind of kept escalating from there really.
>
> *(24 June 2010)*

Humera discussed how Beyond the Veil was set up as a smaller sister organization of Pakeezah, which is also located in Edinburgh and is a community-led group that receives funding from charity organizations. Most of the work is carried out among the volunteers when they finish their paid work or during lunch hours. Humera is also a full-time teacher at her children's primary school as well as one of the main activists within the group, and her work with Beyond the Veil has involved engagement with local schools in Edinburgh, her own school, local police diversity units and interfaith establishments around the Lothian area:

> HUMERA: We target kind of schools and we do workshops there, we do a lot with Lothian Borders Police, we do, erm, diversity training there so we really made a lot of contacts, it's quite good ... we work with the interfaith organization who give us a bit of funding and help but we don't get paid or anything.
>
> *(24 June 2010)*

Beyond the Veil has perhaps grown beyond what was initially expected, but, as can be seen, it was crucial to the development of local community engagement in Edinburgh, with police gaining an enhanced understanding of the workings of these communities. Such groups are vital to performing the community work needed to engage with Muslim women as they actively participate in their everyday local lives. Alongside Humera, the volunteers in the group also bear the responsibility of many Muslim women in the area who have little contact or engagement with the wider general population. The women at both AMINA and Beyond the Veil are carrying out community work with initiatives that are government funded but not government led, and initiatives that receive little funding or none at all. Like Humera, a number of volunteers working for Beyond the Veil do so as a political reaction to the continuing negative social depictions that have been triggered through harmful media portrayal. These are just two examples of the work currently going on within Scotland, with numerous other community groups and organizations working to provide a better framework for community engagement.

Conclusion

This chapter has demonstrated the various ways in which Muslim women are not simply passive and disengaged victims of a patriarchal religion but are engaged actively in contributing to their local communities and to political processes while simultaneously responding to their persistent misrepresentation in the media. Negative media coverage has led Muslim women to reassert themselves within the public sphere and to redefine spaces of civic engagement. In doing so, the participants make it clear that they are empowered in identifying as Muslim women in Scotland. Their 'everyday making' constitutes an important set of engagements with political processes in their local communities and in the Scottish polity more broadly.

Having found that negative media representations were perceived as having a direct impact on the ways in which Muslim women access public services, Muslim women assert political and social agency to develop collaborations with the non-Muslim and Muslim communities in Scotland, with the specific aim of improving perceptions about Muslims and diminishing negative media stereotypes, becoming proactive both by challenging public discourse and stereotypes, and through the ongoing construction of reflective spaces of civic engagement. In particular, we have demonstrated the sensitivity of Muslim women to negative representations of their faith and gendered identities. Furthermore, this sensitivity has been accompanied by a willingness to engage in the public sphere and to participate in everyday making through places of work and volunteering. There is, nonetheless, a long way to go in demarcating negative media perceptions, social attitudes and stereotypes before the Muslim population of Scotland are no longer held accountable for the actions of minority politico-religious movements across the world. The debates surrounding responsibility and allegiance to state nationalism is one that continues to differentiate Muslims within particular media discourses. As outlined in this chapter, these discourses have led to the construction of political spaces in which Muslim women are empowered to think critically about the ways in which they can continue to contribute to civic duties through community-led change and activisms. Further work in this area, including engagements between researchers, communities and those working in the media, could usefully help overturn problematic stereotypes about Muslim women in order that they become less marginalized and stigmatized within British society.

Acknowledgements

We thank the ESRC and the Scottish Government for doctoral funding for this project.

Notes

1 The Runnymede Trust report commissioned in 1997 defined Islamophobia as 'dread or hatred of Islam and therefore .. the fear and dislike of all Muslims'. However, some writers have further described it as 'not irrational, but rather a rational process involving the deliberate demonization of Muslims based upon misinformation used in the post 9/11 context to support the war on terror' (Birt 2009: 218).

2 Aftab's study follows the discourse of a nineteenth-century plea from Muslim women in Punjab, India, to a key politician of the time, Sir Syed Ahmed Khan. The women wrote a detailed letter to Sir Syed requesting provisions to be made for women's education in the area.
3 Video of the attack is available widely on the internet. However, for this chapter the source accessed was BBC News (2009)
4 Rushanara Ali, MP for Bethnal Green and Bow; Shabana Mahmood, MP for Birmingham Ladywood; Yasmin Qureshi, MP for Bolton South East.
5 Bashir Maan, Bashir Ahmed, Mohammad Sarwar, Osama Saeed and Anas Sarwar.
6 This government-funded establishment was set up in 1997 to promote developments in religious, racial and community cohesion alongside aiding women in overcoming barriers to participation through a befriending service.

References

Aftab, T. (2005) 'Negotiating with patriarchy: South Asian Muslim women and the appeal to Sir Syed Ahmed Khan', *Women's History Review* 14 (1): 75–97.

Arat, Y. (1998) 'Feminists, Islamists, and political change in Turkey', *Political Psychology* 19 (1): 117–131.

Archer, L. (2001) '"Muslim brothers, black lads, traditional Asians": British Muslim young men's constructions of race, religion and masculinity', *Feminism and Psychology* 11 (1): 79–105.

Bang, H. P. (2003) 'A new ruler meeting a new citizen: culture governance and everyday making', in H. P. Bang (ed.) *Governance as Social and Political Communication*, Manchester: Manchester University Press.

BBC News (2009) 'Tory Muslim peer pelted with eggs'. Online, available at: http://news.bbc.co.uk/1/hi/england/beds/bucks/herts/8387110.stm (accessed 15 July 2010).

Birt, J. (2009) 'Islamophobia in the construction of British Muslim identity politics', in R. Gale and P. Hopkins (eds) *Muslims in Britain: Race, Place and Identities*, Edinburgh: Edinburgh University Press.

Dwyer, C. (1998) 'Contested identities: challenging dominant representations of Muslim women', in T. Skelton and G. Valentine (eds) *Cool Places: Geographies of Youth Culture*, London: Routledge.

Dwyer, C., Shah, B. and Sanghera, G. (2008) '"From cricket lover to terror suspect": challenging representations of young British Muslim men', *Gender, Place and Culture* 15 (2): 117–136.

Gale, R. and Hopkins, P. (eds) (2009) *Muslims in Britain: Race, Place and Identities*, Edinburgh: Edinburgh University Press.

Glynn, S. (2009) 'Liberalizing Islam: creating Brits of the Islamic persuasion', in R. Phillips (ed.) *Muslim Spaces of Hope: Geographies of Possibility in Britain and the West*, London: Zed Books.

Haw, K. (2009) 'From hijab to jilbab and the "myth" of British identity: being Muslim in contemporary Britain a half-generation on', *Race, Ethnicity and Education* 12 (3): 363–378.

Hopkins, P. (2004) 'Young Muslim men in Scotland: inclusions and exclusions', *Children's Geographies* 2 (2): 257–272.

Hopkins, P. (2008) *The Issue of Masculine Identities for British Muslims after 9/11: A Social Analysis*, New York: Edward Mellen Press.

Hopkins, P. (2009) 'Muslims in the West: deconstructing geographical boundaries', in R. Phillips (ed.) *Geographies of Possibility in Britain and the West: Muslim Spaces of Hope*, London: Zed Books.

Hussain, Y. and Bagguley, P. (2003) 'Citizenship, ethnicity and identity: British Pakistanis after the 2001 "riots" ', Working Paper, University of Leeds.

Kobayashi, A. (1994) 'Coloring the field: gender, "race" and the politics of fieldwork', *Professional Geographer* 46: 73–80.

Kong, L. (2001) 'Mapping "new" geographies of religion: politics and poetics in modernity', *Progress in Human Geography* 25 (2): 211–233.

Maan, B. (2008) *The Thistle and the Crescent*, Glasgow: Argyle Publishing.

Marranci, G. (2007) 'From the ethos of justice to the ideology of justice: understanding radical views of Scottish Muslims', in T. Abbas (ed.) *Islamic Political Radicalism: A European Perspective*, Edinburgh: Edinburgh University Press.

Modood, T. (2009) 'Muslims and the politics of difference', in R. Gale and P. Hopkins (eds) *Muslims in Britain: Race, Place and Identities*, Edinburgh: Edinburgh University Press.

Moghadam, V. M. (2008) *Globalization and Social Movements: Islamism, Feminism, and the Global Justice Movement*, Lanham, MD: Rowman & Littlefield.

Nagel, C. R. and Staeheli, L. A. (2008) 'Integration and the negotiation of "here" and "there": the case of British Arab activists', *Social and Cultural Geography* 9 (4): 415–430.

Naples, N. A. (ed.) (1998) *Community Activism and Feminist Politics: Organizing Race Class, and Gender*, New York: Routledge.

Noble, G. (2005) 'The discomfort of strangers: racism, incivility and ontological security in a relaxed and comfortable nation', *Journal of Intercultural Studies* 26 (1-2): 107–120.

O'Toole, T. and Gale, R. T. (2010) 'Contemporary grammars of political action among ethnic minority young activists', *Ethnic and Racial Studies* 33 (1): 126–143.

Peek, L. A. (2003) 'Reactions and responses: Muslim students' experiences on New York City campuses post 9/11', *Journal of Muslim Minority Affairs* 23 (2): 271–283.

Phillips, D. (2006) 'Parallel lives? Challenging discourses of British Muslim self-segregation', *Environment and Planning D: Society and Space* 24 (1): 25–40.

Phoenix, A. (1997) 'The place of "race" and ethnicity in the lives of children and young people', *Educational and Child Psychology* 14 (3): 5–24.

Pritchett, S. M. (2005) 'Will dualism tear us apart? The challenges of fragmentation in identity politics for young feminists in the New Global Order', in S. Wilson, A. Sengupta and K. Evans (eds) *Defending Our Dreams: Global Feminist Voices for a New Generation*, London: Zed Books, in association with the Association for Women's Rights in Development (AWID).

Runnymede Trust (1997) *Islamophobia: A Challenge for Us All*, London: Runnymede Trust.

Scottish Executive National Statistics (2005) *Analysis of Religion in the 2001 Census: Summary Report*, Edinburgh: Scottish Executive.

Spalek, B. and McDonald, L. Z. (2009) 'Terror crime prevention: constructing Muslim practices and beliefs as "anti-social" and "extreme" through CONTEST 2', *Social Policy and Society*, 9: 123–132.

Tarlo, E. (2010) *Visibly Muslim: Fashion, Politics, Faith*, Oxford: Berg.

Werbner, P. (1997) 'Essentialising essentialism, essentialising silence: ambivalence and multiplicity in the constructions of race and ethnicity', in P. Werbner and T. Modood (eds) *Debating Cultural Hybridity: Multi-cultural Identities and the Politics of Anti-racism*, London: Zed Books.

Wilson, S., Sengupta, A. and Evans, K. (eds) (2005) *Defending Our Dreams: Global Feminist Voices for a New Generation*, London: Zed Books, in association with the Association for Women's Rights in Development (AWID).

Zine, J. (2006) 'Unveiled sentiments: gendered Islamophobia and experiences of veiling among Muslim girls in a Canadian Islamic school', *Equity and Excellence in Education* 39: 239–252.

8

NEGOTIATING FAITH AND POLITICS

The emergence of Muslim consciousness in Britain

Nasar Meer

> It has caused a rupture in conventional political wisdom and remains an enigma to social policy.
>
> (*Atif Imtiaz, Wondering Lonely in a Crowd, 2010*)

Introduction

In the epigraph to this chapter, Imtiaz (2010) could be referring to an intangible phenomenon: neither animal, vegetable nor mineral, elusive in its properties and provenance, but sufficiently generalised as to warrant a high degree of prominence in public policy. He was in fact referring to the emergence of Muslim identity politics in Britain. While it is inevitable that different accounts vary both in their genealogies of the emergence of Islam as a salient marker of minority difference and in their understanding of what this heralds, it has nevertheless become passé to observe that the category of 'Muslim' has only relatively recently assumed the prominence in Britain that we are familiar with today.

Explanations for why this is so vary, but it is at least partly due to the role of disrupting heterogeneity in ethnic, doctrinal and linguistic backgrounds which has historically made up the constituency of Muslims in Britain. Yet the question of how much analytical emphasis to give to this internal diversity is also a political one, and to some extent reflects an earlier unwillingness to recognise that religious affiliation might provide a source for identity articulations akin to race, class and gender (Modood 1994). This is at least one legacy of overly materialist and positivist currents in the social sciences, in so far as 'much migration research has maintained a built-in interpretative bias that has led scholars to see religious identification as a backward or reactionary form of "false consciousness" simply masking objectives and interests that are actually "secular"' (Statham 2005: 164).[1]

Among the South Asian component alone, therefore, the groups that are now designated as British Muslims have also been studied by sociologists, anthropologists and political scientists as black, working-class, Pakistanis, Bangladeshis, Mirpuirus, Sylhetis, etc. (Samad 1992: 508). One of the key arguments of this chapter is that such a shift in semantics reflects important internal developments – specifically, the coming to fruition of a tangible Muslim consciousness among Muslim communities themselves (Meer 2010). That is to say: the ways in which mobilisations as self-consciously 'Muslim' have become ascendant in a manner that is analogous to racial and ethnic self-assertions (Modood 2007). To elaborate this argument, I explore contemporary relationships between Muslim minorities and the British state. Focusing upon structural and cultural dynamics, I discuss the ways in which British Muslims have sought to negotiate the reconciliation (on occasion re-imagination) of faith commitments with citizenship rights and responsibilities. I argue that with differing levels of success this approach is observable as emerging cumulatively across a number of arenas, and that the successes (and obstacles) encountered during these experiences are furnishing Muslim groups with a sense of confidence that offers resilience at times of acute social and political anxiety and hostility.

'Grouping' Muslims in Britain

An immediate issue that needs to be tackled in any discussion of Muslims in Britain is the tension between generality and particularity, namely Muslim group identities. One thoughtful set of objections against 'grouping' Muslims was put forward by the late Fred Halliday. He suggested that studying immigrant communities exclusively in terms of religion was easy.

> But this is to miss other identities – of work, location, ethnicity – and, not least, the ways in which different Muslims relate to each other. Anyone with the slightest acquaintance of the inner life of the Arabs in Britain, or the Pakistani and Bengali communities, will know there is as much difference as commonality.
>
> *(1999: 897)*

Halliday provided a valuable caution against an understanding of Muslims in Britain as a monolithic group. However, such readings ignore how certain concerns span different Muslims, and how these concerns are not outcomes of either a shared faith or shared ethnicity alone, but instead reflect a heightened sense of an 'associational' identity (Modood 1997b). One way of putting this is to say that we might distinguish between faith-based – *Islamic* – and more sociological – *Muslim* – identities. It is suggested here that the relationship between Islam and Muslim identities might be better conceived as *instructive* but not *determining*, something analogous to the relationship between the categorisation of one's sex and one's gendered identity.[2] That is to say, one may be biologically female or male in a narrow sense of the definition, but one may be a woman or man in multiple, overlapping and discontinuous ways – one's gender reflecting something that emerges on a continuum that can be either (or both) internally defined or externally ascribed.

This means that in addition to the scriptural conception, we could view Muslim identity as a quasi-ethnic sociological formation which facilitates a range of factors other than Scripture (such as ethnicity, race, gender, sexuality and agnosticism) to shape Muslim identities. 'Quasi' is used to denote something *similar* but *not the same as*, because ethnic and religious boundaries continue to interact and are rarely wholly demarcated, hence the term 'ethno-religious' (see Modood 1997a: 337). Compared to the purely theological variety, this sociological category might be preferred as a less exclusive and more valid way of operationalising Muslim identity at the level of the social because it includes opportunities for self-definition (such as formally on the census or on 'ethnic' monitoring forms (see Aspinall 2000) or informally in public and media discourse). Equally, it can facilitate the description of oneself as 'Muslim' and take the multiple (overlapping or synthesised) and subjective elements into account independently of or intertwined with objective behavioural congruence with the religious practices outlined earlier. It is maintained that this space for self-definition is a helpful means of conceptualising the difference between externally imposed and self-ascribed identities, with both potentially becoming more prominent at some times and less at others.

The emphasis is on the element of choice in self-definition. For example, one might view Islam as a historical, civilisational edifice that has contributed to modern science and philosophy, and take pride in this, but simultaneously disassociate oneself from the religious teachings. This historical or civilisational role of Islam may be minimised in favour of the elevation and re-imagining of a particular religious doctrine, or way of being a Muslim, based upon an adherence to articles of divine and confessional faith. What is therefore being argued is that when a Muslim identity is mobilised, it should be understood as a mode of classification according to the particular kinds of claims Muslims make for themselves, albeit in various ways.

Observing British Muslim identities

How may these theoretical tendencies be delineated in practice? Greaves (2007) has insisted that an increasing self-identification of second and subsequent generations as 'Muslim' constitutes a reaction to the aspect of their identity believed to be under attack for 'it is likely that the images of Muslim civilians seen to be dying and suffering in various hotspots around the world ... will impact upon the emotive ties inherent within identity construction' (Greaves, 2007: 22). This appears fairly straightforward and perhaps too simplistic when contrasted with the findings of Jacobson's (1997a, b, 1998) ethnographic research among youth of Pakistani and Bangladeshi backgrounds in East London. Her thesis begins by returning to Fredrick Barth's (1969) argument that ethnic groups should be defined according to the boundaries that actors *subjectively* determine themselves, and not simply according to *objective* classifications based upon ascribed cultural features. Jacobson (1997b: 240) takes this to hypothesise that while ethnic and religious cleavages can coincide with one another, they often offer contradictory modes of self-definition. She specifically points to the following tendency among her sample to emphasise a distinction between religious, cultural and ethnic facets of identity construction: 'whereas ethnic boundaries are becoming increasingly permeable and cultural boundaries are (re-) negotiated, the religious boundaries are remaining clear-cut and pervasive and thus serve to protect and enhance attachments to Islam'.

The explanation she offers for this distinction develops from the way in which ethnicity is understood as an attachment to tradition and custom intertwined with cultural practice. Ethnicity here is perceived as non-religious in origin. This allows youth of Pakistani and Bangladeshi descent to distinguish between the universalism of religion and limited locality of cultures that migrated from South Asia with an older generation ('disparate loyalties from a disparate place'). Or else, as Gale and O'Toole's (2009: 151) study of the Muslim youth organisation Muslim Justice Movement (MJM) reports, 'the members of the MJM articulated a commitment to religion which they consciously decoupled from ethnic identification'. They acknowledged a continuing 'connection' to Pakistan, but also 'laid claim to a hyphenated "British Muslim" identity, suggesting that loyalties attached to place of birth and those relating to faith are not mutually exclusive'.

In other words, for those who were brought up in Pakistan or Bangladesh and migrated to Britain as adults, Islam was arguably located in an oral tradition that was much more – though not entirely – linked to life-cycle rituals. This form of Islam was seeped in rural traditions and inevitably influenced by non-Islamic conventions (and over time had more to do with the Pakistan they left behind than with contemporary Pakistan). Among Jacobson's (1997b: 239) British-born sample, a more discrete Islam was consumed and reproduced, and was, by and large, central to their sense of who they were, since 'they affirm their belief in its teachings and regard it as something in relation to which they should orient their behaviour in all spheres of life and which therefore demands of them a self-conscious and explicit commitment'.

In comparison to this mode of Muslim identity, Jacobson argues that ethnicity is more peripheral and is not regarded as a basis from which to frame their experience of the world. It is worth noting too how Knott and Khokher (1993) and Dwyer (1999) have previously shown that in their negotiations young Muslim women draw a distinction between 'religion' and 'ethnicity' in rejecting their parents' subscription to traditions that are less consistent which the aspirations of these young women themselves. This frequently builds upon a self-conscious exploration of religion as a means of promoting advancement in education, career opportunities, and so forth (see also Baggueley and Hussain 2008).

It is argued that shared Muslim concerns are likely to encompass the ways in which to combat anti-Muslim racism, or cultivate a positive public image (heterogeneous or otherwise), or a desire among some Muslim parents to school their children in Islamic traditions, and so on. For example, it is particularly noteworthy that while support for the Labour government decreased among all minorities in the 2005 general election, it did so radically among Muslim groups. The most dramatic example was the defeat of the incumbent MP in the predominantly Bangladeshi London constituency of Bethnal Green and Bow by George Galloway, a former Labour MP who led the anti-war Respect party. One particular issue that this raised is whether a discernible British Muslim identity has given rise to a discernible 'Muslim vote' in Britain, for it is clear that Muslim organisations in that general election campaigned on a distinctive equality agenda that drew attention to the ways Muslims have become the subject of anti-terrorism campaigns and related Islamophobia (Modood 2005).

If we continue with this example, a number of implications can be drawn from these developments, implications that include differences between Muslim and non-Muslim ethnic minority voting patterns, as well as the extent to which Muslim political electoral participation is 'closely connected to the size of the local Muslim population [which] indicates that registration, like turnout, is affected by the forces of [Muslim] mobilisation' (Fieldhouse and Cutts 2008: 333). One example of Muslim electoral mobilisation was much in evidence when the Muslim Council of Britain (MCB) issued a ten-point check card to encourage Muslim voters to evaluate various politicians' positions on matters concerning both domestic and foreign policy.[3] The reception of such a strategy by a former leading Labour politician provides a lucid illustration of the electoral impact of attitudinal and social shifts among contemporary Muslims in his former constituency:

> For more than 30 years, I took the votes of Birmingham Muslims for granted.... [I]f, at any time between 1964 and 1997 I heard of a Khan, Saleem or Iqbal who did not support Labour I was both outraged and astonished....
>
> The Muslim view of Labour has changed....
>
> Anxious immigrants who throw themselves on the mercy of their members of parliament are now a minority. Their children and grandchildren will only vote for politicians who explicitly meet their demands....
>
> In future they will pick and choose between the parties and ask: 'What have you done for me?'
>
> *(Hattersley 2005)*

The central narrative running through this account is that of a confident British Muslim democratic engagement that is further illustrated by Sher Khan of the MCB:

> Our position has always been that we see ourselves as part of this society. I do not think that you can be part of it if you are not willing to take part in electing your own representatives. So, engage with the process of governance or of your community as part of being a citizen of this community. We think it is imperative.
>
> *(Quoted in Carter 2005)*

This ethic of engagement has not been limited to electoral participation, however, for it is also observed in some key areas in which Muslims in Britain have secured forms of state recognition through processes of engagement and lobbying.

Muslims and multi-faith Britain

British Muslim engagement with the state proceeds in a context that is characterised by an internal religious plurality which has been supplemented by the migration of different religious groups over the past two centuries (Filby 2006). To be sure, and in spite of maintaining a Protestant established Church of England, the superior status of the dominant Anglican Church has consistently been challenged by other Christian denominations, not least in Scotland, where the religious majority is not Anglican but Presbyterian, which led to the creation of a Church of Scotland. In England and Wales, Protestant Nonconformists have been vocal; and issues such as education have in the past encouraged many of these groups to 'stand out against the state for giving every opportunity to the Church of England to proselytise through the education system' (Skinner 2002: 174).

The cycles of nineteenth-century migration from Ireland to London, Glasgow and the north of England considerably expanded the Roman Catholic presence in Britain. The turn of the twentieth century, meanwhile, witnessed the arrival of destitute Jewish migrants fleeing both the pogroms and economic deprivation in Russia (Meer and Noorani 2008). Both groups have suffered racial discrimination and civil disadvantage on the basis of their religious affiliation but in due course have come to enjoy some of the benefits initially associated with 'establishment' (the identification of the Church of England with the British state). This includes allowing the Catholic Church to set up schools alongside the state and then, in the 1944 Education Act, to opt into the state sector and receive provisions similar to those enjoyed by members of the established Church – a provision that was soon extended to other religious groups, notably Jewish minorities.

Muslims, then, like Hindus and Sikhs, are the most recent and numerically significant addition to this plurality to have established themselves, with varying degrees of success, as part of the 'new cultural landscape' of Britain (Peach and Gale 2003: 487–488). This is evidenced is several spheres but is made strikingly visible in what Peach and Gale (ibid.: 469) describe as the 'new "cathedrals" of the English cultural landscape'. By this they refer to the creation of Muslim *masjids* (mosques), alongside Hindu mandirs and Sikh gurdwaras, which have emerged through a process of dialogue between minority faith groups and British city planning authorities. One of several points of interest in the creation of these places of worship is that out of the thousand or so that exist, the majority are in fact conversions of disused chapels, churches and other such premises (ibid.: 482). In this context it is not surprising to learn that mosque building is less controversial in Britain than elsewhere in Europe, since Muslims frequently use the 1852 and 1855 Places of Worship Registration Acts.[4] Similar historical settlements explain religious burial accommodations (see Ansari 2004).

One of the most prominent examples of Muslim-state engagement is to be found in the Muslim mobilisations for Islamic schools (see Meer 2012). In this area, Muslim groups achieved a significant breakthrough in 1998 when, after 18 years of a Conservative administration, a New Labour government delivered on a promise in its election manifesto and co-opted two Muslim schools, Islamia School (in Brent, London) and Al-Furqan School (in Birmingham), into the state sector by awarding each "voluntary aided" (VA) status. This status prescribed an allocation of public money to cover teacher salaries and the running costs of the school. It arrived 'fourteen years and five Secretaries of State after the first naive approach' (Hewitt 1998: 22), when Muslim parents and educators had only begun to get to grips with the convoluted application process needed to achieve state funding, and were dealing with a Conservative government that was hostile to the idea of state-funded Muslim schools. By 2011 the number of state-funded Muslim faith schools had risen to 11 (Tinker and Smart 2011), and included Al-Hijrah (a secondary school in Birmingham), Feversham College (a secondary school in Bradford), Gatton Primary School (in Wandsworth, south London), Tauheedul Islam Girls' High School (in Blackburn, Lancashire) and The Avenue School (another primary school in Brent, north-west London).

Elsewhere I have argued that Muslim identities can inform the movement for Muslim schools in a variety of ways, and that where Muslim constituencies are granted greater participatory space and provisions for Muslim schooling, it is evident from the testimonies of Muslim educators and the content of school curricula that a reconciliation between faith requirements and citizenship commitments is a first-order priority (Meer 2009). Yet what is often overlooked in the deployment of Muslim identities in the case for Muslim schools in Britain is how the imagining of a Muslim identity *goes hand in hand with* the imagining of a British identity. This is very evident in the characterisation by the head teacher, Abdullah Trevathan, of the 'ethos' of Islamia Primary, the first Muslim school in Britain to receive state funding:

> This school is about creating a British Muslim culture, instead of, as I've often said in the press, conserving or saving a particular culture, say from the sub-continent or from Egypt or from Morocco or from wherever it may be. Obviously those cultures may feed into this British Muslim cultural identity, but we're not in the business of preserving … it's just not feasible and it's not sensible … it's dead: I mean I'm not saying *those* cultures are dead but it's a dead duck in the water as far as being *here* is concerned.
>
> *(Trevathan, interview with author, 6 March 2006)*

Islamia Primary is not unique in trying to partner the Muslim dimension with the national, so that instead of suffocating hybridity or encouraging reification, for example, the outward projection of this internal diversity informs a pursuit of hyphenated identities. The casualty in this 'steering' of Muslim identity is the geographical origin conception of ethnicity, and the scramble to de-emphasise the 'ethnic culture' in favour of an ecumenical Islamic identity soon gives rise to an important complaint. This includes the lack of provisions within comprehensive schooling to cater for identity articulations that are not premised upon the recognition of minority status per se, but which move outward on their own terms in an increasingly confident or assertive manner. Idris Mears, director of the Association of Muslim Schools (AMS), stresses this position:

> I think a general point which is very important to get across is that state schools do not handle the meaning of Muslim identity well for the children. In actual fact, the way that general society looks at Muslims is as an immigrant minority-ethnic-racial-group and how young people are made to look at themselves through the teaching in state schools tells them, 'You are this marginal group/minority group and have therefore got to integrate with the mainstream.' So there's a process of marginalisation and that often leads to resentment. But in a Muslim school that identity is built upon being a Muslim, *not* an ethnic minority. The impact of being Muslim is very different because the role of the Muslims in any situation is to be the middle nation to take the middle ground and be the model as witnesses of humanity. I think it gives young people a greater sense of who they are and how they can interact in society and therefore learn that Islam is not just a thing that is relevant to minority rights. Islam is relevant to the economy, to foreign policy, etc., which means that we're not getting on to a stationary train but a train that is moving.
>
> *(Mears, interview 1 April 2006)*

This 'train' – which moves between different sites of boundary maintenance – is an articulation of Muslim consciousness. Mears expresses a 'clean' version of Muslim consciousness that is free from ethnic and racial markers and therefore does not correspond to the lived reality, but is expressed as an aspiration to be realised through Muslim schooling environments. It is a desire reflected in the findings of Patricia Kelly (1998: 203), who, in her ethnographic study of schooling choices made by Muslim parents with both secular and Islamic worldviews, concluded that

> as some less-religious families do opt for specifically Muslim education, we can consider this as an example of a decision to selectively emphasise this pan-ethnic (Muslim) group identity, in order to reap whatever benefits – economic, social and psychological as well as spiritual – it offers.

While this emphasises that much of the motivation for Muslim schooling reflects the desire of Muslim parents to instil a sense of a Muslim heritage in all its heterogeneity, this is not incommensurable with what are seen as the liberal democratic norms and conventions in Britain. As Soper and Fetzer (2010: 13) insist, 'it is theologically naïve and historically misguided to assume Islam is any more inherently incapable of making peace with liberal-democratic values than are Christian and Jewish traditions'. An illustration of this point is provided by Mears, who stresses the distinction between a school premised upon an ethnic origin conception of Islam, driven by a desire for 'cultural protection zones', and an Islamically driven environment that moves outward to build upon evaluative criteria already established and in place (Mears, interview). Such nuance, however, is often overlooked in public discussion, which operates within narrow parameters that risk 'rendering Muslims profoundly "invisible"' (Archer 2009: 75). By this, Archer is referring to how the terms of reference and debate within which Muslims are 'allowed' to speak and appear 'remain incredibly narrow' (ibid.).

Self and public representation

It is precisely the force of a narrow frame in mainstream press coverage of Islam and British Muslims, and specifically a propensity for negative portrayals, that have informed the cultivation of alternative Muslim media sources that are 'more aware of and sympathetic to Muslims' in the course of reflecting 'the Muslim or Islamic identity of both its producers and readers' (Ahmed 2005: 111; cf. Morey and Yaqin 2011). Publications such as *Muslim News*, *Q-News*, *Crescent International*, *Impact International* and *Trends*, media committees at the MCB and the Forum Against Islamophobia and Racism (FAIR), and radio stations such as Radio Ummah and Radio Ramadan, as well as the Islam Channel, have increasingly mobilised alternative views to those surveyed above. In truth, this agency is not limited to alternative public spheres but is equally discernible among a plethora of Muslim organisations seeking to challenge the negative representation of Muslims in the mainstream media. As Inayat Bunglawala, formerly of the MCB, put it:

> We've often been in a very uneven playing field in the mainstream media, with the tabloid press often rushing to air the most outlandish voices, the most radical voices, at the expense of ordinary Muslims. Because these are often given huge publicity without a necessary context as to how on the fringe the radical groups are or what their numbers amount to compared to the mainstream Muslim view. So in the end the MCB try to counteract that unfair portrayal of the British-Muslim community at the same time as being the focus of it ourselves!
>
> *(Interview)*

Simultaneously, and as an example of what Nancy Fraser (1992) would term 'subaltern-counterpublics', these Muslim media sources 'represent an expanding social field characterised by more than contested authority and by more than proliferating voices or blurred boundaries; central to this expanding public sphere of Islam are new media and interest profiles they advance' (Anderson 2003: 888). The content and outlook of each of these media committees and news sources are inevitably informed by the background of the producer itself, including the ideological or political stance of its editors and journalists. They are also determined by whether the aim is to provide a current affairs source of information or is more concerned with addressing social and cultural issues. For example, *The Invitation* offers an accessible account of cultural affairs, while others, such as *Q-News*, attach much more emphasis to the impact of British and international politics on Muslims in Britain. The latter was created as a fortnightly tabloid publication before it evolved into its current monthly magazine format under the editorship of Fareena Alam. It describes itself as

> Britain's leading Muslim magazine, providing independent analysis, critique and review of politics, culture and ideas. We are read by second and third generation British Muslims, parliamentarians, policy makers and educators. A third of our readership are not Muslim giving us unique place in the market as a publication which communicates the rich Muslim experience to a diverse audience...
>
> The philosophy of *Q-News* is a combination of style, appeal and relevance to the Muslim community living in the west and around the world. Over the years, *Q-News* has repeatedly set the agenda, rather than react to it. Our chief interest lies in the development of a unique and relevant Western Muslim discourse.[5]

Thus, 'while the media-savvy militants capture the attention, particularly of analysts, a quieter drama is unfolding' (Anderson 2003: 889). In these terms of encouraging a 'Western Muslim discourse', Fareena Alam has herself described the issues that most concerned her before taking editorial control:

> I was struggling with questions of who do I want to be: a Muslim journalist or a journalist who happens to be Muslim?
>
> Islam has an incredible capacity to develop distinct cultural forms and expression while maintaining its universal principles ... I want British Islam to reflect the best of my – and others' – faith and citizenship.[6]

While such publications are a fairly recent emergence, they convey a clear desire to move beyond solely Muslim audiences, with the editor of *Impact International* describing his belief that 'in the course of time, the Muslim media are also going to be part of the mainstream' (quoted in Ahmed 2005: 112). Another publication, the *Muslim News*, epitomises this conviction in its determination to reach out beyond its constituency of Muslim readers, while at the same time taking pride in its role in elevating and accentuating a British Muslim consciousness. It states that 'the *Muslim News* has been one of the pioneers of recognising the Muslim community as a diverse faith group with a common British Muslim identity'.[7]

Part of this process has been mediated by a remit in which the *Muslim News* 'reports on what the non-Muslim media does not report' (ibid.). It insists, for example, that 'in its 15 years of publication, it has exposed media establishments' institutionalised Islamophobia on various issues – politics, education, employment and religion' (ibid.). A more recent and perhaps broader development takes the *Muslim News*' concerns and distils them through a movement named ENGAGE.[8] This collective is oriented towards enhancing the active engagement of British Muslim communities in the fields of politics and the media through such means as running seminars for Muslims on how to engage productively with the media by furnishing Muslim audiences with the means to respond effectively to derogatory and inflammatory news stories. It also organises forums for journalists to interact with local Muslim communities, ensuring greater access to Muslim grass roots. Perhaps most challengingly, it also highlights the work of journalists and other public figures promoting anti-Muslim sentiment.

Conclusions and implications

Over 25 years ago, writing in the magazine *Marxism Today*, the Welsh Muslim writer Merryl Wyn Davies (1985) predicted that British Muslims would be 'prepared to organise for issues as they see them: to create a platform for being Muslims in Britain. But there is no obvious political home for this developing Muslim politics.' This was a prescient observation, for Muslims in Britain have done precisely this, but rather than mobilising through a single platform, they have instead sought to stitch their presence into existing tapestries, as well as creating their own where necessary.

Much of this discussion has proceeded without reference to Muslims elsewhere in Europe, a focus that needs to be cognisant of the reality that there are presently more Muslims than Catholics in the Protestant north of Europe, and more Muslims than Protestants in the Catholic south (somewhere between 15 and 20 million; Pew 2008; Klausen 2005). This demands that while public discourse can often become polarized (especially in the media), social science research on the 'Muslim question' must eschew simple binaries between *optimists* (who stress the possibilities of synthesis and innovation, sometimes through the concept of 'Euro-Islam') and *pessimists* (who warn that higher levels of Muslim fertility and alleged cultural assertiveness will subsume Europe into 'Eurabia') (cf. Ramadan 2004; Tibi 2008; Steyn 2006; and Caldwell 2009). Social scientists instead need to establish a meaningful evidence base from which to conceptualise and chart the sociological features that pertain to the post-Second World War development of large-scale Muslim communities in Europe, and especially in the ways in which Muslim identities provide valuable means of resources, refuge and respect in the negotiation of faith and politics in contemporary European societies.

To this end, one of the core implications that arises from this chapter is the need to renew our interpretation of the sociological data centring on Muslim identities in order to provide a *contemporary* reading that moves us past simple accounts of 'first' or 'second generation'. For example, an initial sociological question asked why an attachment to Islam has not been relinquished, as secularisation theories predicted, during the process of migration, post-migration settlement, or indeed with subsequent socialisation in relatively secular European societies (Nielsen 1984). One salient explanation that emerged was that an attachment to Islam provided resources, refuge and respect throughout the migration and resettlement experience (Modood 1988; Werbner 1994; cf. Hirschman 2004). This appeared to be true – with important variations – across a number of sociological cleavages (age, class and gender) among different Muslim ethnic groups (Cesari and McLoughlin 2005). Hence, the Fourth National Survey of Ethnic Minorities (FNSEM) of 1997 identified the tendency for an overarching 'associational identification' with Islam which reoccurs across first- and second-generation Muslims. The FNSEM was a British survey that has been augmented with similar findings in France, Germany and elsewhere in North-Western Europe, most recently by the Gallup Index in 2010.

This does not mean that self-identification as 'Muslim' in Britain has been either exclusive in not permitting different kinds of hybridity (e.g. as 'British-Muslim') or unchanging (e.g. reflecting a different meaning to young Muslims born and brought up in Luton as compared with its meaning for their parents who migrated from Lahore). Nor does it mean that self-identification as a Muslim in Britain has been anchored in a subscription to a single Islamic doctrine (e.g. a literal reading of the Qu'ran or a branch of Islámic jurisprudence) (Roy 2004).

On the contrary, the precise meaning of 'Muslim' has instead taken on a number of competing public forms, some of which have most recently been accentuated in concerns about violent extremism, for example between public categories of 'moderates' and 'Islamists', Sufis and Salafis, etc. (Modood and Ahmad 2007). The key point is that Muslim identities are being shown to contain many *social layers* that are often independent of scriptural texts. For example, a discernible Muslim presence may be strongly observed in the disproportionate support for a political party (the so-called Muslim vote). The same is true of a subscription to and modification of particular business models (sometimes called 'Islamic finance') (Ansari 2004), or a commitment to equalities and anti-discrimination movements and agendas especially (in seeking to have Islamophbia understood as a form of social and not theological discrimination) (Meer, 2008). The same could be said of the community aspiration for post-compulsory education (contributing to a revision of cultural capital theory to incorporate the assets generated in minority religious groups) (Modood 2004).

The ambiguities in these observations permeate the ways in which Muslims have organised and have continued to appropriate the appellation of 'Muslim' without any unanimity on Islamic matters (precisely as Jewish minorities have historically negotiated and continue to debate what being 'Jewish' means). This point is not widely stressed, and as a consequence the dynamic features of Muslims' identities in Britain can too often be reduced to a subscription to Islamic belief and practice. This has its place, and should not be ignored, but rather the distinction should be stressed so that one is not ignored at the expense of registering the other.

Acknowledgements

My thanks to Waqar Ahmed and Ziauddin Sardar for helpful comments on an earlier draft. For a book length treatment of the arguments in this chapter, see Meer (2010).

Notes

1 One might ask, for example, why it is little recognised that Muslims became the first non-Judaeo-Christians to set up places of worship in Britain – as long ago as 1900 (Ansari, 2004), or why the desecration of the Al Asqa mosque in the Israeli-occupied Arab sector of Jerusalem in 1969 provoked greater protest from Muslims in Britain than the incendiary speeches of Enoch Powell (Hiro 1991). This could be augmented by the observation that while first-generation post-immigrant organisations such as the Pakistani Workers Association (PWA) were concerned with organised workers' representation, one of their earliest priorities was to secure funds to build mosques (Meer 2001). One of the questions directly addressed in this chapter builds upon these others, asking why, while coping with being 'the most socially deprived and racially harassed group', Muslims in Britain were moved to campaign against the publication of a novel by Salman Rushdie (Modood 1992: 261)?

2 It should be stressed that this distinction is problematic, but is adopted as a heuristic device to develop this particular point. See Meer's (2010: 212) discussion of Butler (1990) on this point.

3 See: www.mcb.org.uk/vote2005/ (accessed 1 September 2008).

4 Although it is worth noting that securing planning permission to function as a place of worship or education (or both) under the Town and Country Planning Act 1971 is never straightforward (while registration is not a legal requirement, planning permission is).

5 See the *Q-News* website: www.q-news.com/about.htm.

6 Quoted in the NS Interview: 'The petrodollar-funded literalists think their version is the real Islam. I'm for an Islam that is at home in Britain.' Rachel Aspden, *New Statesman*, 27 February 2006. Online, available at: www.newstatesman.com/200602270020.

7 See 'About Us' at *Muslim News*: www.muslimnews.co.uk.

8 See http://iengage.org.uk (accessed 2 March 2009).

References

Ahmed, T. S. (2005) 'Reading between the lines: Muslims and the media', in T. Abbas (ed.) *Muslim Britain: Communities under Pressure*, London: Zed Books.

Anderson, J. W. (2003) 'New media, new publics: reconfiguring the public sphere of Islam', *Social Research* 70 (3): 887–906.

Ansari, H. (2004) *'The Infidel Within': Muslims in Britain since 1800*, London: Hurst.

Archer, L. (2009) 'Race, "face", and masculinity', in P. Hopkins and R. Gale (eds) *Muslims in Britain: Race, Place and Identities*, Edinburgh: Edinburgh University Press.

Aspinall, P. (2000) 'Should a question on "religion" be asked in the 2001 British census? A public policy case in favour', *Social Policy and Administration* 34 (5): 584–600.

Bagguley, P. and Hussain, Y. (2008) *Riotous Citizens: Ethnic Conflict in Multicultural Britain*, London: Ashgate.

Barth, F. (ed.) (1969) *Ethnic Groups and Boundaries: The Social Organization of Culture Difference*, London: Allen & Unwin.

Butler, J. (1992) *Gender Trouble: Feminism and the Subversion of Gender*, London: Routledge.

Caldwell, C. (2010) *Reflections on the Revolution in Europe: Can Europe be the Same with Different People in It?* London: Penguin.

Carter, D. (2005) 'Muslims test their strength as voters and candidates', *The Times* (London), 22 March.

Cesari, J. and McLoughlin, S. (2005) *European Muslims and the Secular State*, Aldershot: Ashgate.

Davies, M. W. (1985) 'A new Muslim politics?', *Marxism Today*, December: 6.

Dwyer, C. (1999) 'Veiled meanings: British Muslim women and the negotiation of differences', *Gender, Place and Culture* 6 (1): 5–26.

Fieldhouse, E. and Cutts, D. (2008) 'Mobilisation or marginalisation? Neighbourhood effects on Muslim electoral registration in Britain in 2001', *Political Studies* 56 (2): 333–354.

Filby, L. (2006) 'Religion and belief', in 'Equalities in Great Britain 1946–2006' (unpublished), EHRC Consultation Papers, Equality and Human Rights Commission, London.

Fraser, N. (1992) 'Rethinking the public sphere: a contribution to the critique of actually existing democracy', in C. Calhoun (ed.) *Habermas and the Public Sphere*, Cambridge, MA: MIT Press.

Greaves, R. (2007) 'A reassement of identity strategies amongst British South Asian Muslims', in J. R. Hinnells (ed.) *Religious Reconstruction in South Asian Diasporas*, Basingstoke: Palgrave Macmillan.

Halliday, F. (1999) '"Islamophobia" reconsidered', *Ethnic and Racial Studies* 22 (5): 892–902.

Hattersley, R. (2005) 'I took the Muslim vote for granted – but that has all changed…', *Guardian* (London), 8 April 2005.

Hewitt, I. (1998) Final report, *Report: The Magazine from the Association of Teachers and Lecturers*, April: 10–25.

Hiro, D. (1991) *White British/Black British*, London: Grafton Books.

Hirschman, C. (2004) 'The role of religion in the origins and adaptation of immigrant groups in the United States', *International Migration Review* 38 (3): 1206–1233.

Imtiaz, A. (2010) *Wandering Lonely in a Crowd: Reflections on the Muslim Condition in the West*, Markfield, Leicestershire: Kube.

Jacobson, J. (1997a) 'Perceptions of Britishness', *Nations and Nationalism* 3 (2): 165–179.

Jacobson, J. (1997b) 'Religion and ethnicity: dual and alternative sources of identity among young British Pakistanis', *Ethnic and Racial Studies* 20 (2): 238–256.

Jacobson, J. (1998) *Islam in Transition: Religion and Identity among British Pakistani Youth*, London: Routledge.

Kelly, P. (1999) 'Integration and identity in Muslim schools: Britain, United States and Montreal', *Islam and Christian–Muslim Relations* 10 (2): 197–217.

Klausen, J. (2005) *The Islamic Challenge*, Oxford: Oxford University Press.

Knott, K. and Khocker, S. (1993) 'Religious and ethnic identity among young Muslim women in Bradford', *Journal of Ethnic and Migration Studies* 19 (4): 593–610.

Meer, N. (2001) 'The activities of Indian workers' associations and immigrant organisations and amalgamations in Britain 1955–1974', unpublished BA thesis, Essex University.

Meer, N. (2008) 'The politics of voluntary and involuntary identities: are Muslims in Britain an ethnic, racial or religious minority?', *Patterns of Prejudice* 41 (5): 61–81.

Meer, N. (2009) 'Identity articulations, mobilisation and autonomy in the movement for Muslim schools in Britain', *Race, Ethnicity and Education* 12 (3): 379–398.

Meer, N. (2010) *Citizenship, Identity and the Politics of Multiculturalism*, Basingstoke: Palgrave Macmillan.

Meer, N. (2012) 'Misrecognising Muslim consciousness in Europe', *Ethnicities* 12 (2). Online.

Meer, N. and Noorani, T. (2008) 'A sociological comparison of anti-Semitism and anti-Muslim sentiment in Britain', *Sociological Review* 56 (2): 195–219.

Modood, T. (1988) '"Black, racial equality and Asian identity', *New Community* 14 (3): 397–404.

Modood, T. (1992) *Not Easy Being British: Colour, Culture and Citizenship*, Stoke-on-Trent: Runnymede Trust and Trentham Books.

Modood, T. (1994) 'Muslim identity: real or imagined?', CSIC Paper Europe no. 12, Selly Oaks Colleges, Birmingham.

Modood, T. (1997a) '"Difference", cultural racism and anti-racism', in P. Werbner and T. Modood (eds) *Debating Cultural Hybridity: Multi-cultural Identities and the Politics of Anti-racism*, London: Zed Books.

Modood, T. (ed.) (1997b) *Church, State and Religious Minorities*, London: Policy Studies Institute.

Modood, T. (2004) 'Capitals, ethnic identity and educational qualifications', *Cultural Trends* 13 (2): 87–105.

Modood, T. (2005) 'Disaffected Muslims will make their votes count', *Financial Times*, 28 April.

Modood, T. (2007) *Multiculturalism, a Civic Idea*, Cambridge: Polity Press.

Modood, T. and Ahmad, F. (2007) 'British Muslim perspectives on multiculturalism', *Theory, Culture and Society* 24 (2): 187–213.

Morey, P. and Yaqin, A. (2011) *Framing Muslims: Stereotyping and Representation after 9/11*, Cambridge, MA: Harvard University Press.

Nielsen, J. (1984) 'Muslim immigration and settlement in Britain', Research Papers: Muslims in Europe no. 21, Centre for the Study of Islam and Christian–Muslim Relations (CSIC), University of Birmingham.

O'Toole, T. and Gale, R. (2009) 'Young people and faith activism: British Muslim youth, globalisation and the *umma*', in A. Dinham, R. Furbey and V. Lowndes (eds) *Faith in the Public Realm: Controversies, Policies and Practices*, Bristol: Policy Press.

Peach, C. and Gale, R. (2003) 'Muslims, Hindus, and Sikhs in the new religious landscape of England', *Geographical Review* 93 (4): 469–490.

Pew Global Attitudes Survey Report (2008) 'Unfavorable views of Jews and Muslims on the increase in Europe'. Online, available at: www.pewglobal.org/files/pdf/262.pdf.

Ramadan, T. (2004) *Western Muslims and the Future of Islam*, New York: Oxford University Press.

Roy, O. (2004) *Globalised Islam: The Search for a New Ummah*, London: Hurst.

Samad, Y. (1992) 'Book-burning and race relations: political mobilisation of Bradford Muslims', *New Community* 18 (4): 507–519.

Skinner, G. (2002) 'Religious pluralism and school provision in Britain', *Intercultural Education* 13 (2): 171–181.

Soper, J. C. and Fetzer, J. S. (2010) 'The not-so-naked public square: Islam and the state in Western Europe', *Orient: German Journal for Politics, Economics and Culture of the Middle East* 51 (2): 6–14.

Statham, P. (2005) 'The need to take religion seriously for understanding multicultural controversies: institutional channeling versus cultural identification?', in M. Giugni and F. Passy (eds) *Dialogues in Migration Policy*, Lanham, MD: Lexington Books.

Steyn, M. (2006) *America Alone: The End of the World as We Know It*, New York: Regnery Publishing.

Tibi, B. (2008) *Political Islam, World Politics and Europe: Democratic Peace and Euro-Islam versus Global Jihad*, London: Routledge.

Tinker, C. and Smart, A. (2011) 'Constructions of collective Muslim identity by advocates of Muslim schools in Britain', *Ethnic and Racial Studies*. Online.

Werbner, P. (1994) 'Islamic radicalism and the Gulf War', in B. Lewis and D. Schnapper (eds) *Muslims in Europe*, Oxford: Berg.

9

'CREATING A SOCIETY OF SHEEP'?

British Muslim elite on mosques and imams

Waqar I. U. Ahmad

> Mosques have to change 'to survive and to cater for the flocks' as there are 'a lot of angry people who are pissed off' with mosques.
>
> *(Respondent 24, male writer and academic)*

> [Imams] are not allowing individuals to think for themselves and to explore the texts of the Scriptures for themselves and they are creating a society of sheep ... if we remove the middleman, we as individuals would access the Scriptures and take the time, even if it takes 20 years, to think about what it is, to think about the content, make our own decisions and make our own journey and path to God.
>
> *(Respondent 26, female artist)*

> Now all that [mosques as seats of debate and learning, including acting as publishing houses] has been reduced to a kind of monolithic notion of a mosque which is simply for prayer and some of the mosques actually closed [outside prayer times] ... then this is a mosque only for the Wahabis and the mystics should not bother coming in and the women should come from the back ... [It] performs no other function except prayers ... I think the tradition of openness, not just in mosques, but ... within Islam, has basically died down.
>
> *(Respondent 27, male polymath and public intellectual)*

On the basis of conversations with 27 'elite' Muslims – academics, artists, writers, public intellectuals, policy-makers, parliamentarians and senior local politicians – this chapter explores the current role of British mosques. In these conversations, respondents lament the diminution of the mosque to little more than a place for public performance of male piety, divorced from community concerns and largely irrelevant to Muslim women. While some noted welcome changes in the functions and governance of mosques, the desire of many respondents to see mosques as community hubs, seats of learning, spaces for dialogue and contestation, and vital bridges to people of other faiths and of no faith remains a distant dream. However, many noted that Britain offers the political and legal space for theological innovation, and some important provocations in re-imagining the mosque are discussed in the chapter.

Britain is home to around 2 million Muslims, two-thirds of them from the Indian subcontinent, with sizeable populations of Turkish, Arab and African Muslims. Early mosques provided spaces of safety and community-making, and helped to maintain social order and to transmit religion and culture to future generations (Ansari 2003; Biondo 2006; Brown 2008; Humphrey 1987; Reeber 1991; Woodlock 2010). Ansari (2003) notes that the first purpose-built British mosque was created in 1889 in Woking. Today, Britain houses 1,500–3,000 mosques (estimates vary wildly) serving Muslims of different ethnicities and denominations. Against a trend of declining religiousness in Britain (Voas and Crockett 2005), Islam remains an actively practised religion, across generations.

The making of British mosques has not been trouble-free. Conflicts have ranged from open racism and Islamophobia, to campaigns couched in the language of threats to national heritage, assaults on local character, and fears over health, safety, noise pollution and traffic congestion (Ansari 2003; Eade 1989; Gale 2005; McLoughlin 2005; Naylor and Ryan 2002). Much of the British literature links symbolic meanings of mosques with the politics of the built environment and questions of national character, themes also prevalent in North American (Lotfi 2001; Metcalf 1996), Australian (Dunn *et al.* 2007; Humphrey 1987) and European literature on mosques (Cesari 2005; Maussen 2007), with occasional forays into the study of form, functions, or governance of, or the imposition of external agendas on British mosques (Brown 2008; Dyke 2009; McLoughlin 2005; Wardak 2002).

More recently, however, there are hopeful signs of an end to such conflicts in high Muslim density areas of British (McLoughlin 2005) and European cities (Cesari 2005), with only occasional incidents of open hostility towards the creation or expansion of mosques (see, for example, the opposition by the Conservative cabinet minister Michael Gove to the creation of a mosque in Surrey (Taylor 2010)). Construction of mosques, as well as practices such as burying the Muslim dead, 'have helped to create space that demonstrates the changing nature of Muslim "rootedness" within the British environment' (Ansari 2007: 545). Mosques are now as ubiquitous a feature of Britain's cityscapes and townscapes as are churches and parks.

While early mosques were inclusive of ethnic as well as denominational diversity, in a trend also experienced by other faiths (e.g. Sikhs in Bradford – see Singh 1992), fragmentation on ethnic and theological grounds quickly took hold as communities became established. Interestingly, this fragmentation was not confined to the living but also affected the dead. Ansari (2007: 562) notes that Brookwood, one of the early graveyards to cater for Muslim dead, now has 'separately dedicated burial plots for Sunnis, Ithna Ashari, Ismaili and Bohra Shias and, since 1975, Ahmadiyyas'.

While important to religious and social life, mosques are attracting internal and external criticism. Dyke (2009) reports shortcomings along with some positive initiatives, including attempts to engage women. Her report is critical of, among other things, importation of imams, their education and training, mosque governance, children's Islamic education and women's exclusion from mosques. Women's position in Muslim communities, including relation to and relative exclusion from the mosque, is increasingly being challenged by Muslim women (Barlas 2002; Mernissi 1991; Wadud 1999) and men (Sardar 2011b). Dyke reports that just over half of the mosques provided facilities for women and only 2 per cent had women on governance committees. Male interpretations of Islam, based on decontexualised and dehistoricised readings of the Qur'an and selective emphasis on a few Hadith (traditions of the Prophet), are argued to diminish women's position in Islam (see Barlas 2002; Mernissi 1991; Sardar 2011b). Religious leaders are criticised by Ajijola (1998) for the diminution of Islam and its increasing irrelevance to believers' lives.

In recent years the British government has attempted to strengthen links with Britain's Muslim communities, while also introducing policies, in the guise of 'social cohesion', that have alienated Muslims by portraying them in terms of threats to national security (Glynn 2009). In cultivating bridges to the Muslim communities, both the recent Labour and the current (2012) Conservative–Liberal Democratic governments have been promiscuous with their affections, shifting favours from the Muslim Council of Britain (MCB) to the Sufi Council, the British Muslim Forum and, more recently, the Quilliam Foundation, depending on these organisations' willingness to do the government's bidding. The unceremonial ditching of the largest umbrella Muslim organisation, the MCB, by the previous Labour government (and continued by the current Conservative–Liberal Democratic government) shows the fragility of the formal state's relationship with Muslim communities. The closeness to government of the Quilliam Foundation, with its single-issue focus on addressing radicalisation, reflects how the Muslim community is now viewed by the government – first and foremost as a security concern. In this discourse, mosques are seen as both the seats of and a potential solution to radicalisation and Islamist violence (Brown 2008). Recently, the government has established the Mosques and Imams Advisory Board (MINAB) in a bid to regulate mosques and imams. The government has also made pronouncements over gender equality in the mosque (see Brown 2008). However, this interest is not benign (Brown 2008; Glynn 2009; House of Commons 2010). Government's support for women's participation is designed to feminise and pacify mosque space and male radicalism, and to counter the mosques' assumed divisive role in society.

Researchers have reported the *biraderi* control of Britain's mosques by 'babas' (elderly men) with limited education or professional skills (McLoughlin 2005). *Biraderi* forms an important locus of political authority, social and financial support, and personal as well as group identity, and serves as a potential marriage market (Talbot 1998). In the central Punjab area of Pakistan, where I was born, someone without a strong *biraderi* would be referred to as 'having no arms'. A role as chair or member of the mosque governing committee gives these 'babas' status in and outside of *biraderi* both in Britain and in ancestral villages and towns; and it enables them to fight off challenges to their notions of true Islam from the younger generation as well as Muslims of other denominations. Such power will therefore not be easily given away. Foreign, particularly Saudi Arabian, sponsorship of some of Europe's mosques is also noted as a problem (Klausen 2005), propagating a literalist and conservative theology often termed 'Wahabism'. Such sponsorship is not confined to the United Kingdom: Ghosal (2010) criticises Arab funding for the 'assault' on the South Asian 'syncretic and inclusive' Islam. Others have criticised the reduction of Islam to ritualised and uncritical practice of traditions (Barlas 2002; Rahman 1998) – something the mosques reflect and promote.

However, there is some evidence of mosques beginning to change to accommodate worshippers' needs (Ansari 2003; Dyke 2009), such as involving women and young people, providing social welfare services and being more willing to engage in dialogue with non-Muslim communities. And as Samad (1992) noted in relation to the Rushdie affair, mosques do have the power to mobilise Muslim communities on certain issues.

Sociologists have regarded elite studies as providing important windows into the workings of society (Savage and Williams 2008). The views of elite Muslims about challenges facing their communities are not well researched. A recent study (Modood and Ahmad 2007) has explored the views of 'Muslim professionals' in relation to multiculturalism. The study reported here is the first of its kind, exploring the perspectives of Britain's Muslim elite – politicians, intellectuals and policy leaders – on Britain's mosques.

Methods

This chapter is based on qualitative interviews, with 27 prominent or elite Muslims (10 women and 17 men), conducted between late 2008 and mid-2010. Following Scott (2008), I define 'elites' as people in positions of influence because of their formal roles, status within civil society, political or representational power, or involvement in professions or government. Three broad categories of 'elite' – political, policy and academic/intellectual – with considerable internal diversity were interviewed. For example, four of the seven political elite were parliamentarians (representing both houses of Parliament), two were prospective parliamentary candidates, one of these joining Parliament in the 2010 general election, and the remaining one was a senior local politician and a one-time lord mayor of a major city. The policy elite included senior civil servants, local authority chief officers and voluntary-sector leaders. Finally, the academic and intellectual elite included seven senior academics, two writers and an artist.

My analysis is based on two types of insights. First, many of the respondents recount their own experiences of Islam and gender relations in Britain. Their own position as elites is significant here in that they may be important role models for others in the community. Second, they offer their perspectives on what they observe taking place in the Muslim communities around them. As these two types of insights are mutually consistent, I do not distinguish between them in what follows. An earlier article based on these conversations has explored the making and representation of Muslim identity (Ahmad and Evergeti 2010).

Findings

Mosque development was a key concern of first-generation Muslims (see Ansari 2003). Mosques provided a focus for religious activity and identity affirmation, a meeting point and a sanctuary, as well as a vehicle for maintaining social order, replicating tradition and establishing boundaries of identity and behaviour (Ansari 2003; Dunn *et al.* 2007; Wardak 2002). While housed in cramped spaces, they were inclusive institutions, accommodating differences of theology, national origin, region and language. A highly educated and high-profile imam, closely involved in the Federation of Student Islamic Societies in 1960s, has established 16 mosques and welcomed this inclusiveness:

> I founded the [X] mosque. There are 39 different nationalities, cultures and at least 19 or 20 different schools of thought of Islam ... [represented], but all pray together under me – Shia, Sunni, Wahabi, Sufi, all pray with me.
>
> *(Respondent 14, senior imam and scholar)*

However, openness did not last long. Respondent 27 was concerned about an increasing reductivism in Islam – used here in the sense of diminution, curtailment and exclusivity – where a group argues that their way is 'not just the best way but the only way of doing things' (polymath and public intellectual – see also Rahman 1998; Ghosal 2010). The subsequent fragmentation of mosques along denominational, ethnic and linguistic lines reflects both this reductivism and the transplantation of traditions of the worshippers' countries of origin to their new home in Britain. As communities became established, they replicated traditional sectarian and ethnic divides; such fragmentation accelerated and ossified with the appointment of, almost exclusively, imported imams loyal to particular reductive theologies associated with particular regional and ethnic communities (see Singh 1992, for a study of a Sikh community).

Inclusive congregations are now the preserve of a few 'central' mosques such as Regent's Park Mosque in London, or mosques in small towns with small populations of ethnically, linguistically and denominationally diverse Muslims. Here the general inclusiveness also tends to go hand in hand with English as the lingua franca of mosque business, with Arabic remaining the language of formal, ritual prayers. During my years in York, in the early 1990s, I witnessed this diversity in what was then the city's only mosque, where the congregation was mixed ethnically and denominationally, with English as the common language. In contrast, Bradford mosques tended to be denominationally and ethnically more exclusive.

The fragmentation took hold quickly and was sometimes bad-tempered. Many noted that the notion of a collective Muslim Ummah, though more widely espoused by the second generation and powerful in response to adversity (Ahmad and Evergeti 2010; Samad 1992), is insufficient for maintaining cross-ethnic or cross-denominational alliances. This was already a problem by the late 1970s and spilled over into turf wars over mosque ownership and control:

> [For example] Barelvis were buying a place and the Wahabis were coming to take it away. So we didn't have a democratic process. They would bring a truckload of people and beat their opponents and take over.
>
> *(Respondent 14, senior imam and scholar)*

Ethnic and historical differences intersected with denominational subtleties. So, for example, the historical distrust between the Turkish and Arab communities (Turks feeling betrayed by Arabs over the demise of the Ottoman Empire), combined with, respectively, adherence to Sufi or Wahabist theologies created competition:

> So if you're an Arab community trying to represent Islam in one particular place, then the Turkish Muslims feel that that place has been lost. So they try to represent Islam there because they feel that their Anatolian Sufi-orientated Islam is the authentic Islam and the Arabs obviously feel, you know, repulsed by the word ... Sufi and Sufism, so they try to bring in their 'unadulterated' Islam and they feel that that's authentic. So there's definitely a competition between the two.... Muslims are not great at alliances.
>
> *(Respondent 11, male researcher, head of a think tank)*

Equally, the ill feelings between Bangladeshis and Pakistanis over the 1971 separation of Bangladesh from Pakistan, led to tensions between these communities in Bradford:

> [W]e used to live not far from here now, in the Valley Parade area, and in the early [19]80s we saw a lot of Bangladeshis coming in, so [although] we were all Muslims, but as Bangladeshis came in, 'let's move from there', you know.
>
> *(Respondent 1, male head of a social development charity)*

As one denominational group may define its own authenticity in opposition to the presumed corrupted faith of other sects, conflicts over dates for Ramadan or Eid can symbolise this clash between truth and corruption. Further, foreign sponsorship can result in mosques aligning Ramadan or Eid celebrations with their sponsor countries. Bizarre reasons are sometimes offered for fragmentation, noted a Muslim parliamentarian:

> [W]e will blame everybody else [for internal divisions], except ourselves. I invited ... *'ulama e karaam* [respected religious leaders] and asked, 'Why can't we celebrate Eid on one [agreed] day? And you will be shocked that some of them said, 'Americans don't want us to celebrate Eid on one day.'
>
> *(Respondent 7, Muslim parliamentarian)*

While praising the 'first generation' for having established mosques, respondents regarded the continued control of mosques by the 'first generation', coupled with the practice of importing imams from countries of origin, as increasingly problematic.

Relevant to community needs?

Respondents had varying degrees of interaction with the mosque. Women rarely ventured into the mosque. Men who had attended as children did not have warm memories of mosques. An academic and writer remembered the mosque as propagating an Islam of fear and intolerance, involving 'a good *phaintee*' (beating), resenting questioning and emphasising literalist acceptance of traditions, at odds with the 'woolly liberal' experience of school (Respondent 24, male academic and writer). A social researcher who initially attended the mosque with her brothers noted that females were largely absent from the early British mosques, or, if permitted, then only so up to their pre-pubescent years (Respondent 19, female social researcher).

It was generally argued that mosques continue to propagate an Islam in which reductive notions of piety, demonstrated through appearance (beard, scarf), ritual observance and unquestioned acceptance (*taqlid*), are regarded as supreme Islamic virtues, and learning, scholarship, ethics or public service have been excised from core Islamic values; Wardak (2002) notes *sabaq* (Qur'anic 'lessons') and prayers as the two functions of the mosque. It troubled respondents that mosques and imams were 'creating a society of sheep' (Respondent 26, female artist), as opposed to independent critical thinkers able to engage with religion intelligently, as a guide to productive living and the making a contribution to society. Respondent 27 has studied the evolution of Islam and argued that the reductivism has also impacted on the form and function of the mosque:

> Now all that has been reduced to a kind of monolithic notion of a mosque which is simply for prayer, and some of the mosques actually closed [outside prayer times] ... then this is a mosque only for the Wahabis, and the mystics should not bother coming in, and the women should come from the back ... [It] performs no other function except prayers ... Mosques have become very boring, monolithic institutions. And the architecture now reflects that.... I think the tradition of openness, not just in mosques but ... within Islam, has basically died down, and it didn't happen overnight.
>
> *(Respondent 27, male polymath and public intellectual)*

This reductivism has led to the loss of independent thinking (*ijtihad*), the removal of democratic decision-making (*ijma*) and its replacement with imitation or unquestioned acceptance (*taqlid*), argued Respondent 27 and others (see Arkoun 1998; Barlas 2002; Sardar 2003). As religious innovation, equated in Wahabist theology with corruption and pollution of the authentic, has become discredited, all innovation has become suspect. In many Muslim countries, rote learning has radiated from madrasahs into the national educational system as the only means of learning; children, as empty vessels, are filled with inherited, unchanging and never-to-be-questioned knowledge. Ordinary people, especially women, therefore must be stopped from interpreting the Qur'an and traditions for fear of misinterpretation (see Barlas 2002; Sardar 2003: various chapters). Some argued that such fear of misinterpretation is dehumanising and hampers interpretation and formulation of an Islam relevant to our times (e.g. Respondent 26 and 27; see Sardar 2011b). Sardar has argued for democratising the engagement and interpretation of the Qur'an. The control by *'ulama* (Islamic legal scholars) over the power to define has disempowered the Muslim publics, especially women (Barlas 2002; Mernissi 1991; Wadud 1999). This reduced, medieval Islam being propagated by imams, 'these frogs in a well' (Respondent 10, male retired chief education officer), is incapable of connecting Islam to the needs of the twenty-first century. The artist, Respondent 26, argued that we cannot regard this reduction as benign. Engagement with knowledge and society is a religious duty – or 'God's work', according to Respondent 12, a public service leader, and Respondent 11, who heads a think tank – and will only come through the removal of the 'middlemen'. Unlike Christianity (with the pope or the bishops) and Judaism (the chief rabbi), Islam shuns institutionalised religious hierarchy, giving scope to believers to interpret the Qur'an and the traditions – a power that people must wrest from the imams and religious leaders. Imams

> are not allowing individuals to think for themselves and to explore the texts of the Scriptures for themselves and they are creating a society of sheep . . . if we remove the middleman, we as individuals would access the Scriptures and take the time, even if it takes 20 years, to think about what it is, to think about the content, make our own decisions and make our own journey and path to God.
>
> *(Respondent 26, female artist)*

This respondent argued, passionately, that 'a mosque shouldn't just be about safety. God isn't just about creating a safe space.' Mosques have to be spaces for critical dialogue, thinking, learning, connecting and serving; and for dissent and innovation. Respondent 27 noted that mosques were once social and intellectual hubs, often also functioning as publishing houses; books were 'published' through public dictation by authors, noted down by *warraqs* (learned scribes) and, after the author's *ijaza* (approval), reproduced for distribution (see Sardar 1993). The great mosques connected the religious with the social and the natural, including the development of astronomy in the Muslim world (Masood 2009). It is not an accident that some great seats of learning, and not just of religious knowledge, such as the Mustansariya in Baghdad (where Ghazali was a professor, and which may have given western academia the notion of 'chair' as 'professor', as the teacher was the one who had a chair, with learners sitting on the floor) and Al-Azhar in Cairo, developed out of mosques.

For some, the interconnections should extend to celebrating common values between religions and cultures. A female writer and academic who has studied the intertextuality between South Asian religions, with a particular focus on Sufi poetry and its propagation through public performance, lamented the sacralisation of the mosque and the regressive 'profanisation' and 'othering' of much of life, especially music (Respondent 25, female writer and academic). This 'Arabization' has turned, as Ghosal (2010: 69) notes, 'a syncretic and inclusive Islam to a puritanical and exclusivist one under the influence of ideas, norms, practices, and finances flowing from the Arab world'. This has excised fun from the mosque. She thought it ironic that *qawwali* (devotional music popularised in the West by the late Nusrat Fateh Ali Khan), so important in the propagation of Islam in South Asia, continues to be performed in Hindu and Sikh temples but not in the mosque.

So how do British mosques meet the needs of their Muslim communities?

Many respondents regarded Britain's mosques as unfit for purpose. A local government chief officer, a devout Muslim, lamented:

> [T]hey are places for you to worship . . . – what else do they do? They provide madrasahs, they provide Qur'an teaching, usually parrot fashion. . . . When you look at the disturbances on the streets . . ., Burnley, Oldham, Bradford – whatnot – and even the 7/7 bombers . . . they are probably all beneficiaries of our mosque system in this country. They have all done the two hours a day, four days a week for five years to get through and celebrate completing the Qur'an – what difference has it made to their lives in terms of their understanding of their faith, the responsibility it puts on them as a citizen. . .? I would say very little, and the mosque system hasn't understood that and isn't prepared to challenge itself.
>
> *(Respondent 9, male local government chief officer)*

Mosques have failed not only to provide leadership at times of adversity (with some exceptions; see Samad 1992) but even to acknowledge community issues as legitimate concerns for them; lack of leadership from mosques in relation to street disturbances of 2001, the 7 July bombings in London, the 11 September attacks in New York, poor educational outcomes, domestic relations and violence, and unemployment were given as examples of the irrelevance of mosques to major concerns of the day. A senior parliamentarian felt that they were irrelevant to community needs, and another parliamentarian proposed an independent Muslim think tank to provide creative thinking on Islam, as mosques and imams had proved incapable of such thinking (Respondents 1 and 2). The local government chief officer introduced above criticised parents for cynically using mosques to absolve themselves of personal responsibility towards their children's Islamic education:

> Actually we need a new system and parents are to blame, of course, because the parent approaches, 'well, send them off – that's eight hours a week, my duty done . . .' I think probably the best service that mosques could do, and it is quite radical, is to close all the madrasahs. The parents would have to wake up to their responsibility for their children and their Islamic, spiritual education.
>
> *(Respondent 9)*

Disappointed with mosques, many respondents had made other arrangements for their children's Islamic education. An activist and imam's daughter, among others, felt that Islam was best learned on 'mother's lap' or on father's shoulders (Respondent 15, female activist, social entrepreneur and head of a public service charity). Sacralisation of Islamic teaching by relegating it to a mosque was a problem; it separated it from other forms of learning and from domestic and public life. An Arab academic's children attended a language school for Arabic and Qur'anic learning (Respondent 23, female senior academic). Respondent 1, with others, established a weekend school for Arab children, teaching Arab history and citizenship and not just religious education (Respondent 1, male academic). The lawyer daughter of the renowned polymath and public intellectual, Respondent 27, had completed a London University Master's in Islamic studies and Shariah, as part of her religious education; his advice to my children was to do the same.

Mosque education posed other challenges too. Respondents argued that children are exposed to clashes of fundamentalisms: imams abhor the values of the secular West, while schoolteachers despise the 'irrational, medieval teaching' in the mosque (e.g. Respondent 10, retired chief education officer and religious scholar, and Respondent 24, writer and academic). The retired chief education officer faced this as a major challenge in his professional life; he felt that in some areas the situation was no better now.

Key challenges

Foreign sponsorship of mosques, the first generation's unwillingness to shed control of mosques, the training and capacity of imams, and women's exclusion from mosques were highlighted as key challenges.

Foreign sponsorship

Respondents identified Saudi Arabia, Libya and Iran as sponsors of many British mosques, thus potentially influencing their theology and character. Several noted that these countries saw an opening for greater involvement in Britain's mosques following the Rushdie affair. One well-informed respondent (Respondent 14) estimated that the Saudis sponsor around 150 mosques and 120 imams in Britain; Libya and Iran have also sponsored mosques, religious colleges and prominent individuals (the late Dr Zaki Badawi's institution was, and remains, funded by a Libyan foundation). For many, foreign sponsorship was arrogant and cynical – a means of buying influence and robbing Islam of vitality, rootedness and fun. A senior academic summarises this well:

> [T]he problem ... is we still haven't developed our own institutions and broken the link with the governments that have ... failed to provide economic opportunities for us in our home country, but ... they want to control the way we practise Islam in Britain. I have done research on the Saudi links with British Muslims ... one of the detrimental consequences of oil wealth is for the Saudis to engage in this transnational spread of the very, very limited interpretation of Islam that everybody now calls Wahabism.
>
> *(Respondent 23, female senior academic)*

She argues that the Saudi strategy of investment to gain influence over British Muslims has largely failed, given that British Muslims were critical of the Saudi Arabian role in both the Gulf wars. However, given Kibria's (2008) contention that the 'new Islam' of some young people is heavily influenced by conservative, Wahabist theology, in opposition to their parents' more syncretic and regional notions of Islam, this respondent may be underestimating the significance of Saudi sponsorship. Klausen (2005) addressed some of these issues in her Europe-wide study.

The first generation's control of mosques

The mosque elders' poor education and professional skills compromise their capacity to govern, innovate, negotiate with councils, deal with the media, or provide leadership over major challenges. *Biraderi* domination in South Asian-led mosques restricted the pool of potential leaders, argued several respondents (e.g. Respondent 9; Respondent 21, a male senior academic; and Respondent 24; and see also McLoughlin 2005).

> The Birmingham and Manchester mosque model was largely dependent on retired factory workers ... – manual labourers and so on, people with minimum levels of education and a minimum level of understanding of the broader aspects of their faith – ... they ran a mosque in the way that they have always understood it and they couldn't step outside that.
>
> *(Respondent 9)*

And a sociologist respondent described mosque committees as clubs for the elderly and the unemployed (Respondent 21). A number of respondents noted that the first generation believe they have a divine right to lead:

> But these guys have ... to allow younger Muslims to come forward to be imams, to be Muslim leaders ... Somehow, those who come from back home, they have this superiority problem, they think they know it better and ... they have been given a God-given right to lead ... Muslims in this country.
>
> *(Respondent 18, male academic)*

Several noted that control would be difficult to wrest from the first generation; as noted, the mosque power base gives them identity and status both in Britain and in the countries of origin, something they will fight to protect (see also McLoughlin 2005). Others were critical of the lack of strong second-generation leaders coming through (Respondent 3, local politician and one-time lord mayor of a major city). And Respondent 27 criticised Muslim intellectuals and professionals, who were quick to criticise but loath to lead mosques. It is significant that with the exception of the two imams and the head of a think tank, very few respondents, including those with a strong Islamic identity, were involved in the governance of their local mosque.

The trouble with imams

Imams were criticised as ill-educated, conservative men propagating medieval theologies, incapable of interpreting Islam for the present day, and sometimes in the employ of foreign governments. Imams, who continue to be imported largely from the Indian subcontinent and Saudi Arabia, were a bigger problem than poor governance structures. Respondents regarded imported imams as unacceptable, although some made an exception for 'learned imams' (Respondent 2, a parliamentarian). They feared that many imams cannot relate to life in Britain and therefore do not understand issues facing Muslims, far less being able to build bridges with non-Muslim communities. Many have limited and parochial understanding of Islam and cannot relate to the questioning, critical approach of young people. They also import with them the conservative values of their countries of origin. This is happening at the same time as the Muslim community of Britain is developing an understanding of Islam that may be more relevant to life in Britain (Ramadan 2004).

> We have got ... [to the] second or third generation – how are those people going to relate to somebody who comes from wherever – from the Imam University in Riyadh? Who doesn't even speak English who is installed in a mosque in Britain? ... I strongly object to that.
>
> *(Respondent 23, female senior academic)*

A retired chief education officer and religious scholar elaborated on the same point in relation to children's Islamic teaching, arguing that these imams may be doing their best, 'but because of their own ... narrow perspective of life, they don't engage the children into thinking for themselves' (Respondent 10)

Respondent 3, who as a city elder attends different mosques so as not to appear partisan, highlighted some imams' disconnection from Britain. He publicly criticised one imam and his mosque committee; the imam made his 'blood boil' by 'shouting' in his *jumma khutba* (Friday sermon), '*YAD RAKHEN, HAM DIAR-E-GHAIR MEIN REHTAY HAIN*' (remember, we live in a foreign country). This respondent argued that he, and the majority of the congregation, regarded Britain as their home. With about half of Britain's Muslims now being British born, this equation of Britain with a 'foreign country' is becoming increasingly absurd.

Few British mosques have British-born and -educated imams; and even British imam training centres are failing to make theology relevant to Britain. Many respondents had observed the development of imam training centres and were critical of their 'medieval' syllabuses and domination by Jamat Islami, Deobandis and the Tablighi Jamat (e.g. Respondents 14; 17, a radical imam; and 27).

> They insist you must study [the] Gujarati language first, you must study Urdu first, and then they bring out a hundred years old syllabuses in order to teach them in the same language ... 'If a dog died in your pond you would have to take sixty buckets of water out of the pond, then the water will be clean for your ablutions...' – these are outdated books ... written ... by the Tablighi Jamat ... not suitable for England, even if translated into English.... And ... they don't update Islamic knowledge, after the medieval period.
>
> *(Respondent 14, senior imam and scholar)*

Respondents were particularly concerned about making Islam current, relevant and rational – to engage with current issues, such as social change, ethics, the environment and public service through the Qur'anic edicts of *tatafakaroon*, *yatadabbaroon* and *tata'aqaloon* (think, explore, critically reason); see Barlas (2002), Mernissi (1991), Ramadan (2004, 2009) and Sardar (2003).

> I criticise (traditional) training courses ... There's no improvement in the religion, there's no improvement in theology, there's no ... posing questions which we Muslims should ask, because the Qur'an commands us to ponder upon [them] – *tatafakaroon, yatadabbaroon, tata'aqqaloon.*
>
> *(Respondent 14, senior imam and scholar)*

The Friday sermon, designed to link *deen* (faith) with *duniya* (worldly affairs), has also become reduced (Respondents 17, radical imam, and 27). In most mosques the sermon was given in Arabic, and often written by a long-dead religious figure. Once a vehicle for weekly dialogue with and between the community, the *khutba* has become a ritualised recitation of standardised Arabic language sermons understood by few, often not even the imams. In contrast, Reeber (1991) argues that *khutbas* in French mosques were beginning to address, in the 1990s, issues confronting Muslims (largely of North African and Turkish origin), but this has not been the case with Britain's Muslims, who are largely of South Asian origin. And while the imams may precede the formal *khutba* with a speech in Urdu, Bangla, Gujarati, Turkish or, as Dyke (2009) notes, sometimes in English, these speeches often focus on esoteric theological minutiae designed to cement the imam's scholarly credentials, rather than addressing pressing issues of contemporary social relevance.

The senior imam and scholar introduced above (Respondent 14) has argued for the professionalisation of imams, including compulsory registration, but regards the MINAB initiative as inadequate (see Ahmad and Evergeti 2010); in contrast, a Muslim member of the previous Labour government told me that he welcomed this as an important early intervention in regulating imams and mosques.

Mosques and women

Many argued that mosques cannot be inclusive without involving women, while some women regarded this as a 'red herring', arguing that they were more concerned about personal rights, their children's education and well-being, and domestic equality, and that the mosque is peripheral to women's religious performance and identity.

> [I]t's . . . a red herring that takes away from the actual problems of the Muslim community . . . [which] go far beyond the . . . four walls . . . of the mosque. Most of the actual problems of the Muslim community are within education . . . or within the home.
>
> *(Respondent 15, female activist, consultant and head of a public service charity)*

Others argued that, while not satisfactory, there was already greater participation of women in mosques in Britain than in South Asia or the Middle East. Some argued, however, that women's lack of enthusiasm for engagement in mosques reflects the second-class status that mosques accord them (e.g. Respondent 27). A female senior academic who only attended during Ramadan was put off by foreign sponsorship and

> the competition between big men with big egos who want to dominate certain mosques. . . . Then also the differences in interpretations of Islam. You go sometimes, people tell you off because you are praying in a particular way and not according to their way.
>
> *(Respondent 23, female senior academic)*

Even when accommodated, women were confined to peripheral floors or rooms with an entrance from the side or back, and were allowed little if any representation in mosque governance (see also Dyke 2009). The gender-unequal order of the mosque was transferred to Britain from Muslim countries, although respondents noted that in the Ka'ba (the great mosque in Mecca), women are not segregated, and they are visible in religious institutions in Iran, as among some Muslim communities in East Africa. A female artist (Respondent 26) once ventured into the

Regent Park Mosque, only to have an argument with the imam. She never returned to the mosque. A female senior academic argued that even those mosques which employed females did so more as a token of progressiveness than as a reflection of genuine change (Respondent 20, female academic and theologian; Respondent 23). Women rarely occupied roles of significant power in such appointments.

The masculinisation of mosques disadvantaged women in other ways too. An aspiring national politician was stopped from addressing the mosque audience in the run-up to a general election (Respondent 6, then parliamentary candidate for one of the main political parties). She felt that male Muslim candidates and non-Muslim candidates of both genders would have enjoyed such access. The gender-segregated order of the mosque disadvantaged her as a Muslim woman but would not have applied to men or non-Muslim women candidates.

Women's involvement was important to move mosques away from traditional worship patterns and their restricted role, towards mosques becoming a social and community resource:

> I think a lot of women do want the mosque to be a place where women feel comfortable and ... aren't just relegated to a traditional worship pattern ... it is not just about the governance, I think it is also about women wanting space for more social activities.... But ... can [we] get beyond the traditional segregated order of Muslim societies ... and work out something that is mutually beneficial but still reserve the parameters of shame and modesty?
>
> *(Respondent 20, female academic and theologian)*

While Brown (2008) notes that women who desire equal mosque access may not be the liberals that the previous and current government wish to cultivate, respondents regard feminisation of mosque space as vital for creating a compassionate Islam, countering destructive masculinity, including radicalisation, promoting civicness, and connecting the mosque with the home.

> But I think in England there is a real problem about the exclusion of women from the mosque and I think the problem is for the mosque, not for the women ... I am in a way concerned because I actually think that having women in any arena helps enormously in the whole kind of dynamics of living, and these all-men spaces are actually very problematic.
>
> *(Respondent 4, female parliamentarian)*

Changing mosques: a case study

Mosques have to change 'to survive and to cater for the flocks', as there are 'a lot of angry people who are pissed off' with mosques (Respondent 24, male academic and writer). Change would be slow and needs to be forced by women, young people and professionals. External adversity (9/11, 7/7, the Rushdie affair, the 2001 street disturbances), internal challenges and the broader environment of democracy and equality demand change. Respondents argued that mosques need younger and more inclusive leadership, with professionalism and management capacity to become welcoming places for families, women and young people, and for local non-Muslims.

Some examples were given of positive change. A Turkish community-sponsored mosque has opted for a governing committee with a broad gender and ethnic base; interestingly, recognising the potential role of the mosque as a bridge with local people of other faiths, the governing committee also includes a non-Muslim member. A planned mosque in north-west London has South Asian and African Muslim men and women on the organisation committee. Apart from facilities for prayers and Islamic education, the mosque will provide social, entertainment and sport facilities to the diverse local community of those of different faiths and no faith. The professionals engaged in such ventures, it was argued, have a greater and more inclusive understanding of Islam, are better able to address current challenges, bring with them a commitment to equality and democracy, and have the capacity to deal with external stakeholders (see also Dyke 2009).

While change is slow and threatening, Britain enables experiments and provocations that would not be tolerated in Muslim majority countries. I use the interventions of one (in his own words) 'iconoclastic' imam to demonstrate what may be possible and at what cost (Respondent 17). This respondent is a trained imam with a higher degree in history and extensive media experience. He established his small organisation in response to the 'inaction' of his local mosques over 11 September and subsequent significant events. He came into the public eye over his decision to hold non-gender-segregated Friday prayers and, on separate occasions, to invite two women, Amina Wadud (in 2008), and Rahila Raza (in 2009), to lead Friday prayers. Defining himself as a Mutazilite (in a reference to a rationalist sect in the early Abbasid period), he aims to rise above denominational differences ('I was born a Hanafi but will die a Muslim') to 'revolutionise Islam', making it inclusive, rational, progressive and relevant to Britain. The prayers led by Wadud and Raza, although attended by a small handful of people, he regards as important provocations in pursuit of a liberalisation of Islam. Respondents who discussed this formed two camps. Some, while being strong proponents of gender equality, felt that his interventions meddled with religion and could not be condoned (e.g. Respondent 11, male researcher and head of a think tank, and Respondent 18, male academic).

But is it prohibited in Islam for women to have a role as imams? I discussed this in some detail with two other respondents, both scholars of Islam. For Respondent 27, introduced earlier, the Qur'an unequivocally confirms the equality of genders; Barlas (2002) notes that, unlike Judaism and Christianity, the Qur'an rejects the notion of God the Father. Adam's wife, known to Muslims as Hawa, was co-created with Adam, not created from his left rib. Woman in the Qur'an is man's equal, not his derivative (see also King 2009: 309; Sardar 2011b). Given this Qur'anic edict, we cannot deny women the right to lead prayers, this polymath and scholar argues. He welcomes the broader legal and social environment of gender equality and human rights in the United Kingdom, and the appointment of female Muslim chaplains in public services (Ali and Gilliat-Ray 2012). Another senior imam and scholar, Respondent 14, is forceful in his condemnation of patriarchal excision of women from the mosque and community leadership, and noted that the writing of Muhammad's wife Aisha 'has been burned' to diminish her status as a leader. The Prophet Muhammad appointed Umm e Waraqa, a woman, as imam to part of Madina, and

> Muslim theology doesn't stop Muslim women becoming imams. Imam – what is [an] imam? [An] imam is a leader, [an] imam is a teacher, [an] imam is a guide, [an] imam is a ... a helper and adviser ... on all areas of religious, cultural social and political life.... [An] imam is a pastoral carer in relation to marriage, births, deaths ... a guide.

For our 'iconoclastic imam' (Respondent 17), *imamat*, the claim to leading people in prayers, requires only two qualities: *ilm* (broadly defined knowledge) and *taqwa* (God-consciousness), neither being the preserve of men alone. He resented his interventions being belittled by 'reactionaries' and regretted the lack of support from liberal Muslims. This reflected male self-protectionism: 'scratch the surface and you will see patriarchy ... This notion of women's exclusion from the *baitullah* [house of Allah] is a patriarchal, chauvinistic development that is not founded on the Qur'an.'

Mullahs oppose mixed congregations, fearing potential sexual *fitna* (upheaval, chaos or social discord). Woodlock (2010) notes that male mosque-goers once raised concerns with the Prophet Muhammad over the prospect of *fitna* posed by the mosque attendance of a beautiful woman. Supported by a Qur'anic edict, he dismissed their concerns, placing on them the onus for maintaining social order. Woodlock also notes that Caliph Umar was admonished by a woman worshipper over his Friday sermon and returned to the pulpit to withdraw his statements.

Before the interview, I joined this respondent's Friday congregation. Following tradition, the first part of his *khutba*, delivered in English, focused on *deen* (faith or religion) and addressed the purpose of creation, especially *haquq al ibad* (duty towards others), and the second part on *duniya* (worldly issues), including an Afghan woman MP's work with sexually abused women. The congregation of two women and five men arranged themselves on gendered lines, with the women a little distance away from and to the side of men, in a church hall. The younger of the two women, entering the hall unscarved, took out a scarf from her bag and wore it before coming to the prayer mat. A little further away, sitting quietly on chairs with their heads scarved, were an equal number of non-Muslim, largely white women 'friends' of the imam, who later shared refreshments with worshippers. The imam regards concerns over potential sexual *fitna* posed by a mixed congregation as insulting to both women and men. If the two genders can respect boundaries of decency and decorum in schools, educational establishments, the workplace, on public transport and in social life, why would they suddenly become threats to each other's sexual and moral identities in the mosque, he rightly asks. Surely requirements for decorum and decency would be more, and not less, likely to be honoured in the house of God, the mosque? Even if there was a threat of *fitna*, why should it be women who are excluded from mosques rather than men?

This small organisation provides Qur'anic education to children and adults, Friday prayers, lectures, seminars, conferences, study circles and interfaith dialogue. However, while enjoying considerable media visibility, after seven years it still has only a small following, something that fails to daunt him:

AHMAD: So you have been going for ... seven years ... It hasn't really taken off, has it?

RESPONDENT 17: No, but what has happened is that we are known worldwide and in Britain, what progressive Islam is about . . . If we had, say, a budget of £50,000 or £100,000, which is not a big amount, we would revolutionise [Islam in] Britain . . . For an organisation with no money, no paid staff, to make so many waves, I wouldn't agree with you that we haven't taken off.

Conclusion

Both the strengths and the limitations of this study need to be acknowledged. This is not a study of mosques or worshippers who use them, even though many of my male and some of the female respondents were mosque-goers. That would have required different methods and a different focus. Also, these respondents are more 'liberal' and less 'traditional' than would be expected of a cross section of Britain's Muslims, although such binary divisions are artificial and unhelpful. I am not claiming that my sample is representative of the general Muslim population of Britain. The key contribution of this study is that it explores the reflections of influential, elite Muslims on British mosques, their strengths and weaknesses and what they ought to become. The respondents' perspectives and assessments are based on personal experience of mosques; but, importantly, also on their understanding of the full and central role that mosques once played, and ought to play in a vibrant multicultural society. Many of the respondents have closely observed the development of Islam and of mosques in Britain, have a history of conducting research on and with Muslim communities, and have relevant political and policy interests or are scholars of Islam and Muslim history. While acknowledging the contribution of the first generation, respondents are critical of the reductive role of Britain's mosques as places of prayer but not of learning, or for addressing community issues. Mosques and imams are ill-equipped for community leadership or building bridges with non-Muslims. While Muslim communities may be in their second or third generation, mosque leadership remains in the hands of the first generation, including imported imams; thus, the 'first-generation mindset' is constantly being renewed by continued importation of imams trained in Muslim majority countries such as Pakistan, Egypt or Saudi Arabia. And while Dyke (2009) notes sufficient provision of imams trained in Britain, respondents criticise the outmoded teaching and conservative theology that dominate in Britain's Islamic seminaries. The reductivism in Islam has sacralised the mosque space, othering most of life except ritual prayers; respondents argued for a new conception of the mosque – open, inclusive, family-friendly, gender-equal, a seat of learning, a place for dialogue and dissent, and a resource for the whole community, including non-Muslims. Mosques therefore have to be re-imagined as truly British institutions, propagating an empowering Islam far removed from the current focus on literalism, *taqlid*, fragmentation and exclusivity.

While generally true, these criticisms may underplay the change that mosques have already gone through (Ansari 2003; McLoughlin 2005; Dyke 2009). Respondents note that both external pressures and young people's and women's self-empowerment, through closer reading of Islam and greater skills acquired through education or professional roles, will dictate change in mosque leadership and *imamat*. The broader equalities and human rights culture, respondents felt, will also have a positive impact. The trend among public authorities to appoint Muslim chaplains of both genders was welcomed and, as noted by Ali and Gilliat-Ray in Chapter 4, may radiate theological change out into mosques and communities.

Women are providing powerful critiques of common-sense, patriarchalised Islam. Such notions of Islam, they argue, are based not on the Qur'an, the foundational text of Islam, but on secondary sources: weak Hadith (the Prophet's traditions) and patriarchal cultures (see Barlas 2002; Mernissi 1991; Wadud 1999). While respondents rightly criticised the relative exclusion of women from mosques, it should be noted that even the modest gains already made would be hard to contemplate in many Muslim majority countries. And while the experiments with mixed congregations and female imams may seem peripheral to 'mainstream' Islam, they represent important provocations, testing the limits and pace of acceptable change and benefiting from equality and human rights legislation. Such provocations would simply not be possible in most Muslim majority countries, although the remarkable reformation of Muslim family law in Morocco gives some hope of positive change (Sardar 2011a).

Muslim critics have bemoaned the lack of space in Muslim countries for Islamic reformation (Ahmed 2003; Barlas 2002; Rahman 1998). Ahmed (2003) notes that Muslim reformers have often sought refuge in, or belong to, Europe or North America. Among them are women scholars such as Barlas (2002) and Wadud (1999), who provide a progressive theology rooted in critical, integrative and historicised interpretations of the Qur'an and reject patriarchal traditions that justify women's subjugation. Ramadan (2004) argues that European Muslims have the freedom to liberate and modernise Islam, at home in Europe; and Sardar's (2011b) recent intervention focuses on the liberative potential of the Qur'an through developing methods for its democratised reading. While respondents feared certain ossification of conservative Islam, they noted that Britain provides a relatively safe space for challenging religious orthodoxies and experimenting with alternatives. To make this a reality, mosques have to be re-imagined: to be democratically led and to become inclusive, empowering institutions – spaces for personal growth, learning, community-making, citizenship and re-imagining Islam.

Acknowledgements

Respondents for this study were generous in making time for these conversations; Middlesex University provided the time for this research; analyses for this chapter were conducted while I was a Visiting Associate at the Centre for Migration Policy and Society of the University of Oxford during the summer of 2010. Ziauddin Sardar provided helpful comments on an earlier draft of this chapter. To all, my heartfelt thanks.

References

Ahmad, W. I. U. and Evergeti, V. (2010) 'The making and representation of Muslim identity in Britain: conversations with British Muslim "elites"', *Ethnic and Racial Studies* 33 (10): 1697–1717.

Ahmed, A. S. (2003) *Islam under Siege*, Cambridge: Polity Press.

Ajijola, A. A. D. (1998) 'The problem of "*ulama*"', in C. Kurzman (ed.) *Liberal Islam: A Source Book*, New York: Oxford University Press.

Ansari, H. (2003) *The Infidel Within: Muslims in Britain since 1800*, London: Hurst.

Ansari, H. (2007) '"Burying the dead": making Muslim space in Britain', *Historical Research* 80 (210): 545–566.

Arkoun, A. (1998) 'Rethinking Islam today', in C. Kurzman (ed.) *Liberal Islam: A Source Book*, New York: Oxford University Press.

Barlas, A. (2002) *Believing Women in Islam: Unreading Patriarchal Interpretations of the Qur'an*, Austin: University of Texas Press.

Biondo, V. F. III (2006) 'The architecture of mosques in the US and Britain', *Journal of Muslim Minority Affairs* 26 (3): 400–420.

Brown, K. (2008) 'The promise and peril of women's participation in UK mosques: the impact of securitisation agendas on identity, gender and community', *British Journal of Politics and International Relations* 10 (3): 472–491.

Cesari, J. (2005) 'Mosques in French cities: towards the end of a conflict?', *Journal of Ethnic and Migration Studies* 31 (6): 1025–1043.

Dunn, K. M., Klocker, N. and Salabay, T. (2007) 'Contemporary racism and Islamophobia in Australia: racializing religion', *Ethnicities* 7 (4): 564–589.

Dyke, A. H. (2009) *Mosques Made in Britain*, London: Quilliam.

Eade, J. (1989) *The Politics of Community: The Bangladeshi Community in East London*, Aldershot: Avebury.

Gale, R. (2005) 'Representing the city: mosques and the planning process in Birmingham', *Journal of Ethnic and Migration Studies* 31 (6): 1161–1179.

Ghosal, B. (2010) 'Arabization: the changing face of Islam in Asia', *India Quarterly* 66 (1): 69–89.

Glynn, G. (2009) 'Liberalizing Islam: creating Brits of the Islamic persuasion', in R. Phillips (ed.) *Muslim Spaces of Hope*, London: Zed Books.

House of Commons, Department for Communities and Local Government (2010) *Preventing Violent Extremism: Sixth Report of Session 2009–10*, London: The Stationery Office.

Humphrey, M. (1987) 'Community, mosque and ethnic politics', *Journal of Sociology* 23 (2): 233–245.

Kibria, N. (2008) 'The "new Islam" and Bangladeshi youth in Britain and the US', *Ethnic and Racial Studies* 31 (2): 243–266.

King, A. (2009) 'Islam, women and violence', *Feminist Theology* 17 (3): 292–328.

Klausen, J. (2005) *The Islamic Challenge: Politics and Religion in Western Europe*, Oxford: Oxford University Press.

Lotfi, A. (2001) 'Creating Muslim space in the USA: *masajid* and Islamic centres', *Islam and Christian–Muslim Relations* 12 (2): 235–254.

McLoughlin, S. (2005) 'Mosques and the public space: conflicts and cooperation in Bradford', *Journal of Ethnic and Migration Studies* 31 (6): 1045–1066.

Masood, E. (2009) *Science and Islam: A History*, London: Icon Books.

Maussen, M. (2007) 'Islamic presence and mosque establishment in France: colonialism, arrangements for guestworkers and citizenship', *Journal of Ethnic and Migration Studies* 33 (6): 981–1002.

Mernissi, F. (1991) *The Veil and the Male Elite: A Feminist Interpretation of Women's Rights in Islam*, Reading, MA: Addison-Wesley.

Metcalf, B. D. (1996) *Making Muslim Space in North America and Europe*, Berkeley: University of California Press.

Modood, T. and Ahmad, F. (2007) 'British Muslim perceptions of multiculturalism', *Theory, Culture and Society* 61 (2): 143–160.

Naylor, S. and Ryan, J. R. (2002) 'The mosque in the suburbs: negotiating religion and ethnicity in South London', *Social and Cultural Geography* 3 (1): 39–59.

Rahman, F. (1998) 'Islam and modernity', in C. Kurzman (ed.) *Liberal Islam: A Source Book*, New York: Oxford University Press.

Ramadan, T. (2004) *Western Muslims and the Future of Islam*, New York: Oxford University Press.

Ramadan, T. (2009) *Radical Reform: Islamic Ethics and Liberation*, New York: Oxford University Press.

Reeber, M. (1991) 'A study of Islamic preaching in France', *Islam and Christian–Muslim Relations* 2 (2): 275–294.

Samad, Y. (1992) 'Book burning and race relations: political mobilisation of Bradford Muslims', *Journal of Ethnic and Migration Studies* 18 (4): 507–519.

Sardar, Z. (1993) 'Paper, printing and compact disks: the making and unmaking of Islamic culture', *Media, Culture and Society* 15 (1): 43–59.

Sardar, Z. (2003) *Islam, Postmodernism and Other Futures: A Ziauddin Sardar Reader*, ed. S. Inayatullah and G. Boxwell, London: Pluto Press.

Sardar, Z. (2011a) 'Making reform real: Ziauddin Sardar on why uttering "I divorce thee" just won't do'. Online, available at: www.musliminstitute.org/blogs/culture/making-reform-real-ziauddin-sardar-why-uttering-i-divorce-thee-just-wont-do (accessed 23 August 2011).

Sardar, Z. (2011b) *Reading the Qur'an*, London: Hurst.

Savage, M. and Williams, K. (eds) (2008) *Remembering Elites*, Oxford: Blackwell.

Scott, J. (2008) 'Modes of power and reconceptualization of elites', in M. Savage and K. Williams (eds) *Remembering Elites*, Oxford: Blackwell.

Singh, R. (1992) *Immigrants to Citizens: The Sikh Community in Bradford*, Bradford: Race Relations Research Unit, University of Bradford.

Talbot, I. (1998) *Pakistan: A Modern History*, New York: St Martin's Press.

Taylor, M. (2010) 'Michael Gove opposes mosque at centre of "inflammatory" campaign', *Guardian* (London), 10 February. Online, available at: www.guardian.co.uk/politics/2010/feb/12/michael-gove-opposes-mosque.

Voas, D. and Crockett, A. (2005) 'Religion in Britain: neither believing nor belonging', *Sociology* 39 (1): 11–28.

Wadud, A. (1999) *Qur'an and Woman: Reading the Sacred Text from a Woman's Perspective*, Oxford: Oxford University Press.

Wardak, A. (2002) 'The mosque and social control in Edinburgh's Muslim community', *Culture and Religion* 3 (2): 201–219.

Woodlock, R. (2010) 'The *masjid* is for men: competing voices in the debate about Australian Muslim women's access to mosques', *Islam and Christian–Muslim Relations* 21 (1): 51–60.

INDEX

Page numbers in *italics* denote tables, those in **bold** denote figures.

Abu-Lughod, Lila 121
abuse 106
active citizenship 123
activism 86–7, 131–3, 143–4
adl 30
Afshar, Haleh 129, 135
Aftab, T. 143
age, and social mixing 69, 75
agreement, between religious communities 25–6
Ahmad, Waqar 7; and Evergeti, Venetia 175, 176, 184
Ahmed, Leila 125, 129
Ahmed, Sara 124, 128
Alam, Fareena 165
Albrow, M. 104
Ali, M. Mansur 8–10
Ali, Rahielah 6, 10–11
aliens 2
Amin, A. 39–40
AMINA 150–3
Anderson, J. W. 164, 165
Andrews, R. 44
Appadurai, A. 102
assimilation 2
associational identification 167
Attlee, Clement 36

Bagguley, P. 45
Bang, H. P. 141
Banglatown 125
Barlas, Asma 125–6, 186
Barth, Fredrick 158
Bechofer, F. 44
Beckett, C. 124
Begum, Halima 125
behaviour 113–16
Beijing Platform for Action 135
belonging 10, 34–6
bereavement and death 95–7
Beyond the Veil 152
biraderi 173–4
Blair, Tony 40, 42, 46, 48
Bloch, A. 37
Blunkett, David 42
Blunt, A. 106
boundaries: of Britishness 40–1, 43–4, 46–9; public/private 86–9, 94–7
British National Party 41
British state, construction of 35
Britishness 3–4, 15; agenda of 36–8; boundaries 40–1, 43–4, 46–9; conflicting agendas 40–4; context and overview 33–4; essential values 42; ethnic minorities 45–6; exclusion 46–9; identification with 42, 44; Muslims and the agenda 39–40; nation, belonging and place 34–6; Northern Ireland 44–5; and rights 45; summary and conclusions 49; tensions 43; UK as disunited 44–6
broadcast media, religious programming 19, 20–1

Brown, Gordon 1, 33, 37, 41–2
Brown, K. 173
Bunglawala, Inayat 164
Bunting, M. 37
burial 96

Cameron, David 1, 12, 41
campaigning 87
Chakrabati, Shami 48
chaplains 8–10; context and overview 84–5; death and bereavement 95–7; gender 94; and gender relations 89–90; *ijtihad* 90–2; innovating networks 94–7; interpretation 89–92; legal schools 88, 91–2; multiple roles 87–9, 96–7; prayer 93; public/ private boundary 94–7; religious training 88; summary and conclusions 97–8; teamwork 93–4; theological reflection 89–92; troubleshooting 94; *see also* Muslim Chaplaincy Project
Cheong, P. H. 47
Christianity 19, 24
citizenship 4–5, 45; acquisition 47; active 13, 31, 123; conceptualization 132; requirements for 123
citizenship pledge 43
Citizenship Survey 48, 58, 67
civic engagement, and everyday making 150–3
civic integration 123
civic values 48–9
class 3, 6, 14–15
close friendships 72–9, *73*, *76–7*, **78**, 80
clothing 113–16, 120, 129–30, 144–5
Cohen, R. 33–4, 35–6
cohesion 123
colonialism 14
commensality, social participation 57, 62
Commission for Racial Equality (CRE) 37
Commonwealth 36
community cohesion 123
Community Cohesion funding 131
community support 55
conscience 18
consciousness: context and overview 156; and education 162–4; grouping 157–8; observing identities 158–61; political participation 159–60; religious plurality 161–4; self and public representation 164–6; summary and conclusions 166–7
Conservative Party 41
consumerism 18
Convention on the Elimination of All Forms of Discrimination against Women (CEDAW) 133
counter-terrorism 47–8
createdness 25
cultural identity 5
culture: change 14; death by 130; as distinct from religion 26; and religious identity 111–12

Davies, Graham 6
death and bereavement 95–7
death by culture 130
debate 7
decolonization 36
demonization 1
deprivation 39
diasporas 7
diasporic identities 103
difference 2
difference, minorities and social networks 53–4
differentiation 56–8
diversity 2, 26, 47, 156–7
dominance 26–7; English, in UK 35, 44
doubt 20
Douglas, Mary 128
Dowling, R. 106
dress 113–16, 120, 129–30, 144–5
Dwyer, C. 144, 159
Dyke, A. H. 173

economic restructuring 36–7
education 38; and Britishness 41; and identity 162–4; Islamic 180; Islamic schools 162–4; parental choice 39; *see also* faith schools
Ehrkamp, P. 103
elites 7
elites study: challenges to mosques 180–5; changing mosques 185–8; context and overview 171; findings 175–7; imams 182–4; methods 174–5; relevance of mosques 177–80; summary and conclusions 188–9; *see also* mosques
Empire Windrush 36
employment, changes in 36–7
employment status, and social mixing 75
ENGAGE 166
England, dominance 35, 44
Englishness 1, 5, 42, 45
ethnic differentiation 56–8
ethnic minorities, identification with Britishness 45–6
ethnicity 159, 162–3; and friendships 64–5
ethnocentrism, latent 130
Europe, role of Islam 6–7
European Union 36

everyday making 141–2; and civic engagement 150–3; and Muslim women 143–5
exclusion, Britishness 46–9
extremism 47–8

faith, in public life 17–18
faith schools 30, 38
family structure 37
Fanon, Franz 129
far right 41
fear, and truth 128
Fekete, L. 128
feminism 133–4
festivals, recognition 31
Fetzer, J. S. 163
Forced Marriage Civil Protection Act 2007 131
Forced Marriage Unit (FMU) 127
foreign policy, effects of 14
fragmentation, of mosques 175–7
friendship networks 58, 64–5, 79–80; close friendships 72–9, *73*, *76*–7, **78**, 80
funerals 96
fuzzy frontiers 35–6

Gale, R. 142, 150, 159, 161
Gardner, K. 104
gender: chaplains 94; and social mixing 69, 74–5, 78–9, 80; young Muslims 113–16; *see also* Muslim women
gender-blindness 124
gender relations, and chaplains 89–90
gendered sexualized practices 126
Gilliat Ray, Sophie 8–10
global events, and British perceptions 2–3
globalization 102
Glynn, G. 173
God consciousness 25–6
God problem 20
Goldberg, D. T. 123
Goodhart, David 1–2, 37, 43–4
government, links with Muslim communities 173
Greaves, R. 158
grouping 157–8

Habermas, Jürgen 88, 98
Hall, Stuart 122
Halliday, Fred 157
Hanafi 88, 186
Hattersley, Roy 159–60
Heath, A. 44
heterogeneity 54, 56–8, 65–6, 156–7
hijab activism 145
history 5–7
home, concepts of 105–8
homophily **63**, 63–7, *66*, 79
honour crimes 126–8, 133, 135
Hopkins, Peter 6, 10–11, 142, 143, 144
hospitals, chaplains 84, 85
housing, allocation of 39
human rights 135
Hussain, Y. 45
hybridity 167
hypocrisy of Empire 14

identities: diasporic 103, 110–11; distinguishing 157–8; as fluid and dynamic 102, 104, 109; multiple 10; observing 158–61
identity: British 41; and class 3, 6; cultural 5; and culture 111–12; and education 162–4; evolution 11–12; grouping 157; hybridity 167; local 10; of minorities 2; national 34, 35–6; and otherness 2; and race 3, 6; reification of 124; and religion 3, 109–10, 143; religious 11, 19; and religious belief 37; self-definition 8; visible 101; women's role in 121
identity politics, emergence 156
ijtihad 9, 90–1
illiteracy, religious 21
ilm 30
images, of Muslims 2
imams: criticism of 182–4, 188–9; women as 186–7
immigration 2, 36, 122
Immigration Acts 46
immigration policy 33, 46–7
Impact International 165
inclusion 36, 55
income 64–5, 69, 80
Index of Dissimilarity 13
individualism 37
inequality 18, 44
integration 2, 13, 47, 123
Ireland 35
Irish people, in British nation 35
Islam, knowledge of 11, 112
Islamic feminism 133–4
Islamic schools 162
Islamophobia 126–30, 142–3, 149–50
isolationism 64
istislah 30

Jackson, P. 104, 107
Jacobson, J. 40–1, 158–9
Joppke, C. 37–8, 47
Judaism 9, 96

Kanneh, K. 129
Keith, M. 104, 107
Kelly, Patricia 163
Khan, S. 40, 41–2, 47, 160
Khokher, S. 159
Knott, K. 159
knowledge, and ignorance 18
Kundnani, A. 38, 39, 43, 48

labels 2
language 35, 47
latent ethnocentrism 130
leadership, mosques 179–80
liberalism 15, 43
lobbying 87
local, and translocal 103
locality, salience of 103–4
London bombings, 2005 40
London, young Muslims 105–8
loyalty 3

Macey, M. 124
magnetic resonance imaging (MRI), post-mortems 96–7
Malik, Maleiha 126, 127
marginalization 19, 55
Marinetto, M. 44
Massey, Doreen 104, 116
Matar, Nabil 6
McCrone, D. 44
Mears, Idris 163, 164
media, Muslim 164–6
media representations 142–3, 147–50, 164–6
Meer, Nasir 7–8
men: perceptions of 134; view of women 144
mental ghettoes 29
Mernissi, Fatima 125
migrants, locality 103–4
migration, effects of 124–5
migration policy 46–7
minorities: demonization of 1; difference and social networks 53–4
Mir-Hosseini, Ziba 133
Mirza, Heidi Safia 12, 13
mixing, social 4
mobility 37, 104
Modood, T. 142, 156, 157, 158
Moghissi, Haidah 125
Mohanty, Chandra Talpade 130
moral reflection, religion as 22–3
mosques: challenges 180–5; changing 185–8; control of 173–4, 181–2; criticisms of 173; fragmentation 175–7; government view of 173; imams 182–4, 188–9; Islamic education 180; leadership 179–80; re-imagining 7; relevance 177–80; roles and functions 172, 177–8; sponsorship 174, 180–1; women 173, 184–5; *see also* elites study
Multi-ethnic Britain (Runnymede Trust) 14
multi-faith chaplaincy teams 85, 93
multicultural discourse, faith-based approach 123–4
multicultural drift 122
multiculturalism 2, 11, 12–15, 27; concessions to 123; criticism of 37; failure to implement 37–8; liberal version 43; *see also* Muslim women
muscular liberalism 15
Muslim Chaplaincy Project: methods 86; overview 85; public/private boundary 86–9; research questions 85–6; *see also* chaplains
Muslim Council of Britain (MCB) 48, 160
Muslim Justice Movement (MJM) 159
Muslim News 165–6
Muslim vote 160
Muslim women: accounts of lives 143; and everyday making 143–5; everyday making and civic engagement 150–3; and Islamophobia 126–30; marginalization 121–6; overview 120–1; recognition 131–4; summary and conclusions 134–6; as symbolic 120; as victims 141
Muslim women, Scotland 10–11; context and method of project 145–7; context and overview 141; everyday making 143–5; Islamophobia and media representations 142–3; media representations 147–50; summary and conclusions 153
Muslim Women's Network 131
myths, of nationhood 34–5

nation, belonging and place 34–6
nation-states 33, 34
National Front 41
nationalism 44
Nationality Act 1948 46
nationhood 5, 34–5
naturalization 47
networks, chaplains 94–7
New Labour 43
niceness, religion as 22–3
No Recourse to Public Funds rule 131–2
Northern Ireland, Britishness 44–5
Nyhagen Predelli, L. 110

Oath of Allegiance 43
offending others 24–6
Oldham 13
One-Year Rule 131
oppression, gendered 125–6
organized activities, participation in 62–3
Orwell, George 1, 3, 4, 5, 10, 14, 15
otherness 2, 46, 54, 128
O'Toole, T. 150, 159

Parekh, B. 40
participation 29
Patel, Pragna 123–4, 132
patriarchy 125–6, 127–8, 134
Peach, C. 161
Penrose, J. 104
Phillips, Trevor 37
Pile, S. 104, 107
place: and behaviour 116; and identity 10; local and translocal 103; nation and belonging 34–6; theorizing 102–5
Place and Placelessness (Relph) 102–3
places of worship 161
Platt, Lucinda 4, 10, 58
plurality, religious 161–4
policies, multicultural 15
policy attention 53
political activism, women 144
political participation 150, 159–60
political parties: associations with 10–11; and Britishness 41–2
post-mortems 9, 95–7
poverty 18, 55
Powell, Enoch 2
power divisions, gendered 124
prayer 93
Prevent Strategy 48
Primary Purpose Rule 131
prisons, chaplains 8–9, 84, 85
public debate 30
public discourse 17, 54
public life, faith in 17–18
public space: giving offence 24–6; practice 29–31; religious voices 18–19; summary and conclusions 31

Q-News 165
Qur'an, gendered understandings 125–6

race 3, 6, 14–15
racism 121–2
radical secularism 20–1
radicalization 14
Ramji, Hasmita 125
re-imagining 7
reciprocity, social participation 61, 62
reductionism, view of religion 21–4, 175
reflexivity 10
refugees 45–6
reification, of identity 124
religion: and Britishness 42; and identity 3, 11, 143; loss of purpose 28; marginalization 17; and national identity 37; reductive perceptions 21–4; responsibilities of 18–19; self-identification 19
religious affiliation 19
religious communities, agreement between 25–6
religious education 21
religious illiteracy 21
religious mixing 67
religious plurality 161–4
religious professionals 8–9
religious voices 18–19, 31
Relph, E. 102–3
representation, self and public 164–6
research 53–4
right to exit 126–7
rights, and Britishness 45
riots 39, 143
risk-awareness 148
risks, attention to 128
ritual 22
'rivers of blood' 2
Roberts, J. 44
Rushdie, Salman 2
Ryan, Louise 10, 11, 45, 48

sacredness, respect for 25
Sales, Rosemary 3–5, 12, 15
Salim, S. 127, 133
Samantrai, Ranu 132
Sardar, Ziauddin 3, 18–19, 177–8
Scotland *see* Muslim women, Scotland
secular spaces, loss of 123–4
secularism 3, 20–1, 27
Secure Borders, Safe Haven 39, 42, 47
security 47–8, 173
segregation 39
self, and other 2
self-identification, hybridity 167
self-reformation 26
self-renewal 26
separation 13
September 11, 2001 2–3, 40, 142–3, 147, 149
sexuality 130
'She Who Disputes' 131
shura 30

Siddiqi, Hannana 123–4, 132
Simpson, Ludi 13
sin, individual and collective 90
Smith Institute 42, 43
Smith, Jacqui 48
social capital 54–5
social cohesion 47, 48, 173
social contact, as social support 54–6
social mixing 4, 58–9, 67–72, *68*, *70–1*, **72**, 79
social networks: heterogeneity 65–6, 67; minorities and difference 53–4
social participation 59–63, *61*; and welfare 55
social science 166–7
social spaces: close friendships 72–9, *73*, *76–7*, **78**, 80; context and overview 53; data sources 58–9; ethnic differentiation 56–8; friendship networks 79–80; heterogeneity 56–8; homophily **63**, 63–7, *66*, 79; minorities, difference and social networks 53–4; research method 58–9; results 59–79; sample characteristics *60*; social contact as social support 54–6; social mixing 67–72, *68*, *70–1*, **72**, 79; social participation 59–63, *61*; summary and conclusions 79–80; visiting 79
social values 25
Solomos, J. 37
Soper, J. C. 163
space: and identity 10; multicultural 11
Spivak, Gayatri 127
Sporton, D. 109
state, construction of 35
Statham, P. 156
stereotyping 2, 141, 148
Stevenson, W. 43
Straw, Jack 129

taqlid 90–1
Tarlo, Emma 144–5
Terrorism Acts 47
terrorism, perceived threat 47
The Parekh Report: The Future of Multi-ethnic Britain 14, 122
The Satanic Verses (Rushdie) 2
Tiilikainen, M. 111
tipping point 46–7
tolerance 24–5, 46–7
transmodernity 26–9
transnational belonging 108–13
transnationalism 103–4
Trevathan, Abdullah 162
truth 27–9, 128

Unionism 45
United Kingdom 35, 36, 44–6

Valentine, G. 109
values 4, 7, 25–6, 48–9
veil 129–30
victimhood 130
violence, against women 120, 126–8, 134, 135
vision, of British Muslims 7–8
visiting 58, 79
voices, religious 18–19, 31
voting 160

Wadud, Amina 133, 135
Wales 10
Warsi, Baroness Sayeeda 41, 48, 129, 144
welfare, and social participation 55
women: activism 131–3, 143–4; effects of legislation 131–2; as imams 186–7; mosques 173, 184–5; and national identity 121–2; professional roles 8; public roles 11; right to exit 126–7; violence against 126–8, 134, 135
women's organizations 131
Woodlock, R. 187
Working Party on Forced Marriage 134
writing 7
Wyn Davies, Merryl 166

young Muslims: concepts of home 105–8; context and overview 101–2; experience of abuse and racism 106–7; focus of study 104–5; gender 113–16; methods 105; religious identity 109–10; research participants 105; sense of injustice 110; summary and conclusions 116–17; theorizing place 102–5; transnational belonging 108–13
youth politics 39–40
Yuval-Davis, N. 121